FROM

UNDERGROUND RAILROAD

TO

REBEL REFUGE

FROM UNDERGROUND RAILROAD

TO

REBEL REFUGE

CANADA AND
THE CIVIL WAR

BRIAN MARTIN

Cover design: Michel Vrana
Author photo: Morris Lamont
Front cover artwork: "London Canada West" by E.
Whitefield, 1855. Western University Libraries Historic
Maps Collection, 1800–1900.

LIBRARY AND ARCHIVES CANADA CATALOGUING
IN PUBLICATION

Title: From underground railroad to rebel refuge :
Canada and the Civil War / Brian Martin.

Names: Martin, Brian (Brian Gordon), author.

Identifiers: Canadiana (print) 20220229112 |
Canadiana (ebook) 20220229147

ISBN 978-1-77041-638-3 (softcover)
ISBN 978-1-77852-011-2 (ePub)
ISBN 978-1-77852-012-9 (PDF)
ISBN 978-1-77852-013-6 (Kindle)

Subjects: LCSH: United States—History—Civil War,
1861-1865—Participation, Canadian.

Classification: LCC E540.C25 M37 2022

| DDC 973.7—dc23

We acknowledge the support of the Canada Council for the Arts. *Nous remercions le Conseil des arts du Canada de son soutien.* This book is funded in part by the Government of Canada. *Ce livre est financé en partie par le gouvernement du Canada.* We acknowledge the support of the Ontario Arts Council (OAC), an agency of the Government of Ontario, which last year funded 1,965 individual artists and 1,152 organizations in 197 communities across Ontario for a total of $51.9 million. We also acknowledge the support of the Government of Ontario through the Ontario Book Publishing Tax Credit, and through Ontario Creates.

PRINTED AND BOUND IN CANADA   PRINTING: FRIESENS   5   4   3   2   1

MIX
Paper from
responsible sources
FSC
www.fsc.org   FSC® C016245

This book is dedicated to the notion there is always something we can learn from history.

CONTENTS

ACKNOWLEDGEMENTS

I would like to extend heartfelt thanks to the many people who gave of their time to share what they knew about topics covered in this book. Research is so rewarding because, aside from producing much-needed information, it introduces the researcher to many dedicated and helpful guardians of records who invariably bend over backwards to assist. In particular, I would like to acknowledge the help of Shannon Prince, curator of the Buxton National Historic Site and Museum in North Buxton, Ontario, as well as that of Natasha L. Henry, president of the Ontario Black History Society in Toronto. Thanks are also due to Samantha Meredith, executive director and curator of the Chatham-Kent Black Historical Society and Black Mecca Museum in Chatham, Ontario.

In Niagara-on-the-Lake, historian Doug Phibbs was exceedingly helpful sharing information about the history of that pretty town and some of its noteworthy inhabitants in the past. Also there, writer Denise Ascenzo and Shawn Butts of the Niagara-on-the-Lake Museum were valued partners in research. At the Fort Erie Museum, Jane Davies provided a wealth of historical information.

In South Carolina, Nancy Sambets, director of archives at the History Center of York County in York, kindly provided an important image and information about that town and its characters. Also in York and pitching in to help was Zach Lemhouse, historian and director of the Southern Revolutionary War Institute.

A special shout-out goes to Mark Bourrie, with whom this author once committed daily journalism and who has since become a successful, prolific, and bestselling author. Mark kindly provided advice about connecting with folks who might be interested in publishing this book. Things worked out. Eventually. Thank you, Mark.

Also deserving of praise is dear friend and ancestry researcher Diana Copsey Adams, of Denver, Colorado. Her amazing skills at genealogy and help with several of the author's previous books have earned her the affectionate nickname "Sherlocka." In London, Ontario, Joseph O'Neil Jr. and Kate O'Neil kindly shared what they knew about some of the Southerners resting in a London graveyard. London historian Daniel Brock could always be relied on to fill in blanks in my knowledge as needed. A debt of gratitude is owed to Donald Murray, also of London, a longtime friend of the author whose sage advice and editing skills at the early stages of this book helped make it possible. At a later stage, editor Lesley Erickson provided some excellent ideas to help trim the manuscript, fine-tune it, and reorder some of the content. Thanks, Lesley, for helping me make this the best book possible. At ECW Press, co-publisher Jack David was a pleasure to work with and Samantha Chin demonstrated her heroics with copy issues on several occasions.

Here are others deserving of mention. Apologies are extended to anyone who may have been inadvertently omitted.

Photographer Katie Stewart, of KMS Photography, for her fine images taken in and near her community of York, South Carolina

Miranda Riley, Collections Manager, Royal Military College, Kingston, Ontario

John Aitken, historic postcard collector, Oshawa, Ontario

John Lisowski, historian and lawyer, London, Ontario

Theresa Regnier, Archives Assistant, Regional Room, D.B. Weldon Library, Western University, London, Ontario

Jean Hung, Archives Media Assistant, Collections Centre, Western Libraries, Western University, London, Ontario

Paul Culliton, writer, historian, London, Ontario

Mark Richardson and Arthur McClelland, London Room, London Public Library, London, Ontario

Stephen Harding, friend and historian, London, Ontario

Bob Strawhorn, Civil War buff, Woodstock, Ontario

Scott Andrew Collyer, friend and occupant of a historic home in London long occupied by Southerners, which is featured in this book and whose days are numbered

INTRODUCTION

Leafy Woodland Cemetery is the final resting place for many prominent citizens of London, Ontario, including former mayors and business leaders such as the beer-brewing Labatt family. My unexpected discovery of some Americans also interred there was the genesis of this book. Amidst the grand markers for the Labatts and other community leaders can be found a cluster of headstones for some former enslaved people and plantation owners who were born in Charleston, South Carolina, nearly 1,000 miles due south. Why did these Southerners make the long trek to London so long ago? And how is it they rest alongside prominent citizens in a foreign land so far from home?

The grand stones of the South Carolinians stand in stark contrast to the unmarked plot of Shadrach T. Martin, a native of Tennessee who arrived in London in 1854 and became a popular barber. He was the first Black person to enlist with the Union Army shortly after the Civil War broke out, long before "colored" regiments were formed. Martin served on an army gunboat in the Mississippi River for more than two years before returning to the life he had built in London. A pioneer for his race, he enlisted to fight for freedom for Black people and against a system of servitude that provided such a comfortable life for the Southerners who also lie in Woodland.

The final resting place of others who fought in the Civil War, on both sides, can be found elsewhere in Canada. They include enslaved men and women who sought freedom before the war and other fugitives who had entirely different reasons to find refuge in America's northern neighbour once the fighting ceased.

Among the Black people who found freedom in Canada was the model for the lead character in Harriet Beecher Stowe's powerful anti-slavery book *Uncle Tom's Cabin*. Also making the trek north was the white man who inspired the main character in *The Birth of a Nation*, a racially charged film that reignited hatred for Black people and led to the establishment of the modern Ku Klux Klan. Canada tolerated, if not welcomed, all comers from both sides of the conflict, reflecting the complex role played by the colony-turned-country in race relations and politics in North America during the years bracketing the Civil War.

Canada's long history of acceptance preceded the war between the states and is well known. Sometimes Canadians find themselves the butt of jokes for being so civil and polite. Robin Williams, the late American comedian, apparently had a soft spot for Canada and made at least two films north of the border. In 2013, a year before his untimely death, Williams expressed his fondness for The Great White North this way: "You are the kindest country in the world. You are like a really nice apartment over a meth lab."

Williams easily could have referred to Canada as America's "attic." This book suggests the attic analogy in a bid to explain how Canada acted as a refuge in the years leading up to the Civil War, during the conflict itself, and in its aftermath. When things got out of control in the overheated meth lab, a time-out room was nearby. Conversely, it explains why some Canadians went south to contribute to the war effort — on both sides.

From Underground Railroad to Rebel Refuge tells the story of the flight and history of fugitives from south of the border and how Canadians dealt with them over the course of many decades. Before the conflict, an estimated 40,000 formerly enslaved and free Black people settled in what became Ontario. When the war broke out, some American white men, motivated by money, crossed the border to enlist young Canadians to take up arms in Union blue. In all, about 20,000 men from British North America joined the Union and Confederate armies, some as a result of trickery, but others for their own reasons. Buying agents from both the North and South came north to buy supplies to feed their armies and a large number of horses to move them. There were also American spies and operatives who worked from bases in Toronto and Montreal. Some were funded by large amounts of Confederate money to distract the North with daring missions launched from its back door. They too were tolerated by Canadians, if not welcomed. The border proved porous and many who chose to cross it died in each other's country. From their vantage point above the fray that played out below them, Canadians developed sympathies and prejudices in response to events in which they became entangled. An intriguing four-way relationship existed for a time between Canada, the United States, Britain, and the Confederacy, in which Canada (and Britain) developed sympathy for the South and Southerners coupled with distrust, dislike, and fear of the Union. The Civil War helped push Britain's North American colonies toward Confederation for fear that victorious Union guns might be directed north to finish a conquest the aggressive young republic failed to accomplish in the War of 1812.

Following the Civil War, the small community of Niagara-on-the-Lake, a mere stone's throw from the border, became a home for former Confederate generals and other Southerners who might have been tried for treason and hanged had they remained in the United States. North of the border, in the shadow of the American republic, they reconnected with their former president, Jefferson Davis, who found refuge elsewhere in Canada and was hailed by the public wherever he appeared. The high-profile Confederates who were so readily accommodated in Niagara-on-the-Lake and in other communities eventually returned to the United States when they felt it was safe to do so. Other Southerners stayed, however, content with the new lives they found.

Among those who remained in Canada were the wealthy and influential Mazyck and Manigault families of South Carolina. The first Mazyck settled in London in 1866, and other relatives and friends followed, abandoning their genteel way of life, the people they'd enslaved, and large plantations a world away. They were readily accepted by Londoners who likely shared their views about the supremacy of the white race, but were more discreet about it than the well-educated and financially independent newcomers. Two of the fugitive family members played a key role in South Carolina's secession, making it the first state to leave the Union in the prelude to war. Two leaders of the racist Ku Klux organization who were wanted for murder chose Canada, one settling in London, the other in Niagara.

Here, then, is the story of the northward flight of Black people, draft dodgers, the Confederate president and his prominent officials and generals, some leaders of the Ku Klux terror organization, and of wealthy citizens unable or unwilling to accept changes in the lives they had known. All found refuge in a friendly and much calmer place mere steps away from a republic in turmoil. For them, the attic beckoned. And while some refugees remained in Canada only briefly, others adapted to their new surroundings well and chose to live out their days in a land that extended them the welcome mat.

A NOTE ABOUT SPELLINGS, PLACE NAMES, AND OTHER MATTERS

This book employs standard Canadian-British spelling, with a few exceptions. In direct quotes from American sources, usually newspapers, spellings such as "color," "honor," and "center" are used. Some Canadian newspapers also used American spellings of those and other words during the relevant time frame. They have been adopted as written to preserve the integrity of the material quoted.

Canada is the term often employed for British North America. Quebec was known as Lower Canada and Ontario as Upper Canada before becoming Canada East and Canada West. In 1867 the Canadas joined the colonies of New Brunswick and Nova Scotia to become the Dominion of Canada.

Niagara, the town in Ontario, became known as Niagara-on-the-Lake late in the 1800s to distinguish it from Niagara Falls a few miles away up the Niagara River. The post office promoted the name change because of widespread confusion on the part of letter-writers and the amount of misdirected mail. Some American newspapers of the day made the same mistake, confusing the two communities in their reports.

Yorkville, South Carolina, the home of several Southerners whose stories are shared in this book, was renamed York in 1905.

In keeping with the era in which the book is set, miles are used to express distance, rather than kilometres.

The original white supremacist organization that terrorized Black people across the southern United States was established just after the Civil War. It was known as the Ku Klux, sometimes as Ku-klux, although newspapers occasionally appended "Klan" in a touch of alliteration. The KK was driven out of existence in late 1871. In 1915, an entirely new organization of white supremacists emerged, known as the Knights of the Ku Klux Klan, or KKK, or Klan, for short. The author has done his best to apply the correct term to each organization, despite some sources that incorrectly use "Klan" when referring to the earlier group.

PART ONE

THE ATTIC

CHAPTER ONE

AN INCIDENT
ALONG THE NIAGARA

C hloe Cooley's blood-curdling screams reverberated along the steep banks of the Niagara River that cold winter evening of March 14, 1793, just north of the village of Queenston. The young Black woman struggled violently to free herself from ropes as her enslaver, local farmer Adam Vrooman — assisted by his brother, Isaac, and the son of a neighbour — forced her down the steep slope into a small boat. Vrooman's hired hand, William Grisley, helped guide the boat across the fast-flowing and icy cold river. Their destination lay 1,500 feet across the river, on the U.S. side of the international border, where an American — maybe her new enslaver, or perhaps his agent — waited on the rugged shore to take delivery of the feisty human cargo.

Cooley resisted as best she could. She feared that as bad as life had been for her in recent times, toiling for a new enslaver in the United States could only be worse. She and other freedom seekers living in the newly established British colony of Upper Canada had been hearing rumours that slavery would soon be abolished. Lieutenant Governor John Graves Simcoe had ruled the colony for two years since it was carved from the sprawling colony of Quebec, and he was an outspoken abolitionist. But the House of Assembly, a few miles downriver at Newark (the former name of Niagara-on-the-Lake), with which he governed the sparsely populated colony, also included several enslavers among its members, so nothing was certain.[1]

Cooley demanded her freedom, but her resistance was futile. Her fate is unknown, but her screams would make history, reverberating far beyond tiny Queenston, the river gorge, and the Niagara border.

———

While we know nothing about Cooley and her American enslaver, we know plenty about the men involved in her removal. Adam Vrooman was born in Schoharie, New York, and was considered a bit of a black sheep in a large and successful family, which overwhelmingly supported the American Revolution and fought for the rebel cause. Adam, by contrast, joined Butler's Rangers, a band of loyalists formed in 1777 by Connecticut native John Butler.

Before hostilities broke out, Butler worked for the British authorities to maintain the loyalty of Indigenous peoples, which paid dividends when fighting began and Britain needed allies. He was allowed to establish his Butler's Rangers to fight alongside the Iroquois, and his ranks included freed Black men. Vrooman became a sergeant in one of eight companies commanded by Butler in the Mohawk Valley. They took part in several battles, winning nearly all of them, while suffering only light casualties.

Many of his recruits were accused by their "Patriot" neighbours of being "Tories," sympathetic to Britain, and were beaten and persecuted. New York had been rather late to join the revolutionary cause compared to neighbouring states, but New Yorkers soon engaged in the same forms of violence and harassment meted out to suspected loyalists elsewhere.

In 1778, Vrooman was taken before a board of commissioners and charged with giving aid to the enemy (Britain), but proof of his offence fell short, so he was fined 200 pounds and ordered to take an oath of allegiance to the State of New York, renouncing Great Britain and its king, George III. In exchange, he was allowed to return to his Mohawk Valley home.[2]

Under the Treaty of Paris of 1783, hostilities ceased and the border between Canada and the United States was established. In Niagara, the dividing line became the Niagara River, and Britain agreed to surrender Fort Niagara, which lay on the river's eastern shore at Lake Ontario. After fighting ended, Vrooman's fellow loyalists tried to return home, but were banished, jailed, or even murdered. They found post-revolutionary America was no longer home. Many, like Vrooman, decided to migrate to Upper Canada, which was offering free land to induce settlers. The Crown provided land grants of 100 or 200 acres or more in a bid to populate the frontier areas of the sparsely inhabited colony. Officials encouraged settlement so militias could be formed to assist the army in any future border incursions by American troops.[3] Many members of Butler's Rangers, including Vrooman, settled in the community opposite Fort Niagara, which Butler himself helped lay out; it was initially known as Butlersburg. Sometime between late 1784 and July of 1785, Vrooman took the oath of allegiance to Great Britain and its king. Not long afterward, he became a captain in the local militia. (Butlersburg's name was changed to Niagara when it was incorporated as a town in 1792, and soon afterward to Newark, by colonial governor John Graves Simcoe, who chose the town as his temporary capital. After Simcoe left it reverted to Niagara and today is known as Niagara-on-the-Lake. Butler was among the first residents.)

Chloe Cooley was one of two enslaved people Vrooman had on his farm, located just north of Queenston and seven miles south of Niagara. For about a decade he enslaved a man named Tom. He sold him in 1792 to fellow settler Adam Crysler, whose farm near St. David's was just a few miles west of Vrooman's. Crysler was a fellow native of Schoharie, New York. He had been with the British Indian Affairs office before the American Revolution and during hostilities joined the British military effort along with three brothers. He recruited other loyalists and Indigenous people and served leaders such as Captain Joseph Brant (Thayendanegea, Chief of the Six Nations and also a slaveholder). When his property in Schoharie was confiscated by the revolutionaries, Crysler and his family fled to Upper Canada in 1781, where he was granted 700 acres in Niagara Township.[4] He came with two enslaved people.

At about the same time he sold Tom, Vrooman purchased Chloe Cooley. He bought her from Benjamin Hardison, 35, a prominent farmer near today's Fort Erie, yet another American among the overwhelming majority of the first settlers along the Niagara frontier. Hardison differed from newcomers like Vrooman and Crysler in a fundamental way, however. He served on the American side in the Revolutionary War and his trek to Upper Canada was far more complicated.[5]

Born in Berwick, Maine, a village on the border with New Hampshire, Hardison joined the rebel cause at about age 16 and fought the British at Boston during 1775 as a private in the regiment of Colonel Edmund Phinney. That same year, he accompanied Major General Ethan Allen, who captured Fort Ticonderoga from the British on his march northward to take Montreal. But in September Allen's troops faltered at the Battle of Longue-Pointe outside the city and Allen was taken prisoner. A second try by the Americans to capture Montreal was successful on November 13, under General Richard Montgomery. Hardison was with Montgomery's men when they subsequently lay siege to Quebec City, but the British successfully defended the well-fortified city as the year ended. Montgomery was killed and more than 400 Americans were captured or killed.

Hardison must have escaped because the following May he was under the command of Major Henry Sherburne, whose troops attempted to relieve an American garrison manning The Cedars, a fort built along the St. Lawrence River west of Montreal. The fort was intended to prevent the British from retaking the city. But the British and their First Nation allies, the Iroquois, overwhelmed the defenders and when Sherburne's men arrived they were among several hundred American troops taken captive, including Hardison. He was held as a prisoner in Quebec, and likely for a time at Fort Niagara, before being released. For reasons unknown, Hardison decided to remain in Upper Canada and took advantage of the offer of free land from his former enemy. He settled in Bertie Township along the Niagara River, about 20 miles south of Niagara Falls. There he built a fine home at Queen and Niagara streets in what would become the village of Waterloo (just north of the Canadian end of today's Peace Bridge) and began buying additional properties.

By the time he sold Chloe Cooley to Adam Vrooman, Hardison had amassed nearly 1,000 acres and was part owner of a mill.[6] Given his extensive landholdings, he likely kept several enslaved people to help him work the land. Hardison became a member of the local militia and a magistrate and in 1796 was elected to the Legislative Council of Upper Canada. Upon his death in 1823, he owned eight farms and bequeathed one to each of his eight children. His decision to live under the British flag had been a profitable one for Hardison.

———

Hardison, Vrooman, and Crysler were not unique in having enslaved persons. An estimated 2,000 enslaved people were brought to Canada after the Revolutionary War, about 700 of them to Upper Canada. Britain extended legal protection for slavery in a bid to encourage settlement of its North American colonies, a policy reaffirmed in 1790 by the Imperial Act, under which settlers could bring enslaved people into the colonies duty-free.[7] A census taken in 1783 found six enslaved people living in Butlersburg/Niagara. They belonged to Sir John Johnson, who undertook the census and owned 14 enslaved people in total. His close friend Matthew Elliott, who lived in the Western District down by Detroit, may have owned as many as 50 or 60, some acquired in border clashes with American troops.[8]

By 1784 about 4,000 Black people were living in Britain's North American colonies, about half of whom were enslaved. During the Revolutionary War, an informal slave trade had been conducted by several loyalist forces, including John Butler's Rangers. Black people were sometimes seized by them as war booty and then sold on the Montreal market. Others were offered freedom if they deserted their American enslavers and some responded by joining units like Butler's.[9] Accounts vary about how many leaders of Upper Canada held enslaved people at the time of the Chloe Cooley episode. But they included members of the Upper Canada House of Assembly, which consisted of an appointed

Executive Council and an elected Legislative Council. In 1793, at least four of the Assembly's 16 members owned enslaved people.[10]

But because of the influence of abolitionists such as William Wilberforce in the British House of Commons, by the late 1700s there was a growing sense in the country and its colonies that the days of slavery were numbered. Upper Canada's John Graves Simcoe was a passionate promoter of abolition and retained that view when he was appointed colonial governor in 1792, cutting short his time as a British Member of Parliament. In the colony there was growing recognition that slavery was becoming unacceptable and it was rife with rumours that legislation to ban the practice was under consideration, especially after the arrival of Simcoe.

Adam Vrooman was among those enslavers who worried any such law would render his "property" worthless. He decided to sell Chloe Cooley and recover some of his investment before it was too late. He found an American buyer who had no such concerns; the State of New York was still six years away from its first steps to curb slavery with its Act for the Gradual Abolition of Slavery.[11] Besides, Cooley had proven to be a handful for him in the few months of her servitude. She hated being subjugated by a white man and was often rebellious. It was said her behaviour was unruly and included stealing property, refusing to work, and running away for brief periods. By March of 1793 Vrooman was doubly motivated to rid himself of her.

No doubt attracted by her screams, people witnessed the rough handling of Cooley on the evening of March 14. Exactly a week later, one of them, Peter Martin, along with Vrooman's hired hand Grisley, travelled about eight miles north to Newark to file a complaint about the incident. Martin, a Black man who had served with Butler's Rangers, and Grisley appeared before Simcoe and his Executive Council at Navy Hall on March 21. Martin described the "violent outrage" committed by Vrooman, whom he'd seen "binding her, and violently and forcibly transporting her across the River, and delivering her against her will to certain persons unknown." Grisley confirmed his story and said he was working for Vrooman that day when he declared his plan to sell his "negro wench to some persons in the States." That evening,

Grisley said he saw her tied with rope and placed in a boat. Vrooman asked Grisley to join the enslaved woman and the men in the boat, but Grisley insisted he would take no active role in handling Cooley. He told Simcoe she was delivered to a man on the American side of the river. He said he understood other owners of enslaved people were planning to do the same and that during the incident he saw a Black man bound in a similar fashion along the Canadian shore.

After hearing the men, the Executive Council resolved "to take immediate steps to prevent the continuance of such violent breaches of the public peace" and proceeded to have Vrooman prosecuted.[12] A charge of disturbing the peace was filed at the Court of Quarter Sessions in Newark, but Vrooman responded with a petition arguing he didn't break any law.[13] He insisted he was acting within his rights and that Cooley had none. The case was dropped, but the colonial governor wasn't prepared to leave the matter there.

Simcoe was growing determined to end slavery, despite opponents who argued that Upper Canada must comply with British law, under which enslaved people had no rights. The disturbing incident along the Niagara River acted as a catalyst for him. It was as though he was tormented by the pitiful screams of Chloe Cooley and determined to ensure such a scene would never be repeated.

The colonial governor would have been familiar with the famous British case *Somerset v. Stewart*, from which he might have drawn some satisfaction and inspiration. Charles Stewart, a customs collector from Boston, had purchased an enslaved man named James Somerset from a Virginia plantation owner and took him along on a business trip to England in 1769. Somerset managed to escape but Stewart found him, put him in chains and incarcerated him on a prison ship. Stewart, it was said, planned to take Somerset to Jamaica and sell him there. Fortunately for Somerset, he had godparents in England who enlisted Granville Sharp, a leading abolitionist, who in turn assembled a team of lawyers to free him. They argued that no law whatsoever authorized slavery in England and that Somerset must be freed.

Stewart's lawyers replied that property rights took precedence over human rights and an enslaved person was merely property. And they warned about the danger of freeing the 15,000 persons then enslaved in England. A decision on the case was rendered in 1772. In his famous ruling from The Court of King's Bench, Lord Mansfield said the practice of slavery is so "odious" that no law could possibly legitimize it. Consequently, he added, "as soon as any slave sets foot upon English territory, he becomes free." As a result, Somerset was immediately freed. Slavery managed to persist in Britain for another 60 years, but the Mansfield decision was a step in the right direction and helped turn public opinion against the practice.

In the American colonies the decision was also noted, particularly in the South. It merely added to the growing hostility toward Britain and pushed even more Patriots to become revolutionaries.[14] But the Somerset decision had no legal effect within Britain's North American colonies.[15]

John Graves Simcoe, the British governor of Upper Canada, was the driving force behind legislation in 1793 that gradually brought an end to slavery in the colony, the first jurisdiction in the British Empire to do so. (PAINTED BY GEORGE THEODORE BERTHON, GOVERNMENT OF ONTARIO ART COLLECTION, ID 694156)

At the direction of Simcoe, John White, the Attorney General of Upper Canada, introduced a bill in the House of Assembly on May 31, 1793, that would abolish slavery on a gradual basis. It received first reading on June 19. White then shepherded it through the Legislative Council where it "met much opposition but little argument," he noted in his diary.[16] At the time, the chamber included slaveholders James Baby of Sandwich (Windsor), Peter Russell of York, and Richard

Cartwright of Kingston. Opposition to the bill also came from merchants who had acquired enslaved people from Indigenous people at low prices and were hoping to turn a profit, and from farmers looking to import enslaved people for another two years.

White and Simcoe were effective advocates for the legislation, however, and within two weeks the bill received unanimous approval and then royal assent on July 9. In approving the legislation on behalf of the king, Simcoe said he was pleased that those men and women now enslaved "may henceforth look forward with certainty to the emancipation of their offspring."[17] The bill did not end slavery or free anyone immediately, so it fell short of what Simcoe really wanted. But it was the result of compromise aimed at gaining acceptance for a ground-breaking measure and it was a good start.[18] Abolition would begin slowly and be completed over a period of years. In its preamble, the cumbersomely worded Act to Prevent Further Introduction of Slaves and to Limit the Term of Contracts Within This Province noted "that it is unjust that a people who enjoy freedom by law should encourage the introduction of slaves; and . . . it is highly expedient to abolish slavery in this province, so far as the same may gradually be done without violating private property . . ."[19]

Known more commonly as the Act to Limit Slavery in Upper Canada, the legislation promised no "Negro or other person who shall come or be brought into this province . . . shall be subject to the condition of a slave or [bound to] involuntary service for life." It did not, however, prevent the sale of enslaved people within the province or across the border to the United States.

Among its provisions were the following:

- slavery would continue for every enslaved person who had previously been lawfully brought into Upper Canada;
- every child born after the passing of the act would be considered free upon reaching the age of 25;
- offspring of those children would be free from birth;
- any enslaver freeing an enslaved person had to provide

security to ensure he or she would not become a burden on the public purse [a clause that may have been a disincentive for some owners];

- no enslaved people could be imported from the United States or other British colonies;
- no voluntary contract for service, or indenture, could have a term exceeding nine years.

It was the first legislation anywhere in the British Empire banning slavery and was susceptible to appeal because it rescinded the Imperial Act. Technically, it is doubtful any legislation enacted by a colony could have legally overridden legislation adopted by the House of Commons, the supreme legislative body in the mother ship of the Empire. But Britain didn't bother to challenge it, perhaps sensing the colony was on the right path.[20] Within a generation slavery disappeared in Upper Canada.

In the colony, Attorney General John White was criticized for his role in pushing through the bill and was not re-elected in 1796. That same year an ailing Simcoe returned to Britain and the colonial capital was relocated from Newark across Lake Ontario to York (later renamed Toronto). Two years later, an attempt was made in a newly elected House of Assembly to pass legislation allowing newcomers to bring enslaved people with them, a backward step. Driving that effort was Christopher Robinson, a loyalist originally from Virginia who represented the Eastern District riding of Addington and Ontario and who himself held enslaved people. But the bill never proceeded to third reading and enactment, so it died quietly. Simcoe's law survived and remained the law of the land in the colony, whose population was approaching 70,000.

———

By 1798, five American states had abolished slavery. Vermont was first, in 1777, followed by Pennsylvania in 1780, Massachusetts in 1781, New Hampshire in 1783 and Connecticut a year later. Maine never allowed slavery. New York's bill to gradually abolish slavery wasn't enacted until 1799 and its provisions were similar to those in Upper Canada.[21]

During these years, a patchwork of legislation emerged with sometimes bizarre consequences. In 1787, the United States passed the Northwest Ordinance, which outlined the process under which new territories were to be added to the growing union. The purpose was to treat all states and territories equally. The ordinance protected civil liberties and outlawed slavery.[22] Because of this legislation, an unforeseen situation developed at the western end of Upper Canada in 1805 when nearby Michigan was incorporated as a territory of the United States. Before then, slavery was discouraged but still continued. As of 1805, however, the practice was formally outlawed, prompting enslaved people in the Western District of Upper Canada to flee across the Detroit and St. Clair rivers to Michigan.

Among them were eight of the estimated 60 enslaved people held by abusive enslaver Matthew Elliott, who had been a member of the Upper Canada House of Assembly for several terms, at his estate south of Windsor at Amherstburg. So many escaped to Detroit, a city surrendered to the Americans in 1796, that a company of militia consisting entirely of enslaved people who had fled Canada was established in 1806 to help defend the newly admitted Michigan Territory.[23] It wouldn't be long before that flow was reversed and enslaved people seeking freedom would follow the North Star to Canada for sanctuary in growing numbers.

Britain abolished slavery throughout its empire on August 1, 1834. The Imperial Act of 1833 freed about 800,000 slaves in 16 colonies and compensated their former enslavers. The landmark British legislation made no mention of Upper Canada whatsoever, reflecting the belief among lawmakers in the House of Commons that the colony had abolished slavery long before.[24] Doubtless, John Graves Simcoe would have smiled at that omission, an affirmation of his pioneering work in Upper Canada. But he had died in 1806.

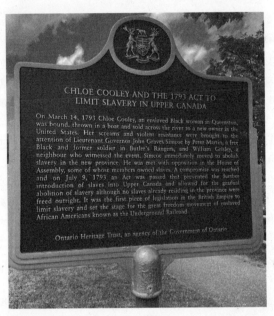

At this spot on a dreary late winter day like this one, enslaved woman Chloe Cooley was forced down the bank of the Niagara River near Queenston by her enslaver and delivered by boat into the hands of a new American owner on the far side. Her screams of protest attracted witnesses and led to the introduction of legislation in Upper Canada to phase out slavery, the first such law in the British Empire. A historic marker, seen near the white car, marks the spot where she struggled with her enslaver and his helpers. (PHOTOS BY CHIP MARTIN)

Simcoe's contribution to bettering the lives of enslaved Black people is well known, imperfect as his compromise legislation may have been. Meanwhile, few Canadians are aware of the young woman whose pitiful screams moved him to act. Chloe Cooley deserves her place in history. A marker alongside the Niagara River where she was forced into a boat so long ago hardly seems adequate.

In 2021, Canada's Parliament declared August 1 Emancipation Day. The gesture recognized Britain's abolishment of slavery in 1834, not the lead Simcoe had taken in Ontario's former colony 13 years before that. But Simcoe continues to be widely revered as an enlightened leader whose surname graces a major lake in central Ontario, the adjacent county, and a large town in the province's southwest, among other places.

By contrast, Chloe Cooley, who inspired him to do the right thing, has only a plaque. But her impact was huge. Within decades of her rough handling along the Niagara River, thousands of freed Black people and freedom seekers from the United States sought refuge in Canada, a nearby attic or safe house, where they were guaranteed their freedom by the British Crown.

CHAPTER TWO

SLAVERY AND FREEDOM IN A BRITISH COLONY

In the 1620s, a Black boy about age five was brought to New France from Africa. British adventurer and mercenary David Kirke acquired the boy in 1628 from an Englishman who found him in Madagascar. (That same year Kirke and his brothers helped capture Tadoussac, a St. Lawrence River settlement northeast of Quebec City. The following year the Kirkes helped take Quebec City.) Kirke sold the boy at a tidy profit to French colonial clerk Olivier Tardif before he returned to England. Three years later, Tardif gave the boy to Guillaume Couillard, a father of 10 who arranged to have the lad and one of Couillard's adopted Indigenous girls taught by Father Paul Le Jeune, the newly arrived Superior of the Jesuit Order for Quebec. When baptized in 1632, the boy adopted the surname of the Jesuit who had provided his rudimentary education and religious training. He took his first name from Tardif. During his baptism as Olivier Le Jeune, the youngster was assured that all men are one when united in Christianity, to which he retorted: "You say that by baptism I shall be like you: I am Black and you are white, I must have my skin taken off then in order to be like you."[1] Paul Le Jeune recorded the unexpectedly insightful comment in his diary. Young Olivier already understood that as an enslaved Black person he differed fundamentally from others in New France. He became the first Black student in Quebec. He died in 1654 at the age of 31, believed by then to have been freed. Upon Le Jeune's death, his occupation was listed as a "domestique," and he was still living with the Couillard family.[2]

———

Olivier Le Jeune wasn't the first enslaved person in the New World and wouldn't be the last. He was simply the best documented of the earliest. A Portuguese explorer apparently held "Indian" enslaved people (likely from India, but possibly Indigenous) when he put ashore in Labrador or Newfoundland as early as 1501. An anonymous Black person died of scurvy in Port Royal in 1606, and an unnamed Black servant was toiling in Acadia in 1608.

By the time of Olivier Le Jeune, France was more enlightened than England when it came to slavery. To the British, enslaved persons were considered personal property. Under Louis XIV, however, attempts were made by France to recognize enslaved people and codify their treatment. Jean-Baptiste Colbert was a powerful figure and influential in trying to grant some rights to enslaved persons. He served as comptroller general of finance, was secretary of state for the navy and charted a course of economic reconstruction that helped France become a dominant power in Europe. Colbert encouraged emigration of enslaved people to New France and authored commercial and criminal legislation. He is responsible for the Code Noir of 1685, which contained 60 articles regulating the life, purchase, marriage, death, punishment, religion, and treatment of the enslaved in all French colonies, including conditions necessary for them to achieve freedom. The Code wasn't particularly praiseworthy, however, because one of its first articles banned Jews from the colonies.[3] Four years later Louis XIV undermined it by allowing the importation of enslaved people into New France in a bid to boost agriculture.

France was constantly at war during this time, and in 1704 Paris decreed that its colonies existed to serve France. It discouraged any competitive industry, commerce, or population growth in them that could come at the expense of the mother country. This policy effectively forced New France to return to the fur trade, which was in decline, thereby curtailing the need for enslaved labour, although some remained on farms that served local needs.[4]

Slavery was generally accepted, and by 1760 around 1,100 Black people lived in New France, mainly in the Montreal area. Most served as farmhands or as household servants, but it's unknown how many were free and how many were not.[5] Some of the enslaved were not Black at all, but were actually First Nations people who were called *panis* ("slaves"). Unlike Britain, which had ready access to enslaved people in the West Indies and brought them to its American colonies to toil on vast plantations in the South, France had no such ready access to Black people, perhaps explaining the use of the word *panis*.

———

With the British conquest of New France, recognized by the 1763 Treaty of Paris, the practice of slavery acquired a new life. Following the War of Independence, some loyalists came north with the people they enslaved, boosting the Black population. The first Americans to seek refuge under the Union Jack were those anxious to remain loyal to the British Crown. Known as United Empire Loyalists, they were soldiers, enslaved people, clerks, farmers, craftsmen, labourers, clergymen, and lawyers. They may have been motivated by their persecution as "Tories" by their neighbours, by fear of change, by emotional bonds or simply out of self-interest. Generally, loyalists distrusted too much democracy, which they felt led to mob rule and a breakdown of law and order. Those who remained in the Thirteen Colonies were branded as traitors by their neighbours, who called themselves Patriots. Any loyalists who spoke out could see property and goods stripped from them and face banishment. Under Patriot control of government, loyalists were not allowed to vote, sell land, sue debtors, or hold jobs as teachers, lawyers, or doctors.[6] When their persecution became intolerable, many loyalists eventually joined those who had already fled to Britain's neighbouring colonies.

During the war, the British had actively encouraged the enslaved to escape from their American enslavers with the promise of freedom under the Crown. Those who jumped to the British side were put to work as labourers, boatmen, woodsmen, buglers, and musicians. Sir Guy Carleton, commander of all British troops in North America, helped relocate Black people to the British West Indies as well as to Britain's northern colonies. Some of them decided to exercise their newfound freedom by fighting for the king. One corps of soldiers, the Black Pioneers, consisted entirely of Black people who had gained their freedom. Most of the enslaved brought into Britain's North American colonies were domestic servants. Owning enslaved people was a sign of wealth and success but were not essential to the northern economy, as they had become in the southern United States.[7]

By 1784, following the American Revolution, the number of Black people living in British North America stood at 4,000. About half were enslaved. Then came the Imperial Act of 1790 and its duty-free provisions for the enslaved, a bid to boost settlement. In 1793, the United States Congress bowed to pressure from southern states and enacted the first Fugitive Slave Act. Southern states were angry at losing enslaved labour to the free states of the North, a situation that pitted states against each other. The new act authorized enslavers and their agents to pursue freedom seekers in northern states with penalties of $500 for anyone harbouring or concealing escapees.[8] Most northern states neglected to enforce the law, but lingering fear that the situation might change at any time became an incentive for some of the formerly enslaved to forsake "safe" states for Britain's nearby colonies.

Unlike south of the border, where most enslaved people toiled on labour-intensive plantations, by the early 1800s Black persons in British North America, both free and enslaved, could be found in trades, employed as blacksmiths, carpenters, millwrights, caulkers, coopers, apprentice printers and acting as waiters.[9] The colonial government accepted them as citizens, regardless of whether they had been born free, had been granted freedom, or had escaped slavery. Black people could own land, on which they paid taxes, they could vote and they were encouraged to join the militia. When the War of 1812 erupted between the United States and Britain, Upper Canada in particular was thinly settled, and Britain was unable to mount a strong defence militarily. The militia was called upon to help defend the borders.

By then, most Black men old enough to fight had been freed under Upper Canada's slavery-ending bill of 1793. They and newer arrivals helped defend not only their homes but a country that had treated them well. Some of the American fighters were surprised to face armed Black fighters on the British side and stories about them found their way back home to the States. In Niagara, the "Coloured Corps" was established to help defend the border and ensure that the British prevailed in the battles of Queenston Heights and Stoney Creek. When hostilities ceased and the Americans gave up their bid to capture Britain's colonies, many skilled Black craftsmen served at heavily damaged Fort George until they were discharged in 1815.[10] Two-thirds of the Coloured Corps were rewarded with land grants in Oro Township, near Lake Simcoe, and elsewhere.

Following the war, Britain inched its way slowly toward abolishing slavery because of growing public distaste for the practice. In 1807 it passed the Act on the Abolition of the Slave Trade in the British Empire, which banned "all manner of dealing and reading in the purchase, sale, barter, or transfer of slaves or of persons intending to be sold, transferred, used or dealt with as slaves, practised or carried in, at, or from any part of the coast or countries of Africa." It also applied to Black people originating from the Caribbean and America. Ships found violating the act could be seized and condemned while enslavers were liable to fines of 100 pounds sterling for each person enslaved or intended to be. Africans liberated from such ships were not freed, however. They were enlisted in the British Army, Navy, or Royal Marines for unlimited service, as though they had done so voluntarily. Women and children were apprenticed to landowners and to the military and local government as labourers and domestics.[11] Britain reached a treaty with Spain in 1817 to expand the law's reach, and later with Portugal and the Netherlands. By the 1860s, diplomatic pressure and anti-slavery patrols along the western coast of Africa finally ended the cross-Atlantic slave trade. But the legislation of 1807 did nothing to free enslaved people within Britain itself. The United States passed its own act to ban the importation of enslaved people in 1808, although the trade of the enslaved continued among American ports along the Atlantic Ocean. This legislation imposed heavy fines on international traders but there was no impact on the domestic slave trade.[12]

———

By the early 1800s, freedom seekers sought refuge in Upper Canada in growing numbers and they tended to cluster just over the border, the bulk of them in the western part of the colony. Generally, they had no funds to travel farther into the interior of the colony and besides, if the situation changed dramatically back home and they wanted to return, they wouldn't have as far to retrace their steps. They settled primarily on fertile lands similar to those they'd left behind. Formerly enslaved people settled in the Niagara area including Ridgemount (which became known as Little Africa), Bertie Hill, Snake Hill, St. Catharines, and Welland, and across from Detroit at Sandwich, Windsor, Amherstburg, and Colchester. Those who ventured farther inland were found in clusters at Dresden, Chatham, London, and Woolwich. Among the early settlements, Amherstburg, along the Detroit River south of Sandwich, was particularly successful for Black migrants initially. Freedom seekers from Virginia teamed up with a white man from Kentucky to establish a flourishing tobacco operation there in 1819. Within two years they were exporting high-quality product to Montreal. Yields of 2,000 pounds of tobacco per acre were recorded. But by 1827 the market was glutted and a drop in quality caused prices to tumble, and local white farmers moved in to take over as Black farmers focused their efforts on traditional crops. That same year, nearly 600 Black people lived in the Amherstburg and Colchester areas. Sandwich, lying directly opposite Detroit, was also attracting a good number of new arrivals, boosted by an 1833 race riot in Detroit.[13] Missions were established for them in Sandwich, Malden Township, and Toronto, among other centres.

Free Black people made their way to southern Ontario, often along the Underground Railroad, a network of anti-slavery activists stretching across several states. Many newcomers established all-Black communities in Oro, Wilberforce, Dresden, and Buxton, while others settled in existing communities like Sandwich (Windsor), Amherstburg, Colchester, Chatham, London, Hamilton, St. Catharines, Niagara, and Toronto. (MAP BY CHIP MARTIN)

Perhaps fittingly, the first organized settlement specifically for Black people was established in Simcoe County, which took its name from the colonial governor who'd enacted the first anti-slavery legislation in the British Empire. The government of Upper Canada was behind the settlement in Oro Township, northeast of present-day Barrie and near the western shore of Lake Simcoe. Beginning in 1819, Black people were provided free 100-acre grants of land by the colonial government. Many of the first settlers were from the Coloured Corps that served in Niagara during the War of 1812. The area became known as the Oro Settlement and it grew slowly, reaching a population of only 100 by 1831 when white people were allowed to settle there as well. By 1825, rules had been changed to restrict free land grants only to loyalists and to Black people with military service, while others had to purchase the land. By 1831 many of the earlier Black settlers had left, discouraged by land that was of poor quality compared to more fertile regions to the south. The influx of white settlers, however, drove up land prices and many of the Black settlers who still remained sold their lands and moved away. (By 1900, the Oro Settlement had virtually disappeared.[14] The colony's first bid to encourage a permanent Black agriculture-based settlement had failed.)

In 1829, another Black settlement was founded on the site of today's village of Lucan, 17 miles north of London and far to the southwest of Oro. The Wilberforce Settlement, named after leading British abolitionist and politician William Wilberforce, differed significantly from Oro, however. It was established by Black people themselves, the first attempt of its kind in Upper Canada.

The roots of Wilberforce lay 400 miles away in Cincinnati, Ohio. Cincinnati lies on the Ohio River, which by 1787 had become the border between pro-slavery and free states. If southern enslaved people could make it to the north side of the river at Cincinnati they'd be free, although Ohio's government nominally supported the Fugitive Slave Act of 1793. Possible apprehension under that legislation remained a constant worry for the runaways. The state passed similar legislation in 1803 and went even further in 1804 with the enactment of the Black Codes, even though Ohio had abolished slavery itself in 1802. Aside from making it even easier for enslavers to recapture the enslaved, the codes required Black travellers to produce papers, if challenged, proving they were free men and women and not escapees. Any Black person entering the state after 1807, the year the Black Law was enacted, had to provide a $500 bond guaranteeing they were solvent and economically self-sufficient so they wouldn't become a burden on local governments. The documents were to be signed by local court clerks who affixed official seals, making them impossible to forge.[15] And no employer could hire Black workers unless they had certificates showing they were legal residents of the state. Life was becoming difficult for Black inhabitants of Ohio.

Some members of the Black community may have heard about Upper Canada having abolished slavery, perhaps from returning soldiers and Black people who accompanied them during the War of 1812 and told of facing armed Black British militiamen. Black people were coming to the conclusion that life in Michigan, Pennsylvania, or New York wouldn't be much different than Ohio because of the reach of the federal fugitive slave legislation, even though those states professed to be free. Further laws were enacted in Ohio that curtailed the civil rights of the Black population. No Black or mulatto person was allowed to give sworn evidence in any court case if the opposing party was white, for instance.

Hostility toward Black people increased in Cincinnati during the ensuing years and violence flared as the Black population rose from 200 in 1815 to nearly 3,000 by 1829, accounting for nearly 10 percent of the city population.[16] The newcomers found inexpensive quarters, often near the riverfront, upsetting neighbouring merchants who feared their presence would hurt business. And the arrivals competed for low-level, unskilled jobs, antagonizing unskilled white residents with whom they competed. At one point, as discrimination against the Black community grew, the local newspaper *Liberty Hall* complained: "The rapid increase of our black population, to say nothing of slavery itself, is of itself a great evil."[17] Politicians responded by rigidly enforcing the Black Law of 1807, which failed to distinguish between vagrants and industrious Black people, or between freedom seekers and those formerly enslaved. City leaders sought to prevent further immigration into Cincinnati. In the civic election in the spring of 1829 hard-line politicians prevailed, sending a chill through the Black community, whose members had already begun to consider emigrating to escape an increasingly hostile environment. On June 30, 1829, the *Cincinnati Daily Gazette* printed a worrisome official notice that all Black residents must enter bonds as required under the 1807 act and do so within 30 days or face expulsion from the city.

This was seen by the Black community as a significant threat of mob violence. That same month it delegated two men to explore options for emigration, one of them being to Upper Canada. Black leader James Charles Brown appealed to the city to delay by three months any plans for stepped-up enforcement. In the same newspaper, he sought to calm white readers and buy time for his people, saying plans were underway for local members of the Black community to migrate to Upper Canada.[18] Two members of Cincinnati's Black community, Israel Lewis and Thomas Crissup, had already been dispatched to the colonial capital at York to discuss plans for a Black settlement in Upper Canada. They received a warm welcome from Sir John Colborne, the new Lieutenant Governor of the colony. "Tell the Republicans on your side of the line that we Royalists do not know men by their colour," Colborne reportedly assured them. "Should you come to us, you will be entitled to all the privileges of the rest of His Majesty's subjects."[19]

Cincinnatians were in no mood to wait. Beginning August 15, 1829, white mobs attacked Black people where they lived, burned their homes, destroyed their businesses, and assaulted residents. Most of the rioters were white and working-class, but men of greater means supported them. As many as 300 white men continued their rampage every night until August 22, and while police failed to act initially, they arrested white and Black alike as the violence continued.[20]

The Cincinnati riots forced organizers to act hastily. Following the week of violence, anywhere from 1,100 to 1,500 Black people fled the city for various destinations, among them a small group heading for Canada.[21] A few hundred of them made their way to Lake Erie and crossed by boat to Upper Canada, arriving at Port Stanley, midway along the northern shore. They discovered the colony was heavily forested and that Wilberforce lay another 40 miles to the north along a primitive road. Many of the new arrivals, tired from the journey, opted instead to travel southwest to an established community in Colchester Township, where they would encounter a rather chilly reception. A small group of determined families continued north to Wilberforce, however, arriving in October, and immediately set about clearing land so they could plant crops the following spring. It was a start, but the settlement never grew much beyond a population of 200, although as many as 800 of them would eventually settle in the general area.[22] Swelling their numbers somewhat were free Black people from Boston, Rochester, Albany, and Baltimore. Once assured racial tensions had eased back in Cincinnati, however, some of the original settlers returned home.

By 1836 it was clear that Wilberforce was failing. The inhabitants had little background in agriculture and struggled to make a living from their rather small plots, despite the fertile soil. And they had no hunting skills to help them feed their families. Two schools had been established to provide good basic education because that was seen as the key to success in the new land. Two churches had been established although only the Baptists erected a building. There was also a gristmill and stores and solid homes constructed of logs. But leadership of the small settlement was weak.

It came in the form of Austin Steward, born into slavery in Virginia, who had escaped and moved to Rochester, New York, where he became a successful grocer. In Rochester, he was approached for funds to help the settlement in Biddulph Township, which he found impressive.

Steward decided to move to Wilberforce with his family in 1830, joining the 50 Black people already settled in. Steward was responsible for establishing a board of managers to run the colony and he was appointed its president. But he soon clashed openly with Israel Lewis, one of the founders. Money was still owing to the Canada Company, which aided immigrants as part of its land-development mission, and additional funds were needed for other purposes such as a planned college or seminary. So two emissaries were sent on fund-raising missions, founder Lewis and Nathaniel Paul. Lewis canvassed northern states for nearly a decade but refused to turn over any money he raised to the settlement. He was accused of embezzling the funds that he raised to support a lavish lifestyle, and was let go and taken to court. Lewis battled not only Steward but the Canada Company over money owing for land. For his part, Paul travelled to England to tout Wilberforce and raise funds, aligning himself with the British abolitionist movement and lecturing about the plight of Black people in the United States. He spent four years overseas but when he returned it was discovered he'd spent the $8,000 he'd raised. He too was let go. Not considered dishonest like Lewis, Paul was simply poor at handling money. Both men failed to live up to expectations placed on them, and the Wilberforce settlers were infuriated.[23]

The damage the disputes caused to the reputation of the settlement prompted the Quakers and others to withdraw their financial

A mural on a downtown wall in Lucan, just north of London, recalls the Wilberforce Settlement. Black people from the Cincinnati area established the colony, which failed to thrive for want of necessary farming and other skills. The settlement suffered from poor leadership and there is little trace of it left today. Among those descended from the Wilberforce pioneers was Peter Butler III, whose likeness is featured in the mural, which was unveiled in 2020. He became the first Black police officer in Canada. Mural artist is Andrew Gillet of London. (PHOTO BY CHIP MARTIN)

The mural saluting Wilberforce in today's Lucan includes an excerpt from the memorable welcoming quote from Upper Canada Governor Sir John Colborne, directed to Black people: "We do not know people by their colour . . . come to us [and] you will be entitled to all the privileges of the rest . . ." (PHOTO BY CHIP MARTIN)

support.[24] And, soured by their dealings with the dishonest Lewis, the Canada Company decided it would no longer sell land to Black settlers, a fatal blow to the colony that prevented any further growth. A disillusioned Steward and his family gave up on Wilberforce and in 1837 returned to Rochester, where he later wrote about his seven-year experience and the financial toll on him.[25]

Irish settlers began arriving in significant numbers by the 1840s and more than took up the slack in Biddulph Township. They were anxious for land and to displace those who had preceded them. Feeling elbowed out, many Black people sold to the Irish and relocated southwest to the Chatham and Amherstburg areas. The Wilberforce experiment was noble in origin and enjoyed some success, but it was plagued from the start by the unexpected rush to establish it, too few participants to create a critical mass of settlers, the immigrants' lack of important skills, loss of support from the Canada Company and the shortcomings of its leadership.

———

Meanwhile, a secret network of Americans determined to abolish slavery was helping freedom seekers escape to northern states and to Canada in growing numbers. The abolitionists were originally based in Philadelphia, many of them Quakers, but their network soon spread and they became highly organized. By the late 1830s, their network had become known as the Underground Railroad.[26] It was the largest anti-slavery operation in North America, helping an estimated 30,000 to 40,000 Black freedom seekers follow the North Star to reach British North America, which many called Canaan, the promised land.

The organization was both clandestine and efficient, linking abolitionists and safe houses from southern states such as Maryland, Virginia, and Kentucky to northern states and into Canada. The abolitionists and their sympathizers included free and enslaved Black, white, and First Nations people. The Quakers were joined by Baptists, Methodists, urban dwellers, farmers, and men and women on both sides of the border. Rail terminology was used throughout the operation. Escapees were known as "passengers," "cargo," "package," and "freight" stealthily delivered to "stations" or "depots." Stations located in cities and towns were known as "terminals." The network operated mainly at night, with rest time during the day. These refuges were sometimes identified by lit candles in their windows, strips of cloth, or lanterns out front. Safe houses were operated by "station masters" who provided meals, a change of clothes and sometimes money, but primarily sanctuary. Persons who helped freedom seekers following routes known as "lines" were called "conductors," while "ticket agents" helped runaways by connecting them with station masters or conductors. Finally, those who contributed funds to help the enslaved escape were known as "stockholders."[27]

Major points of entry to Upper Canada included the ferry dock at the village of Waterloo, at the north end of today's Fort Erie, lying directly across from Black Rock, near Buffalo. Upon arrival, families who had escaped along the Niagara Freedom Trail were provided accommodation at Bertie Hall until sympathizers could help them find jobs and permanent places to live. At Lewiston, seven miles north of Niagara Falls, many citizens hid freedom seekers in their basements before helping them cross the river to Queenston and freedom. One riverfront home, owned by Amos Tryon, had a multi-level basement with interconnecting rooms ideal for providing refuge for the enslaved and their families as they awaited taking the last leg of their trip across the river to Canada at what was dubbed "Freedom Crossing."[28]

At the far western end of the colony, the crossing from Detroit to Windsor and adjacent Sandwich Township was a busy one. There were at least seven known lines of the Underground Railroad in Michigan that brought freedom seekers to Detroit. In all, it was believed there were about 200 stops on the railroad across the state. Once refugees reached Detroit, there was no shortage of abolitionists willing to help them with safe shelter and crossing the Detroit River. One important conductor was Seymour Finney, owner of the Finney Hotel, who provided accommodation for weary travellers while they waited. Dr. Nathan Thomas, founder of the Michigan Republican Party and a Quaker, helped from 1,000 to 1,500 freedom-seekers at his office and home. Another Detroiter, George de Baptiste, was born a free Black man in Virginia but had relocated to Detroit, where he became a respected businessman and owner of a bakery and barbershop. A devout abolitionist, he purchased a steamship to secretly carry runaways across the mile-wide river. His church, Second Baptist, founded in 1836 as the state's first Black congregation, became an important oasis as a last stop on the Underground Railroad and assisted about 5,000 enslaved people over the course of 30 years.[29]

———

The mild climate of Essex County was appealing to freedom seekers and few ventured very far from the border, establishing Black communities in Malden, Anderdon, Colchester, Gosfield, and Maidstone townships as well as in Sandwich Township, farther north near Windsor. Some opted to remain in towns but most settled on farms, some venturing east to Kent County and Chatham as time passed. The first Black to own land in Essex County was James Robertson, a veteran of Butler's Rangers, granted a lot in Colchester Township in 1787.[30] By 1840 Black people were a growing presence across the colony and some white settlers who had welcomed them began to grow wary that even greater numbers would arrive and be unable to find work, requiring possible government assistance.[31] Britain's anti-slavery legislation of 1834 further enhanced the flow of freedom seekers from the United States generally and Underground Railroad "traffic" increased.

Black men were encouraged to join local militias and were called upon by the colonial government to help suppress the rebellions of 1837–38, which were led by reformers seeking greater democracy and an end to the ironclad grip on colonial affairs held by the elite Family Compact. Like many white people, they were alarmed at the rise of republican notions seeping into Upper Canada from south of the border, where slavery was still tolerated.

One member of the militia was Josiah Henson, born into slavery in Maryland, who found freedom in Upper Canada in 1830 and established a Black settlement in Dawn Township, north of Chatham. "The coloured men," Henson said, "were willing to defend the government that had given them a home when they had fled from slavery."[32] Henson was a captain in the Second Company of Essex Volunteers, which helped defend Fort Malden at Amherstburg for six months ending in May of 1838. In one of his memoirs, Henson said that in January 1838 he helped capture the schooner *Anne*, a ship that supplied the rebelling colonists.[33]

At the other end of the colony, Black men fought alongside British troops early in 1838 as they bombarded Navy Island, Canadian territory three miles above Niagara Falls. Rebel and newspaper editor William Lyon Mackenzie and about 300 to 400 followers, many of them unemployed Americans, had taken refuge there as the 1837 rebellion fell apart. MacKenzie, who had fled his home in Toronto, proclaimed himself leader of the New Republic of Canada, with Navy Island its capital. Weapons and money had been provided him from sympathizers in nearby Buffalo and from Hunter's Lodges, secretive American societies near the border that hoped to overthrow the Crown and convert Upper and Lower Canada to republican government.

British troops and their supporting militia, 2,500 men in all, assembled at Chippawa Creek opposite the island. Under cover of darkness, a company of men left the British position in seven boats, rowed across the river, and captured the steamer *Caroline*, then docked on the American shore near the island. The American vessel was being used to ferry men and supplies to Navy Island. The raiders overpowered the men who rushed to face them, then untied the *Caroline* and set her on fire. They watched as she drifted downriver toward Niagara Falls, but the vessel grounded on rocks before she could plunge over.[34] The subsequent bombardment of the rebel-held island forced Mackenzie and his men to forsake it for nearby Grand Island, in American territory. There, he became a headache for the United States government, which was trying to develop good relations with the neighbouring British colonies.[35] Years later, Sir Francis Bond Head, governor of Upper Canada during the rebellion of 1837, praised the contribution of Black men to the assault on Navy Island, writing:

> When our coloured population were informed that American citizens, sympathizing with their sufferings, had taken violent possession of Navy Island, for the double object of liberating them from the domination of British rule, and of imparting to them the blessings of republican institutions, based upon the principle that all men are born equal, did our coloured brethren hail their approach? No, on the contrary, they hastened as volunteers by wagonloads to the Niagara frontier to beg from me permission that . . . they might be allowed to be foremost to defend the glorious institutions of Great Britain.[36]

Black settlers, both free and formerly enslaved, found many ways to contribute to their new homeland. Their willingness to join the militia to help defend it must have come as a shock to the Americans who played the freedom card in a bid to woo or at least neutralize them. But memories of what lay south of the border remained strong and they weren't about to be fooled by anyone.

They knew precisely what they had escaped and why, and were grateful for their freedom in America's attic. They were free, not just from servitude, but to experiment with radical ideas such as living in their own communities or alongside white people, and getting their children educated. For them, it was an entirely new world.

CHAPTER THREE

LIFE IN A SAFE HARBOUR

Among the freedom seekers who swelled the population of Chatham was the formerly enslaved Tom Elice (likely Ellis), who in 1854 penned a touching letter to a special friend named Mary Warner somewhere in the South.

Dated July 9 in "Chatum," it reads in part:

> I hav saw the moste of the folks from our parte of the Cuntry and I think it is one of the best country I eve wos in thare is lots of colord people hear and a coming every day more or les O Dear Mary how I should like to see you I would giv all of the world to see you and I would com but I cant be a slave agane tell my master that I should like to see him and mistress and all the reste of the folks but give me my liberty before all the world give my beste respects to all inquirrings freinds but giv my lov all to your self wright to me to Windsor C. West and let me no how all the folks are agitting along I remain your truly til Death so may god bles you Dearist . . .[1]

The affection for Mary and his old friends (even his former enslaver) shines through, as does the writer's happiness with his new situation and determination to never again be enslaved.

In the decades before the Civil War, Canada had become a safe harbour, a place where the formerly enslaved and abolitionists experimented with radical new ideas such as segregation and integration. Black people were free to live as they chose — among themselves, or in existing white communities. Estimates vary widely on how many fled to Canada and remained. By 1850, for instance, estimates placed the number living in Canada West (formerly Upper Canada) alone at nearly 8,000. Some were free, while others had been enslaved.

At the time, the best known of all freedom seekers on both sides of the border was Josiah Henson, born on a Maryland plantation in 1789. A Methodist preacher and eloquent speaker, he inspired Black people to escape to Canada after establishing an educational institution and a Black community in Dawn Township, near the southwestern community of Dresden. His memoirs, published in 1849, became the inspiration for a book called *Uncle Tom's Cabin*, an anti-slavery story that became the best-selling novel of the century for author Harriet Beecher Stowe.[2]

———

Henson had been owned by a succession of men and suffered a broken arm and two broken shoulders when beaten by a white man, injuries that left him maimed for life. At age 18, he heard his first sermon in Kentucky and was so moved he became a Christian and a Methodist preacher. In 1829 he tried to buy his freedom, but his owner betrayed him and instead arranged to sell him to a new owner in New Orleans. On the trip south, his old enslaver's son took ill, so he and Henson returned to Kentucky. Soon afterward, Henson gathered his wife and four children and made a break for freedom north of the border, travelling to Cincinnati and then walking northeast nearly 450 miles to Buffalo. There, the Hensons took the ferry from Black Rock across the Niagara River to the dock at the tiny village of Waterloo, later renamed Fort Erie.

Arriving on British soil on October 28, 1830, Henson promptly threw himself on the ground "giving way to the riotous exultation of my feelings, to execute sundry antics which excited the astonishment of those who were looking on."[3] Among the bystanders was Colonel John Warren, head of the local militia and operator of the ferry service, who inquired if Henson was having some sort of "fit." In response, the jubilant new arrival "jumped up and told him *I was free.*" Henson then hugged and kissed his wife and children "with a vivacity that made them laugh as well as myself."

Henson found a job with Pennsylvania-born farmer Charles Hibbard, whose large farm was located about six miles west at Ridgemount. Hibbard had several buildings on his Bertie Township property and provided accommodation for his new employee and his

Once Black people crossed the Niagara River from New York, they were welcomed at Bertie Hall, just to the north of the ferry crossing in what is now Fort Erie. Here they were provided food, clothing, and accommodation until they could find work in the area or move on. (PHOTOS BY CHIP MARTIN)

family in a modest shack. The Hensons remained there for three years, during which time Hibbard provided some basic schooling for Tom, Henson's oldest son, while the local schoolmaster provided additional instruction "so that my boy learned to read fluently and well."

Henson himself had never been educated and had memorized Bible verses and chapters he had heard so he could repeat them during his sermons and Bible "readings." He hid this deficiency so well that his 12-year-old son was astounded to discover his father could neither read nor write. "Why, father, *I'll teach you*," the youngster said, as Henson recalled later. "I can do it, I know. And then you'll know so much more that you can talk better and preach better." Henson's son was so earnest there was no resisting him. In about 1833, the family moved a few miles away to a farm owned by a man named Riseley, where Henson began reflecting on his life and what he hoped to accomplish in the new land.

"I was not the only one who had escaped from the States and had settled on the first spot in Canada which they had reached," he recalled years later. There were several hundred fellow Black people who worked for farmers in the area, but few seemed willing to become independent landowners. His new employer permitted Henson to hold meetings at his farmhouse to discuss the future with his fellow runaways, and all agreed the time had come to begin buying land for themselves. "It was precisely the Yankee spirit which I wished to instill into my fellow-slaves, if possible . . . ," Henson recalled in his first autobiography.[4]

He was assigned the task of finding a suitable location for a settlement that could help the formerly enslaved become masters of their own destiny. On foot, Henson scoured the fertile region to the west, lying between Lake Erie and Lake Huron, eventually finding a promising opportunity in Colchester at the westerly end of Lake Erie. An extensive tract of land had been cleared there, but the farmer had failed to live up to certain obligations needed to obtain clear title from the government. In 1836, the farmer agreed to rent land to Henson and about a dozen other families. Not long afterward, Henson realized that paying rent to someone who did not legally own the land was unwise. He appealed to the colonial legislature to challenge the rents that he and his fellow settlers were paying; the legislature was sympathetic and waived their rent. Meanwhile, cultivation of wheat and tobacco was underway.

Henson and the others remained at Colchester for about six years despite a cloud over their heads, knowing their situation could change at any time under a new landowner. During their time in Colchester they failed to expand much beyond the production of tobacco because it attracted such high prices, but the market became glutted and financial returns failed to live up to expectations. Henson had hoped they would diversify into other crops that could be grown on the fertile land.

While at Colchester, Henson met Reverend Hiram Wilson, a Congregationalist missionary from Massachusetts who'd been sent to minister to the Canadian Black population by the American Anti-Slavery Society. The two men bonded and Wilson, a white man, became a supporter of the local Black community and of Henson.

Wilson was able to attract financial support from a philanthropic friend, James Cannings Fuller, a Quaker living in Skaneateles, New York. Henson and Wilson formulated a plan to establish a community for Black people in Dawn Township, helped by funds from Fuller, friends of Wilson in Ohio, and Unitarians in Boston.[5] Two hundred acres were purchased for the new community, which was to be centred on the British-American Institute, a school for children of all ages, providing them a general and manual education as well as courses to train teachers. Black pupils were being excluded from some schools in the colony and Henson wanted to address that worrisome and growing trend by strongly emphasizing education. He purchased another 200 acres alongside the Institute and moved his family there in 1842, the same year the school opened.

Henson never led the community in any official capacity, but sat on the executive committee and became the public face for Dawn on his speaking tours in New England, New York, the Midwest, and Britain, and acted as a spokesperson for the Black community in Canada. Wilson served as administrator for the first five years, dealing with day-to-day operations while Henson travelled and raised money. Henson was the spiritual and symbolic leader of the Dawn Settlement, which expanded to include farms, a sawmill, a gristmill, a brick-yard, a horse-breeding operation, and a community church where he preached. At its peak, the school reached an enrolment of 50.

Maryland-born Josiah Henson escaped from slavery and found his way to Ontario, where he helped establish the Dawn Settlement at Dresden. His life story was the basis of the popular book by Harriet Beecher Stowe, Uncle Tom's Cabin. *He is buried in Dresden, not far from his storied cabin.* (LIBRARY OF CONGRESS)

Settlers at Dawn grew wheat, corn, and tobacco and exported locally grown black walnut lumber to the United States and England. The walnut was of such high quality that in 1851 it won a medal at the Great Exhibition held at the Crystal Palace in London, England. Eventually, about 500 Black people lived at Dawn, which became an important destination on the Underground Railroad.[6] Meanwhile, Henson personally returned to the United States and led 118 enslaved people to freedom.

Henson also travelled to Boston, where he was invited to preach, and met Samuel Atkins Eliot, a leading abolitionist, former mayor of Boston and a Massachusetts state legislator. Eliot was so impressed by Henson and his work that he offered to produce a memoir that Henson could dictate to him. Their collaboration worked well and in 1849, a Boston publisher released *The Life of Josiah Henson, Formerly a Slave, Now an Inhabitant of Canada, as Narrated by Himself.*

Henson's book sold well among abolitionists in the northern states, one of them Harriet Beecher Stowe, who was planning to write a novel critical of slavery. It is believed she met Henson in Boston during one of his visits.[7] Stowe's work first appeared in 1851 as 41 instalments in a Washington-based anti-slavery paper. It was so popular with readers that it became a book, *Uncle Tom's Cabin*, published by John P. Jewett and Company the following year, quickly becoming a bestseller. The book also sold well in Canada, where for many years it was required reading in schools.

Stowe tells the story of two enslaved men of a Kentucky plantation owner who is in arrears and decides to sell them. One of them, a boy named Harry, flees with his mother north to Canada. The other, Uncle Tom, is taken down the Mississippi River to Louisiana where he is sold to a vicious plantation owner. There, Tom encourages two women to escape to Canada. Refusing to reveal where they have gone, he is beaten to death. His former enslaver's son tried to purchase Tom back but arrived too late to do so. Back in Kentucky, the son is disconsolate and decides to free all his late father's enslaved people, encouraging them to remember Tom's sacrifice whenever they see his old cabin. The novel generated significant backlash, especially in the South, where it was dismissed as Northern propaganda. Stowe admitted freely that she wrote her book "to awaken sympathy and feeling for the African race." In that respect she succeeded spectacularly well, adding significant fuel to the fire in the bellies of the growing number of abolitionists in her country.

Stowe fought back against her critics, two years later releasing a large annotated bibliography of the sources upon which she said she relied for *Uncle Tom's Cabin*. This was an odd response to criticism of what was considered a novel, rather than a work of non-fiction. But she felt strongly about her work and was angered it had been dismissed unfairly by some readers. Her rebuttal was cumbersomely titled *The Key to Uncle Tom's Cabin: Presenting the Original Facts and Documents Upon Which the Story Is Founded, Together With Corroborative Statements Verifying the Truth of the Work*. In it, she insisted there were several models for Uncle Tom. "The character of Uncle Tom has been objected to as improbable; and yet the writer has received more confirmations of that character, and from a greater variety of sources, than of any other in the book," she asserted in a chapter devoted exclusively to him. Stowe discusses several of them and on page 42 concedes: "A last instance parallel with that of Uncle Tom is to be found in the published memoirs of the venerable Josiah Henson . . ."[8]

While there were some similarities between Stowe's Uncle Tom and Henson, the Canadian preacher was still very much alive and accepted the recognition accorded him, although he never explicitly claimed he *was* Tom.

———

In 1849, two years before *Uncle Tom's Cabin* appeared, white Presbyterian minister and abolitionist William King established a fourth communal settlement in Raleigh Township, southwest of Chatham. It was better planned, executed more carefully, and led more effectively than Oro, Wilberforce, and Dawn, becoming home to about 1,000 Black people in its heyday. But King's settlement would be the last such organized and segregated community. Descendants of the original settlers still reside in the area today, and several structures from the community can be found in the national historic site established at North Buxton.

In 1841, Irish-born William King had married Mary Phares, the daughter of an owner of a large plantation north of Baton Rouge, and upon her sudden death he inherited 15 enslaved people, estimated to be worth $9,000. But King disliked slavery and placed them on a neighbouring plantation where they would be paid for their services. Not long afterward, he was sent to Canada West as a missionary for the Free Church of Scotland.

King's conscience bothered him about being a slave holder and he came up with a plan to bring his enslaved people north, which would automatically free them. He believed they would need support to adapt to the British colony, so he made them the nucleus of a community he'd establish strictly for Black people. He incorporated the non-sectarian Elgin Settlement Association "for the settlement and moral improvement of the colored population of Canada, for the purpose of purchasing Crown or clergy reserve lands in the township of Raleigh and settling the same with colored families resident in Canada of approved moral character."[9]

A stock company was established to buy land and act as legal agent for the community. The Elgin Association was directed by 24 well-known and capable businessmen and 126 stockholders, who agreed the company would cease to exist when all the land it purchased was occupied by settlers. A school would be established but it would not teach trades, King believing such skills could be acquired readily on-site at the settlement's gristmill, sawmills, blacksmith, cobbler, and carpentry shops. Instead, it focused on literacy training. Settlers were required to become British subjects to counter any suggestion they were merely transients likely to return to the United States when conditions improved.[10]

When Kent County neighbours learned of King's plans for a Black community in their midst, political and public opposition grew. A public meeting was held in the county town of Chatham in August 1849 that passed a resolution condemning the proposed settlement. A ban was called for on the sale of land "to foreigners, the more so when such persons belong to a different branch of the human family and are black."[11] A "vigilance committee" was established to monitor developments and seek funds for the fight from area townships. Chief among the opponents was British-born Edwin Larwill, the outspoken Member of Parliament for Kent and a real estate speculator. He argued Black people should not be allowed in Canada West because they would crowd out Europeans who were better settlers, might intermarry, and possibly trigger a war with the United States. And he warned that property values would tumble. At Larwill's urging, Raleigh Township approved an anti-Black petition that requested a poll tax on Black residents, and also that they be barred from schools and denied the right to vote.[12]

King found himself the subject of threats. He shared them with his superiors in the church, citing one particular instance in Chatham:

When it was known that I intended to settle a colony of coloured persons in the Township my popularity fell rapidly. The next time I visited the town I got the cold shoulder, scarcely anyone would speak to me; one man came to me when I was riding down King Street on horseback and told me as a friend that my life was in danger, and that I should not expose myself after dark in the town.[13]

Despite the opposition from Larwill and others, King settled on his property at the Elgin Settlement in 1849 and opened the Buxton Mission, named after famed abolitionist and British parliamentarian Sir Thomas Fowell Buxton. The Elgin Association had purchased a tract of land about six miles by three miles, consisting of 9,000 heavily forested acres, about 13 miles southwest of Chatham. The land was flat but swampy in places and required drainage ditches, but the soil was excellent, much of it a rich black loam. The first and most challenging task was clearing the land of the tall stands of maple, oak, hickory, ash, beech, and elm trees. King discovered that the new arrivals were proficient with axes and wasted no time converting deep forest into productive farmland.[14] Each family of settlers could buy 50 acres, at $2.50 an acre, and spread payment over 10 years. Minimum standards were set for the homes, which were erected from the ready supply of logs. Each year, King awarded prizes for the best-kept home and grounds in a bid to encourage a tidy appearance for the community.

King's formerly enslaved people were among the first to settle and were soon joined by a rush of others when the American Fugitive Slave Act of 1850 became law. He held church services in his home until the church was completed and tended to the spiritual and educational needs of the community.

In April of 1850, the school doors opened for the first time, welcoming both Black and white children. King established a night school for adults anxious to learn to read and write, and he helped early settlers plan and erect log homes. That same year, Canada West established separate schools for Black children, but they were not as well funded as "common" or district schools. The quality of education provided at the Elgin Settlement school was so good, however, that an increasing number of white children attended and their parents sought forgiveness from King for their initial opposition to Buxton. Initially education was free, but eventually a small fee was imposed to help defray costs. In time, the district school closed and King's school prevailed, with Black and white children learning and playing together.

By 1854, a total of 74 homes had been erected, eight of them exceeding minimum requirements. Also by then, Buxton boasted a two-storey brick hotel, a general store, an office, a mission, and King's large home, which contained his personal office and the largest library between Windsor and London, Ontario. Presbyterian King was aware that religious factionalism had plagued the Dawn Settlement and sought to avoid it, so he encouraged other denominations to operate within the Elgin Settlement, including the Methodist, Baptist, and

This is a typical home built by the formerly enslaved at the successful Elgin Settlement at North Buxton, just southwest of Chatham. Many Black people still live in the area to this day, and the Buxton Settlement is a national historic site. (PHOTO BY CHIP MARTIN)

Roman Catholic churches, even though he personally disapproved of the latter denomination.[15]

Growth of the Elgin Settlement throughout the 1850s was steady and to it were added a steam-powered sawmill, a brickyard, and blacksmith, shoe, and carpentry shops. A factory converted the hardwood from ash trees felled on-site into lye, potash, and a more pure form of potash known as pearl ash, used as a leavening agent in breads.

———

The growth of Black settlements led to the appearance of Black newspapers in Canada West that supported abolition and debated the issue of integration. The first, *The Voice of the Fugitive*, appeared in 1851, published in Windsor by Mary and Henry Bibb. The colony's first newspaper for Black readers reported extensively on the Underground Railroad and encouraged further Black migration to Canada. It attacked racial bigotry, called for the abolition of slavery everywhere, and urged Black integration into Canadian society through temperance, education, and agriculture.

Henry Bibb was born into slavery in Kentucky in 1815. After several failed attempts to escape, he made it to Detroit by the 1840s and became active in the abolition movement. Enactment of the Fugitive Slave Act in 1850 prompted the Bibbs and thousands of other Black newcomers to cross the border. Many settled in Sandwich, the community alongside Windsor.[16] Bibb funded the biweekly paper and also acquired land with proceeds from his bestselling autobiography published in 1849, *Narrative of the Life and Adventures of Henry Bibb, an American Slave*. In his newspaper, Bibb stressed the value of education for Black people. In the January 15, 1851, edition of *The Voice of the Fugitive*, he wrote:

> We regard the education of colored people in North America as being one of the most important measures connected with the destiny of our race. By it we can be strengthened and be elevated — without it we shall

be ignorant, weak, and degraded. By it we shall be clothed with a power which will enable us to arise from degradation and command respect from the whole civilized world: without it we shall ever be imposed upon, oppressed and enslaved . . .[17]

Bibb contributed many articles to leading abolitionist journals, and as a compelling writer and powerful orator he did much to improve the lot of the Black population. At a convention in Sandwich in 1851 he supported a plan by the Refugee Home Society to acquire land from the government to create a Black agricultural community in Essex County.[18]

The issue of whether Black people should create their own communities would become a divisive one in Canada West. Bibb and those who had promoted the settlements at Oro and Wilberforce felt it was best to have their people rely on each other and on agriculture in a communal living experience, away from urban neighbours and any potential racial prejudice. After some time in a mutually supportive environment, he argued, inhabitants could move on and become part of the larger (overwhelmingly white) communities across the colony.

The offer of free or inexpensive land in such settlements had acted as an inducement for some Black people to escape to Canada in the first place. But many others arrived without plans or money, settling in existing communities near the border or a few miles inland. Many were finding success through integration.

A leading advocate for integration in existing communities was Mary Ann Shadd, the tireless anti-slavery campaigner and editor of the *Provincial Freeman*, established in 1853. Born in the State of Delaware in 1823, she was the first child of prominent Black abolitionist Abraham Doras Shadd and Harriet Parnell. Abraham Shadd, a free man born in Delaware, was among those abolitionists who established the American Anti-Slavery Society in Philadelphia in 1833. He helped freedom seekers travel the Underground Railroad, but feared for his large family and began to consider his options. The following year Shadd purchased land near Buxton, onto which he moved his family and several others from Pennsylvania, including a freeborn mulatto named Osborne Anderson, 22, who would become a printer for his daughter in Windsor.

Mary Ann was educated at a Quaker boarding school and became a teacher in Black schools in Pennsylvania, New Jersey, and New York. Shadd published her first pamphlet in 1849, in which she urged Black people not to mimic the conspicuous materialism displayed by white people and to push for anti-slavery reform themselves rather than wait for white action. Motivated by the 1850 Fugitive Slave Act, like so many others, she migrated to Canada West and was soon based in Windsor, where she opened a school supported by the American Missionary Association. Shadd encouraged other Black people to move to Canada while she continued attacking the separatist approach of Bibb, Henson, and others.

She touted her assimilationist views in pamphlets, lectures and the *Provincial Freeman*, published first in Windsor and then in Toronto and Chatham, where she moved and continued teaching students, both Black and white. Shadd has the distinction of being the first female African-American newspaper editor in North America, although she sometimes obscured that fact by crediting male associates as editor in a bid to gain wider acceptance for the journal.

Shadd was passionate in her views and even went so far as to break with organized religion because she felt churches were segregationist. The Refugee Home Society, for instance, with which Bibb was connected, relied heavily on donors in Michigan and its key agent was a white man. Bibb and Shadd had a fundamental philosophical difference about the best way for Black settlers to get established in Canada, so they often clashed.[19]

The two newspaper publishers promoted diametrically opposed approaches to how Black newcomers could best achieve their destiny in a new land. After fire destroyed Bibb's printing office in late 1853, ending the run of *The Voice of the Fugitive*, he continued his efforts with a one-page newsletter until his untimely death at age 39, less than a year later. Bibb's life was short but his influence was substantial. Shadd continued her advocacy after Bibb's passing and became tremendously influential in the growing Black community. She tirelessly criticized Josiah Henson and others for their Black settlement in Dawn Township, north of Chatham.

———

As a leader of the Dawn Settlement, there's no doubt Henson fell short. He was intelligent and energetic, a natural leader, imaginative and independent, but was not without his flaws. He could be vain, possessive, and anxious for praise. He left the day-to-day operations of the settlement to the Congregationalist Wilson, who was followed for a short time by a Black man, Baptist preacher Samuel H. Davis. While Henson's fame was growing and he travelled widely to raise funds and promote abolition, Dawn began to struggle and suffered from a lack of stable leadership.

Wilson was a poor team player and proved to be careless with money. Like Henson, he had a high opinion of himself and could be devious at times. Wilson clashed with Reverend Isaac Rice, a Free Will Baptist from Amherstburg, about funds raised by anti-slavery groups. He and Henson also scrapped with Black Baptist preacher William P. Newman, who for a time was in charge of the sawmill at Dawn and sat on the executive committee of the British-American Institute. By the time Wilson resigned in 1847, the settlement was deep in debt. Funds from Britain had dried up, partly because the famine that gripped Ireland had diverted relief money there. And in Canada, the ongoing conflict at Dawn and its management woes hurt its reputation and support dwindled.[20] Because of criticisms levelled against its leadership, donations from the United States tailed off.

Henson went to England in a bid to raise funds from the British and Foreign Anti-Slavery Society and hoped to persuade them to take over the British-American Institute. When he arrived, Henson found that handbills denouncing him had preceded him to England, distributed by his enemies back home and labelling him an "imposter." The British organization supported Henson but decided to investigate

Josiah Henson's home is the featured attraction at the Josiah Henson Museum of African Canadian History. (PHOTO BY CHIP MARTIN)

the situation first-hand by sending its secretary, John Scoble, to Dawn before taking any steps to assist.

Scoble, a white man, became its administrator on behalf of the British anti-slavery group, but his appointment didn't end controversies that plagued what had been an ambitious communal experiment. Scoble, who was described as "aloof and cantankerous" and often angry, appropriated the best house in the settlement, was paternalistic, and disliked sharing responsibility with Black men. Scoble was repeatedly censured for mismanagement and in one of his retorts to a damning assessment, he blamed Black people for his woes, lending credence to complaints that a racist lurked under his abolitionist facade. Despite this, Scoble lasted for 15 years as the sun slowly set on Dawn.[21]

Things grew worse for Henson and Dawn when editorship of the *Provincial Freeman* passed from Shadd to William P. Newman, the same Baptist preacher and critic of Henson who'd operated the sawmill at Dawn and afterward bad-mouthed Henson and the settlement from south of the border. Adding to these woes, Scoble and Henson became antagonists. In about 1858, Scoble sued Henson for money he claimed he was owed and three years later won a lawsuit against Henson over 80 acres of land.[22] The spiritual leader of the settlement was at loggerheads with its administrative head, a situation that did nothing to improve the reputation of the deeply troubled settlement.

At Dawn, the ill-fated British-American Institute closed its doors and the land was sold, with proceeds used to establish the Wilberforce Educational Institute for Black and white children in Chatham.[23] Despite the high-quality education and training the Institute provided and the welcome and support extended to newly freed Black people, the noble experiment at Dawn ultimately joined Oro and Wilberforce as failures of organized Black settlements set apart from their white neighbours. In 1859, Shadd's paper folded because of financial difficulties and she continued teaching at an interracial school in Chatham.

———

Josiah Henson remained at Dawn and preached every Sunday at the British Methodist Episcopal Church in Dresden. In his later years, he was received by both Queen Victoria at Windsor Castle and by U.S. President Rutherford B. Hayes at the White House. He died at age 93 on May 5, 1883. He is buried under a tree in the Henson family cemetery adjacent to the Josiah Henson Museum of African Canadian History, which was established there in 1964. The house where he was living when he died is a key feature of the site, relocated slightly from its original location. A historical marker nearby notes Henson's success and how his fame grew with the publication of an extraordinary novel that helped change history. "Henson's celebrity raised international awareness of Canada as a haven for refugees from slavery," it reads. And a haven it had been, whether such newcomers chose to live among themselves or in the communities of a new land. It may not have been Canaan, but it was a far better place than the country they had escaped.

CHAPTER FOUR

ABOVE THE TROUBLED FRAY

In September 1858, Chatham's Vigilance Committee felt compelled to swing into action. The group had been established to protect the formerly enslaved from American bounty hunters who ventured across the American border, 50 miles to the west. Members of the committee were alerted to a possible abduction and asked to check the welfare of a young Black on an incoming train. They learned that Elijah Leonard reported from the train station in London, 60 miles to the east, that he had seen "a dandy sort of a fellow pacing up and down the platform with a bright negro boy at his heels, acting as his body servant, and sending the little innocent to buy his papers and cigars." Leonard was a stout abolitionist and was concerned for the boy, who had stopped in London with the older white man while travelling from Niagara Falls. "I was afraid that boy was going into slavery," he later wrote in his memoirs. Leonard shared his concern with Black porter Anderson Diddrick and gave Diddrick money to telegraph some of his friends in Chatham to see if they could intervene at the station there. "When the train stopped at Chatham, sure enough there were nearly a hundred colored men and women with clubs and staves who surrounded and boarded the train and demanded the boy."[1] He was released to the crowd without incident.

The boy, Sylvanus Demarest, found sanctuary with Mary Ann Shadd and her family in Chatham before he relocated to Windsor.[2] She later carried a story in the *Provincial Freeman* about their rescue of Demarest. The *Chatham Planet* and the *Toronto Globe* reported later that the man with Demarest was not a bounty hunter after all, but a travelling salesman out of New York and Rochester named W.R. Merwin. He had convinced the lad to work for him until he could take Demarest to the South and sell him into slavery.[3]

Leonard, a former mayor of London, felt compelled to act, but not all Londoners felt the same. Some supported the South and its institutions. Amelia Ryerse Harris, a member of the city elite and one of its oldest families, kept a diary in which she recorded the events and people of London. The widow of John Harris, a former British military officer and local treasurer, she was accustomed to having housekeepers, cooks, and other servants to operate elegant Eldon House, her grand home overlooking the forks of the Thames River. There, she entertained other members of the local gentry as well as visiting dignitaries, and leaders of the colony and its businesses, such as the Grand Trunk Railway. On September 30, she described what she called "a great outrage" inflicted on a "southern gentleman [who] was passing through with a slave boy 10 years old." She said she learned that when the train stopped in Chatham, a "mob of 300 . . . took the boy forcibly from his master although the child cried and did not wish to go." Her account reflected her sympathy for Southerners. Harris said she learned a manager of the railway intended to prosecute those involved to the full extent of the law. She seemed to approve, expressing concern that such incidents "will turn the American travel from Canada."[4] In years to come, other members of the city's upper crust would extend a warm welcome for moneyed and well-educated former slaveholders who fled the South following the Civil War.

———

By 1850, the South was complaining bitterly about the ongoing flight of the enslaved and that northern states were failing to enforce the Fugitive Slave Act of 1793. Meanwhile, new territories and states such as California, Utah, and New Mexico were being added to the Union following the Mexican-American War of 1848. Which states would become pro-slavery and which would be designated as free ones became a pressing and divisive question, forcing Congress to act. It came up with what was known as The Compromise of 1850. California was declared a free state, while Utah and New Mexico could decide the issue for themselves.

To appease the South, where talk about seceding had emerged as early as the 1840s, new legislation was enacted to curb escapes. The result was a new federal Fugitive Slave Act which compelled citizens to help capture freedom seekers. Fines of $1,000 and sentences of six months in jail would be imposed on anyone interfering in any attempted capture. It also denied runaways the right to trial by jury. Instead, individual cases were to be heard by commissioners who were paid more to return enslaved people than to free them.[5]

Effectively, the new law extended the reach of slavery into northern states, including those which had abolished the practice years before. Anyone providing food, shelter, or other help could be charged and fined. Federal agents were hired to enforce the new law, and the more warm bodies they apprehended, the more they were paid — even if they captured free men and women.

Suddenly, all Black people ran the risk of being abducted and sold into slavery, without the benefit of any semblance of unbiased process. Needless to say, fear spread among Black populations in the North about the new legislation, which was intended to mollify southern states. As a result, as many as 20,000 African-Americans fled to Canada between 1850 and 1860, bringing their total population in British North America to about 60,000.[6] These were the busiest years for the Underground Railroad. The new law was not popular in northern states and met with limited success, like the 1793 act. By 1860, after a decade in force, only about 330 Black freedom seekers had been captured and returned to southern slaveholders.[7]

———

Harriet Tubman became a leading conductor on the Underground Railroad after 1850, helping about 70 enslaved people from Maryland reach Canada in the 13 trips she made before the outbreak of the Civil War in 1861. She was dubbed "Moses" by abolitionist William Lloyd Garrison for her effective work in leading so many of her fellow Black people to the promised land of Canaan (Canada).[8]

Born into slavery in Maryland about 1820, Tubman escaped her plantation by way of the Underground Railroad to Philadelphia, about 90 miles to the north, in 1849. There, she enjoyed her first taste of freedom but found her work as a housekeeper unfulfilling, and she grew determined to help free other members of her family and other enslaved persons back in Maryland. Tubman befriended abolitionist Quakers in Philadelphia, including one of the movement's leaders, Frederick Douglass. Enactment of the Fugitive Slave Act in 1850 suddenly made her job helping enslaved people escape far more risky, but she managed to avoid detection by the authorities. Just to be safe, she carried a pistol for self-defence, or to "encourage" any passenger having second thoughts about the arduous trek undertaken mainly on foot and at night. It was said she never "lost" a passenger.

For 10 years Tubman lived in St. Catharines, a community just west of Niagara Falls, where she helped newcomers get established. She retained her place in Philadelphia and continued to work closely

Born into slavery in Maryland, Harriet Tubman became a leading advocate for Black people. She personally led dozens of enslaved people to freedom in Canada along the Underground Railroad. For about a decade Tubman's base of operations was in St. Catharines, on the Niagara peninsula. With the outbreak of the Civil War she returned to the United States, where she became a nurse and a spy for the Union side. (LIBRARY OF CONGRESS)

with Douglass, who provided safe haven for Underground Railroad passengers at his home in Rochester, New York.[9]

Like Tubman, Frederick Douglass was also born on a plantation in Maryland, but two years earlier. He escaped at about age 20 and settled in Massachusetts, where he joined the abolition movement. Having taught himself to read and write, Douglass educated other Black men, became a powerful orator and a leading member of the anti-slavery movement. He moved to Rochester, where his home became one of the last stops on the Underground Railroad before Canada. It was said he could hide 10 or more runaways at any given time. He published anti-slavery papers and travelled widely, speaking to abolitionists in Canada, Great Britain and Ireland.[10] In February of 1851, Douglass attended the founding meeting of the Anti-Slavery Society of Canada, held in Toronto, which attracted a good crowd. The main topic on the agenda was immigration to Canada. Afterwards, Douglass became a regular speaker at society meetings.[11]

———

In the years immediately before the Civil War, Black colonists in the colony faced challenges not encountered by earlier freedom seekers who arrived when the economy was booming in Canada West with new arrivals from the United States (both white and Black) and from across the British Isles, lured by inexpensive farmland. At that time, American settlers heading for the western reaches of their own country by cutting across the colony sometimes abandoned their treks upon seeing the amount of fertile land that was so readily available.

An additional boost to the economy came in 1854 with the completion of the Great Western Rail Road (later Railway) that linked the Niagara region to Windsor (rather than more populous Sandwich next door), by way of Hamilton, London, and Chatham. Meanwhile the Crimean War from 1854 to 1856 pitted Britain against Russia for control of the Ottoman Empire and, because Britain could no longer import wheat from Russia, it turned to its colonies to supply it. As a result, wheat and other agricultural products from Canada

West were in demand, fetching high prices and further heating up the economy. By 1857, however, things changed abruptly after peace was reached in Crimea and the agricultural boom across the region quickly went bust.[12]

That same year, a sudden economic downturn hit the United States, triggered by the collapse of the country's largest insurance company. Banks failed, railways went bankrupt, and factories closed. More than 5,000 American businesses failed in the panic and economic collapse that spread throughout British North America, Europe, South America, and the Far East, the effects of which lasted nearly two years.[13]

The railway construction boom in Canada West had ended and widespread crop failures and unseasonable frosts crippled the farm economy. During 1857 and 1858, fully three-quarters of the businesses failed in agriculture-dependent London, which dropped from a population of 16,000 in 1855 to 11,000 by 1860.[14] Economic malaise had a firm grip on the southwestern region of the colony.

Black people who easily found employment in cities and towns across the region during boom times, primarily in lower-skilled positions, suffered even more than white people. Many of them were labourers, but others were skilled tradespeople: carpenters, cooks, shoemakers, tailors, and barbers. And one in every 10 ran a business like a grocery or tobacco store — or were ministers.[15]

By the 1850s, outsiders had found most Black people were doing reasonably well in Canada. Boston journalist and abolitionist Benjamin Drew toured Canada West in 1855 and looked into the condition of formerly enslaved people in 14 towns, villages, and Black settlements. He interviewed 129 inhabitants about their treatment and the conditions they faced. The following year, he published *The Refugee: Or the Narratives of Fugitive Slaves in Canada*, which detailed his findings. Drew also spent some time in Buxton, whose population then was about 800, and spoke at length with King. He described how the settlement had grown, the land cleared and crops planted, noting "the health of the settlement continues good; peace and harmony reign among the people." He said 150 children were attending school.[16]

Another outsider's view of the situation facing Black people in Canada West was delivered a few years later by white American physician and abolitionist Samuel Gridley Howe, a member of the American Freedmen's Inquiry Commission, which was established to determine what assistance the enslaved needed to transition to freedom.

Howe and his fellow commissioners travelled through the colony to see how formerly enslaved people were faring. They visited large towns and cities, including Toronto, Hamilton, St. Catharines, London, Chatham, Colchester, and Windsor, as well as Black settlements such as Dawn. The commission interviewed both Black and white people, along with local mayors, constables, schoolmasters, and clergy, in their homes, shops, and on their farms. Howe's report would come as music to the ears of Mary Ann Shadd. He wrote that when Black people move into an inhabited and civilized country they "should not be systematically segregated in communities . . . Experience shows that they do best when scattered about, and forming a small proportion of the whole community."

Howe said living in a segregated colony supported by outside donors, such as at Dawn, "does prolong a dependence which amounts to servitude" when they should be more self-reliant. "Taken as a whole," Howe concluded, "the colonists have cost somebody a great deal of money, and a great deal of effort; and they have not succeeded so well as many who have been thrown entirely upon their own resources." Black people, he found, had proven themselves capable of "self-guidance and support." He noted, however, that when they congregate in large numbers in white communities and establish their own schools, "they not only excite prejudices of race in others, but develop a spirit of caste among themselves and make less progress than when they form a small part of the local population."

Howe found that the newcomers contributed to their communities and were valuable citizens. One of his final conclusions was "that it is not desirable to have them live in communities by themselves."[17] This was certainly not what Josiah Henson, Henry Bibb, and other promoters of communal living wanted to hear.

Canada West was not without its troubles as the Black population continued to rise and discrimination increased. Schooling became a flashpoint. In 1850 the colony had permitted Black people to open their own schools, but the decision became unexpectedly controversial when white people began to *demand* that separate schools be created for Black students because they didn't want their own children learning alongside them. Access to quality education sometimes decreased for Black children as a result.

Toronto had a population of 47,000 by 1855 but only about 1,000 people were Black. Schools in the provincial capital were not segregated. In Buxton, the Black school prevailed over the common school because it provided superior instruction. In Essex County, schools for Black students were established in Amherstburg, Gosfield, and Sandwich, and while poorly funded, they were still able to provide the education upon which their students relied for advancement.

In Windsor, a complaint was lodged that a chicken coop measuring 16 feet by 24 feet was pressed into use for a Black school that accommodated 35 pupils, while a nearby white school had plenty of empty seats.[18] By 1855, when Benjamin Drew visited Canada West, he found Mary Bibb, the widow of Henry, was operating a successful private school in Windsor with 46 pupils, seven of them white.[19]

Next door in Sandwich, however, Drew detected strong prejudice against the Black population. A few years earlier, he was told, school trustees there had imposed school taxes on wealthier residents, who responded by sending their children to the tax-supported common school. "As these sat down, the white children near them deserted the benches: and in a day or two, the white children were wholly withdrawn, leaving the schoolhouse to the teacher and his coloured pupils."[20] In Chatham, where Black people already had separate schools and churches by 1855, town council went so far as to gerrymander a school district boundary to exclude an area that was primarily Black. Drew was not alone in finding that discrimination by white people increased where Black communities were large.

In London, schools were open to all, regardless of colour, well into the 1850s. From 1854 to 1859, the Church of England operated an integrated school that was free to attend in one of the frame infantry barracks of the British garrison. The barracks also served as temporary quarters for several hundred formerly enslaved people who had joined the growing Black community in London. Some child refugees had faced prejudice in existing schools, and the church responded to a plea for an integrated school from Reverend Samuel Ward. The result was a fully integrated school in which Black and white children were treated alike and taught by Black teachers.[21]

As the Black population increased in London in the early 1860s, school officials proposed a segregated school for them. Opposition to any such move was led by successful Black pharmacist Alfred T. Jones, a father of eight, who fought any effort to remove Black children from a common school and place them in one strictly for Black students. A literate and intelligent man who had purchased his freedom in Kentucky — Jones studied Latin so he could better read prescriptions from doctors — he quickly became a prominent opponent of any segregated school. He understood the value of a good education and was upset it might be denied to his offspring. Jones said he was a British citizen and his children "don't believe in anything else but the Queen." He warned the schooling issue was creating hatred for their country and denying them their rights. "I don't believe in 10 years from this time you will see a colored man in this country," he told a Freedman's Inquiry interviewer. "We won't stay here after this [Civil] war is decided. . . ."[22] Jones died not long afterward and his family remained in London, likely because the school he so bitterly opposed never proceeded.[23]

By 1860, the Black population in southern Ontario varied from one community to another. Nearly 4,000 lived in the Windsor-Amherstburg area, 1,000 in Toronto, 700 in St. Catharines, nearly 500 in Hamilton, and 300 in London. Fully one-third of Chatham's population of 6,000 was Black.

Canada West attracted not just Black people and bounty hunters pursuing them, but abolitionists as well, along with writers anxious to tell the story of successful lives in the convenient attic maintained by sympathetic Britain. Among the abolitionists was anti-slavery zealot John Brown, a white man whose willingness to resort to violence to achieve his aims was already known when he appeared in the colony nearly 18 months before his raid on Harper's Ferry, Virginia — his bid to free the enslaved with his "army of emancipation."

In Chatham, Brown held a secretive convention on May 8 and 10, 1858, ostensibly to discuss forming a Black Masonic Lodge. Osborne Anderson, a printer from the *Provincial Freeman*, was among those present, writing later that Brown "made a profound impression upon those who saw or became acquainted with him."[24] The gathering was held at the First Baptist Church and chaired by William C. Monroe, a Black preacher, attracting 34 Black people and 12 white ones. Brown had been in Chatham since April 29 and he unveiled a daring plan that had nothing to do with the Masonic Lodge — he billed the gathering as "a quiet convention . . . of true friends of freedom." His notion was nothing short of revolutionary. Brown talked about raiding the giant armoury for the United States Army, located at Harper's Ferry, and seizing the weapons stored there. Then, with a large number of supporters he would lead an armed insurrection into the South, arming and freeing enslaved men who would then operate from fortified sanctuaries in the Appalachian Mountains, completely demoralizing enslavers and bringing an end to slavery. He said he needed money and supporters willing to join him.

Brown presented a "Provisional Constitution and Ordinances for the People of the United States" to the Chatham gathering, which contained 48 articles that were discussed and adopted. He said the constitution would guide him as commander-in-chief of the new government he'd establish after the insurrection.[25] During his time in Canada West, Brown raised funds for his raid and also spoke to the Black population in London and St. Catharines, conferring with Harriet Tubman in the latter community.

Abolitionist John Brown attended a convention in Chatham in 1858 where he revealed his plans to overthrow the American government by force and abolish slavery. Brown spent time drumming up support for his plan and raising funds during several appearances across southwestern Ontario. His raid at Harper's Ferry the following year was a failure and resulted in his hanging. (LIBRARY OF CONGRESS)

Born in Connecticut in 1800, Brown was a man of action and no stranger to violence. He'd led anti-slavery guerrillas in Kansas in 1855, helping his sons battle armed pro-slavery supporters who were determined to make Kansas a slave-holding state. Following an attack by pro-slavers in May of 1856, Brown led a retaliatory raid on a settlement at Pottawatomie Creek, where five men were dragged from their cabins and hacked to death. Brown's willingness to engage in violence to end slavery made him feared among all those who sought to retain or expand it.[26]

After his convention in Chatham, Brown was urged by his supporters in the United States to quietly bide his time there for a while before launching his revolution at Harper's Ferry. The delay may have diminished some of the ardour among his supporters, who failed to materialize in the numbers he'd hoped to assemble for the actual attack. The following September, Osborne Anderson, the printer from Chatham, was among the men who joined Brown and others at a farmhouse a few miles from Harper's Ferry, which served as a staging area.

Also joining the group was a white Canadian, Stewart Taylor, 22, who had met Brown in Iowa in 1858 and had stayed in touch. He has been described as having his "heart and soul in the anti-slavery cause." Taylor was born in Uxbridge, just northeast of Toronto, and was a spiritualist.[27] On the night of October 16, 1859, Brown launched his raid on the federal arsenal with an armed group of 16 white and five Black abolitionists, capturing several enslavers and the armoury itself. The next day, United States Marines under the command of U.S. Army Colonel Robert E. Lee arrived on scene and forced Brown and his men from the armoury and into a nearby engine house used to store firefighting equipment. Lee and his men overwhelmed the raiders who had barricaded themselves inside, including a wounded Brown.

Ten of Brown's followers, including two of his sons and Taylor, were killed in the firefight. Lee arrested the survivors and took them to the courthouse in Charles Town, Virginia. Osborne Anderson and a companion witnessed the capture of Brown from their position nearby and realized the situation was hopeless. He wrote about his experience three years later, saying he "concluded it was better to retreat while it was possible . . . than to recklessly invite capture and brutality at the hands of our enemies."[28] The two men were among five raiders who escaped the bloody scene. In a trial the following month, Brown was convicted of treason and was hanged on December 2, at the age of 59.[29]

Even some of Brown's supporters felt he had gone too far and in the South he was reviled as evil incarnate. Some Southerners began to fear there were others of his ilk in the North who might be inspired to launch similar deadly raids. Brown's case helped fuel the growing notion that secession might be the best way for the South to protect a way of life that was increasingly under fire.

In Canada, the reaction to the Harper's Ferry raid was mixed. Some supporters hailed him as a hero and raised funds for his widow, while others denounced him. Tories and their pro-slavery newspapers excoriated Brown in no uncertain terms. The *Globe* newspaper in

Toronto, however, took a different tack. Its editor, George Brown, no relation to the abolitionist, knew about the Chatham convention the previous year and wrote on November 4, 1859, that Brown would be remembered as "a brave man who periled property, family, life itself, for an alien race." Later that same month on the eve of Brown's execution, the *Globe* opined, with great insight, that if the tension between the North and South continued, a civil war was inevitable. It added: "No force that the south can raise can hold the slaves if the north wills that they be free."[30] The words would prove prophetic.

Canada's involvement in Brown's preparations for his ill-fated raid became known south of the border, prompting widespread criticism of the colony and of Britain. Henry A. Wise, the governor of Virginia, complained that a "compact of fanaticism and intolerance" was harboured on British soil and that the colony had helped hatch a "predatory war."[31] He suggested Canada should be taken militarily and that he could do so with only 10 men, an assertion scoffed at by raid survivor Osborne Anderson in a pamphlet he published in 1861 in which he described the ill-fated raid and the events leading up to it.[32] In the North, Brown became a martyr and Union troops would sing "John Brown's Body" while marching into Civil War battles, a tune that included the lyrics, "John Brown died that the slaves might be free, but his soul goes marching on." It was reworked later to become the Battle Hymn of the Republic.[33] The Union eventually triumphed and the enslaved were freed, so Brown's work was not in vain.

—

A growing divide between North and South existed even before John Brown announced his plan in Chatham or took up arms at Harper's Ferry. A decision rendered by the Supreme Court of the United States in early 1857 had seen to that. It came in the case of Dred Scott, a Virginia-born enslaved man who had been fighting for his freedom in the courts for 11 years. As an enslaved person, he had been taken by his enslavers to free states for various lengths of time, and his lawyers argued that once Scott entered a free state he automatically gained his freedom forever. The case worked its way up to the highest court in the land. The Supreme Court denied his freedom yet again in what some constitutional scholars consider the worst decision ever made by the court.[34] It ruled that Black people were not citizens of the United States so they couldn't bring cases to federal court.

Chief Justice Roger Taney, a Southerner, wrote the majority opinion and went on to say the Fifth Amendment to the American constitution protected the rights of enslavers to their legal property, which included enslaved people. Going even further, he said legislation Congress enacted to determine which states could uphold slavery and which could be free was unconstitutional. Consequently, the federal government had no power to prevent the spread of slavery.

The Dred Scott decision outraged abolitionists and northern states alike. The *New York Tribune*, whose founder was the abolitionist Horace Greeley, attacked the decision in several editorials: "Downright and bare-faced falsehood is its main staple. Any slave-driving editor or Virginia bar-room politician could have taken the Chief Justice's place on the bench." Concurring justices, it added, had demonstrated "an impudent recklessness of truth and their own reputation."[35] The following day the *Tribune* said the decision established the fact that slavery is a national phenomenon. "Now, wherever the stars and stripes wave, they protect Slavery and represent slavery," it complained. "It is most true that this decision is bad law . . . that it does not at all represent the legal or judicial opinion of the Nation; that it is merely a Southern sophism clothed with the dignity of our highest Court."[36]

For its part, the *New York Times* said the decision would "paralyze and astound the public mind." It complained slavery was now a national institution and that states' rights had been trampled. The *Times* added, "It has laid the only solid foundation which has ever yet existed for an Abolition Party; and it will do more to stimulate the growth, to build up the power and consolidate the action of such a party, than has been done by any other event since the Declaration of Independence."[37]

The South was jubilant that slavery was now enshrined as the law of the land and that the North had to acknowledge that. In Augusta,

Georgia, the *Daily Constitutionalist and Republic* dismissed the hand-wringing by northern newspapers, some of which it quoted, insisting: "These insane and indecent ravings of the abolition press . . . will not be approved by a large portion of the people of the North . . ." The Dred Scott decision, it conceded, "will not take away the occupation of demagogues, or cure the madness of the anti-slavery fanatics of the North."[38] The two sides, fanatical or otherwise, were clearly entrenched well before John Brown's raid, and fears were growing about the future of the frayed Union.

———

As the United States inched toward war, the trial of a Black man in Toronto late in 1860 became an overnight sensation in Canada West. John Anderson came to symbolize the plight of the Black people in America and the evils of slavery. Many members of the public rallied to support him. He'd fled from his enslaver in Missouri in 1853 and found his way to Windsor along the Underground Railroad late that same year. During his flight, he stabbed a Missouri enslaver who tried to stop him. Anderson didn't know the man later died of his injuries. He made his way to Chatham and then to the small community of Caledonia, not far from Brantford, where he became a Mason and plasterer. He did well and by 1858 bought a house there. He befriended another freedom seeker named Wynne, who became his confidant, but for some reason the relationship between the men soured, prompting Wynne to inform a local magistrate in 1860 that Anderson was a fugitive who had stabbed his way to freedom. Anderson was arrested and soon learned he faced a charge of murder back in Missouri.

A hearing was held in Brantford to determine whether Anderson should be extradited to Missouri, pursuant to provisions of the Webster-Ashburton Treaty of 1842 between Britain and the United States, which governed such matters. The local judge ordered his return, but the final decision was left to Attorney General John A. Macdonald, who instead referred the case to the Court of Queen's Bench in Toronto, the colony's highest court. There, Anderson's lawyer argued that an individual could legitimately break any law that denied him his freedom. In anticipation of the judgment, rendered December 15, the Osgoode Hall courthouse was packed with supporters of Anderson, while police and troops, some with bayonets fixed, stood by to discourage violence on the part of the large crowd.[39]

Chief Justice John Beverley Robinson ruled that the extradition of Anderson could not be denied, but a strong dissent was registered by Justice Archibald McLean, a staunch abolitionist, who said he would never decide in favour of any law "which can convert into chattels a very large number of the human race." McLean's view was more aligned with prevailing public sentiment, which viewed any law supporting slavery as a bad law.

Robinson's decision provoked outrage, but no violence, and Anderson was sent back to jail in Brantford to await extradition. Public meetings were held and passionate arguments made that Anderson would never get a fair trial as a Black man in Missouri, and that sending him back there to face justice amounted to a death sentence.

The decision was immediately appealed to the Court of Queen's Bench in Britain, which issued a writ of habeas corpus and ordered Anderson's release. That ruling was upheld by British Prime Minister Lord Palmerston, a stunning rebuke for colonial justice. The British decision was rendered moot in mid-February, however, when the Court of Common Pleas in Toronto declared the initial warrant for Anderson's arrest was too vague, and therefore unenforceable. Anderson was released on February 16, 1861, prompting followers of his case to celebrate in the streets of Toronto and other cities in the Canadas.

In the aftermath of the Anderson case, Britain passed a law to limit its interference in colonial justice in future, while Canada West assigned extradition cases strictly to superior courts. For his part, Anderson delivered speeches in Canada and Britain supporting abolition, and a book about his life was published in 1863.[40]

———

It came as a surprise to American abolitionists when the Canadian provinces did not automatically support the North when the Civil War eventually broke out. The British colonies feared that if the South was defeated, an emboldened Union Army would then march north in a bid to annex Canada. Such concern was pervasive and helped promote unity within the colonies, a significant factor in the push for the creation of Canada as an independent nation in 1867.[41]

Meanwhile the population of the Buxton Settlement began to decline in the early 1860s and its final annual report was issued for 1873. The Presbyterians kept William King on salary until his retirement in 1880. His efforts to help freedom seekers had been a success when compared to earlier ones, a tribute to King's perseverance, patience, and leadership skills. But by creating Black utopias he and others may have delayed integration rather than promote it, as argued by Mary Ann Shadd, Samuel Gridley Howe, and others.

Mary Ann Shadd died in Washington in 1893. Her father remained in the Buxton area where he died in 1882, at age 79. Today, the main road running through the former Buxton Settlement is named A.D. Shadd Road in honour of his significant contributions to the area. Harriet Tubman was recruited by the North when the Civil War broke out, became head of a spy network and helped create Black regiments. Dred Scott was freed by his enslaver in 1857, the same year as his infamous court case, but he died a year later. John Anderson, who so mobilized abolitionists with his Toronto trial, moved to Liberia and was never heard from again.

As for Josiah Henson, his experiences in Canada not only increased awareness of Canada as a refuge; *Uncle Tom's Cabin* influence on the Civil War cannot be overstated. According to circulation records at the Library of Congress in Washington, United States President Abraham Lincoln borrowed *The Key to Uncle Tom's Cabin* on June 16, 1862, and returned it 43 days later. On September 22, Lincoln released his preliminary proclamation, under which enslaved people in rebel states were to be freed. The final version was released on January 1, 1863, and helped convert the war Lincoln originally insisted was about preserving the Union into one focused on the abolition of slavery.[42] It was a deft move intended to keep Britain from supporting the South, because of British opposition to slavery, and also provide new troops for the North from an untapped reservoir of Black people, some only too happy to fight to ensure freedom for family and friends back south.

To what extent the president was influenced by Stowe's powerful work of fiction will never be known, but having it close at hand while he penned his ground-breaking and pivotal declaration is more than coincidence. Lincoln was already quite familiar with *Uncle Tom's Cabin* because his Republican Party had distributed 100,000 copies of it during his 1860 presidential campaign in a bid to win support from abolitionist voters. As Republican Senator Charles Sumner aptly declared, "Had there been no *Uncle Tom's Cabin*, there would have been no Lincoln in the White House."[43]

Henson succeeded as a symbol and inspiration, by giving a face and powerful voice to the anti-slavery movement from his base in Canada.

Neither Henson nor the settlement he fostered were perfect. Far from it. But when Josiah Henson finally went to meet his maker, the world was a far different place — and much better for Black people — than nine decades earlier when he was born into slavery on a Maryland plantation.

Had Josiah Henson not escaped to Canada, history might have been quite different.

PART TWO

A HOUSE TORN ASUNDER

CHAPTER FIVE

"A TRIFLING DIFFERENCE OF OPINION"

William Seward fully expected to become the next president of the United States following the election of 1860. The senator from New York and former governor of the state was an outspoken abolitionist. A lawyer, Seward had been a member of the Whig Party, but after it splintered he became one of the most prominent politicians to join the new Republican Party, which was founded in 1854 and attracted many abolitionists.

In 1856, Pennsylvania Democrat James Buchanan was elected president as the battle between pro- and anti-slavery forces reached a boiling point in what had become known as "Bloody Kansas." Buchanan wanted Kansas admitted to the Union as a pro-slavery state, but Democrats were split about how to proceed, some preferring to let Kansas determine the issue for itself by public vote.

The Dred Scott decision was handed down in 1857 and Seward denounced it in strong terms, accusing Buchanan of colluding with Chief Justice Roger Taney. The economic collapse of 1857 hammered the North, but the South was relatively unscathed as cotton exports remained strong and helped bolster the national economy. Supporters of slavery pounced upon that as proof of their superior system, among them Senator James Hammond of South Carolina, who asserted in early 1858 that cotton exports saved the economy from total collapse, so the South must be heeded. "Cotton is King," he boasted. "What would happen if no cotton was furnished for three years? England would topple headlong and carry the whole civilized world with her, save the South." He and other southern politicians fought all efforts by their northern colleagues to protect the industrial North with high tariffs on foreign imports.[1]

Seward, a gifted communicator who held little back, especially after a drink or two, became increasingly outspoken and by the end of 1858 was arguing the South should receive no more concessions from the North, which had been terribly shortchanged by the Dred Scott decision. In one fiery speech, he claimed the South had started an "irrepressible conflict" with northern states. "The United States must . . . become either entirely a slave-holding nation or entirely a free-labor nation," he declared. Seward was not alone among Republicans in arguing the status quo could not remain.

Meanwhile, a largely unknown lawyer who was campaigning for a Senate seat in Illinois expressed the situation in more memorable terms: "A house divided against itself cannot stand." Abraham Lincoln did not win that Senate race, but his profile was growing and plenty more would be heard from him in months to come. Seward was widely criticized for his inflammatory suggestion that war with the South was inevitable, so he accepted the advice of supporters and took a trip to Britain and Europe, hoping his comments would be soon forgotten and upon his return he could cast himself as a more conciliatory figure.[2]

———

Seward's abolitionist views may have found sympathetic ears in Canada, but not another of his most strongly held ones. He believed in Manifest Destiny, the long-held notion that all of North America should be owned or controlled by the United States. He disliked Britain and felt her colonies should be annexed. He helped push through the Reciprocity Treaty of 1854, which dropped tariffs and brought about greater economic integration with British North America, a move he hoped might be a prelude to political integration. By 1860, Seward was becoming even more blunt about his aspirations to take over America's northern neighbours. "It is very well you are building states to be hereafter admitted to the American union," he said in a speech delivered in St. Paul, Minnesota, but directed at Canadians.[3]

His audience across the border may have been alarmed, or amused, by this sort of talk from a leading American politician. Alarmed because Seward was among those expected to become even more prominent in the politics of his country, or amused because his own nation was showing signs of falling apart. Regardless, the crafty political opportunist Seward was no friend of Canada. He thought Britain was ruled by snobs. The distaste was mutual and the Brits dismissed him as loud, brash, and belligerent. Seward advised them to stay out of American domestic affairs regardless of what lay ahead, warning that if Britain recognized the South in the event of secession, the United States would consider that an act of war and invade Canada. He believed a foreign war would prompt all American states to rally together against a common foe, uniting again as one nation under the Stars and Stripes.[4]

At the time of Seward's sabre-rattling, Canada was poorly defended, a virtual sitting duck and ripe for the taking. Little effort

William Seward, the United States Secretary of State under President Abraham Lincoln, often urged the annexation of Canada and was involved in negotiations when relations between Britain and the United States grew frosty. Initially a rival of Lincoln, Seward became a valued partner of the president during the Civil War.
(LIBRARY OF CONGRESS)

had been made to improve its forts and other defences following the War of 1812, and by 1860 there were only about 4,500 British troops spread across Canada East, Canada West, and Nova Scotia. The Canadian militia was poorly trained and equipped, with about 8,500 men.[5] Britain had committed additional troops to its North American colonies after the Crimean War ended, but there was little chance of repelling a determined invasion by the Americans. Britain found itself caught between needing troops at home because of increased tensions in Europe and the desire to guard its "back door" in North America from an expansionist-minded American republic.

Seward managed to alienate much of Britain's political elite, including Prime Minister Lord Palmerston, who condemned him as a "vapourizing, blustering, ignorant man" whose ego threatened Anglo-American relations.[6] Generally, the British prime minister didn't like Americans at all, calling them "totally unscrupulous and dishonest." Partly because of concern about Seward and other Americans with expansionist notions, Palmerston sent another regiment of British regulars to Canada. He insisted they be equipped with the most modern weapons so the Americans would know Britain would not surrender its colonies without a serious fight. At the same time, Palmerston reinforced the vaunted British fleet along the American coast and in the Caribbean.[7]

Meanwhile, Lincoln, the homespun lawyer from Springfield, Illinois, was seen as far more moderate than Seward and supporters began to suggest he was an ideal Republican presidential candidate for 1860. At the same time, the Democrats had to find someone to replace James Buchanan, who wasn't seeking a second term. In April of 1859, about 630 delegates of the Democratic Party convened in Charleston, South Carolina, as talk of secession gained ground in the South. Delegates who favoured secession demanded the party endorse a platform providing federal guarantees for slavery in all new states and territories. But northern Democrats preferred the status quo and voted down the pro-slavery platform. This split prompted about 50 delegates from cotton states to walk out of the convention, leaving the party in shambles and without a nominee.

The following month, the Republicans gathered in Chicago to select their candidate, no doubt pleased at the schism within in the ranks of Democrats. Seward was confident about winning the nomination, but the convention was in Lincoln's home state and his supporters effectively mounted a campaign featuring his "Honest Abe" persona, his personal success story, and his more moderate views on slavery. Lincoln won his party's nomination on the third ballot.[8]

The Democrats held a second convention in June in Baltimore, but many Southerners did not attend. The Democrats who attended from the cotton states favoured John C. Breckinridge, Buchanan's vice-president, who sought to preserve both the Union and slavery. A Kentuckian, he walked a fine line because he was also willing to support secession. His state was a key border state and its inhabitants generally backed the South and slavery. Breckinridge became the nominee of southern Democrats. But northern Democrats chose Illinois Senator Stephen A. Douglas, who had drawn the greatest support at the Charleston gathering. So the Democrats fielded two candidates to face Lincoln and his Republicans. Meanwhile, a third party, the Constitutional Union Party led by John Bell, entered the fray with a platform based solely on preservation of the Union.[9]

During the election campaign, both Lincoln and Breckinridge opted for low-key strategies for fear of further stirring up passions about slavery and secession. Lincoln delivered no stump speeches and Breckinridge made only one. Northern Democrat Douglas campaigned widely throughout the North and the South, however, passionately defending the Union and speaking against secession. Douglas was willing to let new states decide for themselves on the issue of slavery.

On election day, November 6, Lincoln captured less than 40 percent of the vote, but won a majority in the electoral college to take the presidency. He swept the North (except New Jersey) and won in California and Oregon, but failed to win any southern state that would soon join the Confederacy. Douglas took nearly 30 percent of the vote, placing second in several states but winning only one, pro-slavery Missouri. Breckinridge had 18 percent of the vote and won most of the southern states along with Delaware and Maryland. Third party candidate Bell won Kentucky, Tennessee, and Virginia, with 12.6 percent of the vote.[10] A great divide had set in: The North was Republican and the South was solidly Democratic, and would remain so for some time.

The South was unhappy with the results of the election, coming only four days after John Brown was convicted of murder, treason, and conspiring with the enslaved to rebel. The verdict came as welcome news to Southerners, but fears lingered that other abolitionists in the North might act with similar intentions. Northerners, they felt, were determined to destroy what they euphemistically called their "peculiar institution," the practice of slavery, upon which the South was built and had progressed. On December 2, Brown was hanged. His raid was a significant precipitating factor in the Civil War, but Lincoln's election was seen as the final straw for the South.[11] The day after the election, the *Mercury* newspaper of Charleston, South Carolina, declared on its front page that the Union was "gone." It noted Southern hopes had rested on Breckinridge but they had been dashed, adding "a final severance of this Confederacy is imminent . . . the sooner we arm and organize the better . . . we are about to launch forth upon the stormy sea of a political revolution."[12]

British consul Robert Bunch was living in Charleston at the time and filed reports to Lord John Russell, Britain's foreign secretary, who was closely following the turmoil in America. Bunch described the scene when residents of the port city learned of Lincoln's election:

> People poured out of their homes and offices clam-
> ouring for immediate secession, calling for the creation
> of a great Southern Confederacy. A huge red flag waved
> above Broad Street with a yellow palmetto on it, the

symbol of South Carolina, and a lone star, for independence . . . . A state of things has arisen since the election of Mr. Lincoln very nearly akin to a Revolution.[13]

Two weeks later, Bunch reported: "The violent agitation which has prevailed throughout the State of South Carolina during the last fortnight seems to increase day by day in intensity." He said mobs of "Minute Men" were being formed to fight as needed and they were preying upon anyone expressing abolitionist sentiments. In another message, Bunch said South Carolinians and residents of pro-slavery states had convinced themselves their very lives were at stake if they remained in the Union.

Britain's senior diplomat in Washington, Richard Bickerton Pemell Lyons, known as Lord Lyons, wrote in his post-election report to Lord Russell that "it seems impossible that the South can be mad enough to dissolve the union," even though South Carolina had already announced that it would hold a special convention to consider secession. News of that plan sent shares tumbling on the New York Stock Exchange, which was battered further when it was reported that a merchant vessel had pulled out of Charleston harbour on November 17 flying only the official state flag, rather than the mandatory Stars and Stripes.[14]

William Gist, the outgoing governor of South Carolina, further inflamed passions. He told the legislature in late November he'd like to see trade ended with the North, particularly New York, and replaced by direct trade with Britain and Europe. Gist proposed rolling back even the very limited rights that had been extended to the Black population and called on the people of South Carolina to take up arms. Warhawk Gist said his state would "infinitely prefer annihilation to disgrace."[15]

───

South Carolina had a long history of rebellion that dated back to 1719, when colonists rose up against the Lords Proprietors of Carolina, eight British noblemen who in 1663 had been granted the land that comprises today's North and South Carolina by King Charles II. None of the eight aristocrats ever set foot in the colony, and like most noblemen of the day they enjoyed comfortable lifestyles funded by their landholdings. The independent-minded colonists felt the Lords failed to support the security of the colony and had high-handedly vetoed colonial law. In December 1719, they revolted and asked the British Crown to take direct control. An interim royal governor was appointed and by 1729 the proprietors' ownership was ended.[16] When Carolinians joined the American Revolution in the 1770s, they drew inspiration from their successful revolt against the British noblemen.

Because of enslaved labour, South Carolina had become reliant on cotton and rice by the 1820s, making it the wealthiest of all the cotton producing and exporting states. Since 60 percent of its people were enslaved, South Carolina delegates to the Constitutional Convention of 1787 insisted the new country's constitution maintain slavery. To accommodate the practice and appease the South, the founding fathers agreed to provide pro-slavery states additional representation in Congress, using a formula that counted three-fifths of their enslaved population. South Carolina didn't allow citizens to vote directly for president, leaving that task to the state legislature.[17]

By the 1830s the state was embroiled in a dispute that generated the first talk of secession. The issue was tariffs. South Carolina relied on free trade for its massive exports, but the move toward tariffs to protect northern states was seen as an existential threat. Robert Barnwell Rhett and his *Charleston Mercury* continued playing up that threat into the 1840s, but other southern states expressed little interest in joining South Carolina. During the federal fight over which new states and territories could have slavery, a convention was held in Nashville in 1850 where South Carolina urged other states to band together to protect slavery and oppose Northern aggression. Still, no takers could be found. So strong was the state's reliance on slavery that in 1856 the governor pushed unsuccessfully to reopen the international slave trade.

When the Democrats were split after their conventions in 1860, a group fearing the election of Lincoln was established to lead South

Carolina out of the Union. The "1860 Association" represented people of all political persuasions determined to preserve their way of life in a separate nation. By then, there were four million enslaved people in America. Slaveholders and farmers without enslaved labour united in common cause, fearing a possible insurrection by the Black population if the abolitionist Republicans came into power and trampled the state's right to determine its own destiny.[18]

Abraham Lincoln's election as President of the United States was the last straw for many southern states, unhappy at the growth of anti-slavery sentiment in the North. Months before Lincoln was sworn in, South Carolina became the first state to secede from the Union.
(LIBRARY OF CONGRESS)

The general assembly of South Carolina convened at the state capital of Columbia in November to vote for presidential electors and, upon learning Lincoln would become the next president, decided to hold a special state convention to consider secession. Within days, South Carolina's two senators resigned from the United States Senate. Governor William Gist and Francis W. Pickens, his newly elected successor, contacted the governors in Alabama, Mississippi, Georgia, and Florida, who promised their states would hold similar conventions. On December 6, South Carolina voted for representatives to attend its convention, mainly planters who backed secession. They included state senator Alexander Mazyck, owner of a large rice plantation in Berkeley County just northwest of Charleston, and Gabriel Manigault, who had a plantation in Charleston County. Both were members of prominent and wealthy families of French Huguenot stock who were among the earliest settlers in South Carolina. Mazyck and Manigault were related through marriage, Alexander Mazyck being the brother of Manigault's father-in-law. The two men couldn't possibly have known the vote they were about to take would ultimately prompt them to flee to Canada and never return. In London, Ontario, where they found refuge, they would be buried alongside some of the city's most prominent families.

The delegates for the secession convention gathered in Columbia on December 17, but relocated to Charleston when an outbreak of smallpox was discovered. Half of the delegates were more than 50 years of age, many of them well-known like Mazyck and Manigault, with more than 60 percent owning at least 20 enslaved people. They gathered at Institute Hall, the same venue used by the Democrats for their failed convention the previous April, but soon moved to the smaller St. Andrews Hall for closed-door deliberations. On December 20, all 169 delegates approved the "Ordinance of Secession" and assigned two members to draw up an explanatory resolution. They then reconvened at Institute Hall, later to become known as Secession Hall, where each of the delegates signed the ordinance to the applause of spectators invited to witness the historic event.

"The Union is Dissolved," declared the headline in the *Charleston Mercury* as citizens took to the streets to celebrate, accompanied by fireworks and bonfires. "To describe the enthusiasm with which this announcement was greeted is beyond the power of the pen," it reported. "The high, burning, bursting heart alone can realize it," the ardently secessionist *Mercury* added in purple prose. "A mighty voice of great thoughts and great emotions spoke from the mighty throat of one people as a unit."[19] It continued:

> During the evening several of our fine military compa-
> nies, and processions of private citizens paraded the

streets, accompanied by bands of music, but in many instances the sounds of the latter were drowned by the stentorian shouts of the jubilant populace. The excitement was kept up during the entire evening, and it was long after midnight before the city resumed its wonted quiet, and our exultant citizens sought their pillows on which to take their first rest in the Free, Independent, and Sovereign State of South Carolina.[20]

The explanatory "Declaration of the Immediate Causes Which Induce and Justify the Secession of South Carolina from the Federal Union" was published on Christmas Eve. It complained about the failure of northern states to fulfill "constitutional obligations," but it was clear the main reason was the federal government's unwillingness to recognize and support slavery.[21]

British consul Robert Bunch slipped into the hall to watch the signing ceremony, standing off to the side in the shadow of a pillar. Afterward, he sent a dispatch to the foreign secretary: "My city is wild with excitement — bells ringing, guns firing, and scarcely one man in a thousand regrets the dissolution."[22]

After so many years of trying, South Carolina had finally seceded from the Union. By February 1, following similar conventions, the states of Mississippi, Florida, Alabama, Georgia, Louisiana, and Texas did so as well.

———

When Abraham Lincoln was sworn in as president on March 4, it was to lead a much-diminished nation. His election had been a catalyst and the threat of war hung heavily over Washington. He promised not to interfere with slavery where it existed in a bid to keep border pro-slavery states in the Union. But he stood firmly against secession and the seizure of federal property, insisting, "We are not enemies, but friends. We must not be enemies." Lincoln also appealed to "the better angels of our nature" to avoid conflict.[23] But the clouds of war continued to gather.

Secession came at an immediate financial cost because the South owed more than $200 million to the North, mainly to New York City interests. The city's ties to the cotton states were so strong that it was said some banks accepted enslaved people as collateral. Predictably, the financial community panicked when some southern businesses used secession as an excuse to repudiate their debts, prompting the *New York Post* to complain: "The city of New York belongs almost as much to the South as to the North."[24]

On February 9, the newly established Provisional Congress of the Confederate States of America chose as its president Jefferson Davis, a Democrat who had been a U.S. senator from Mississippi. He was inaugurated on February 18 in Montgomery, Alabama, and expressed a simple goal for his new country: to be left alone. One of the most pressing concerns facing the rebel states was the status of federally owned property. The Confederacy seized most of it, occupying forts, customs houses and arsenals across the South, leaving in federal hands only three forts in Florida and one, Fort Sumter, that guarded the mouth of the harbour at Charleston.

Major Robert Anderson, commander of the Union garrison at Charleston, feared a possible attack on Fort Moultrie on nearby Sullivan's Island, and in late December moved his men to the much stronger Fort Sumter, construction of which was still underway. Sumter had been planned in the 1820s but was not yet finished and remained a construction site. The five-sided structure had brick walls five feet thick and could house as many as 650 defenders, with 135 guns trained on the shipping channels leading to the harbour, but only 15 cannons had been mounted by late 1860. Anderson brought with him 87 officers and enlisted men. The Confederates promptly demanded he evacuate Fort Sumter, but Anderson, a Kentuckian devoutly loyal to the North, refused.

Onshore, about 3,000 militiamen gathered under the command of an ambitious Louisiana-born Creole named Pierre Gustave Toutant-Beauregard, who had just resigned as superintendent of the United States Military Academy at West Point in New York to join the Confederacy as a general.[25] Among the men serving with Beauregard was Gabriel Manigault, the plantation owner who was among the 169 men who signed the Ordinance of Secession. Manigault had become a colonel in the ordinance department of the new army of the Confederate States of America and was in charge of placing batteries for the bombardment of Fort Sumter.[26] Manigault also came up with plans for the defence of the 20 harbours, inlets, and river mouths along the 200 miles of South Carolina's coastline in a document called "Sea Coast Defences," which today can be found in the Library of Congress in Washington.[27] The federal troops at Fort Sumter were denied access to the city that ordinarily supplied it with food and ammunition.

Democrat James Buchanan was biding his time as outgoing United States president and believed secession was illegal, but felt there was nothing he could do about it. Despite being from Pennsylvania, he had sympathies for the South and readily allowed South Carolina to seize other federal properties. In January, Buchanan dispatched a paddlewheel steamer to take provisions and 200 troops to reinforce the garrison at Fort Sumter, but at the entrance to Charleston harbour Confederate batteries opened fire and the ship hastily retreated to the north.

When Lincoln took office, the Fort Sumter standoff landed in his lap, but he made no mention whatsoever of the Confederacy in his inaugural address.[28] Newly appointed Secretary of State William Seward suggested he appease the South by abandoning the fort. Such a move, he argued, would prevent further attempts to secede. But Lincoln preferred to supply the fort and communicated with new South Carolina Governor Francis Pickens, rather than Jefferson Davis, because he felt contacting Davis would be seen as recognizing the legitimacy of the Confederacy. Lincoln warned Pickens that if supply ships were fired upon, he would order federal troops onto South Carolina soil in response. After carefully weighing the potential consequences during the month following his inauguration, on April 4 Lincoln dispatched a small fleet of vessels from New York to take supplies and 200 reinforcements to Fort Sumter.

The Confederates had grown weary of waiting and on April 12 twice asked Anderson to evacuate the fort, which was running out of food. Both times the Union major refused. In a bid to buy some time, Anderson said he'd wait until noon on April 15, when he'd surrender. Beauregard was in no mood to wait any longer, however, warning Anderson that bombardment would soon begin. At 4:30 a.m. the following morning Confederate guns erupted and Sumter found itself surrounded by hostile fire, including from Confederate-held Fort Moultrie. To save precious powder, Anderson withheld return fire for two and a half hours. At 7 a.m., he ordered his second-in-command, Captain Abner Doubleday, to open fire with about 20 guns, half as many as the Confederates had trained on the fort.

In April of 1861, Confederate General Pierre Gustave Toutant-Beauregard ordered the shelling of Union-held Fort Sumter in the harbour of Charleston, South Carolina. These were the first shots fired in the Civil War, a bloody conflict which eventually claimed more than 600,000 lives.
(LIBRARY OF CONGRESS)

Despite the heavy bombardment and return fire, no one had yet been killed, and about three hours later the defenders were able to find some grim humour in their plight. Captain Truman Seymour relieved Doubleday's troops with fresh men, reportedly first asking: "Doubleday, what in the world is the matter here, and what is all this uproar about?" — his tongue firmly planted in cheek. Doubleday was ready, replying: "There is a trifling difference of opinion between us and our neighbours opposite, and we are trying to settle it." Seymour responded, "Very well, do you wish me to take a hand?" Doubleday agreed: "I would like to have you go in." Seymour's men took over and fighting continued.[29] The gallows humour helped the men cope with what appeared to be a hopeless situation. (Doubleday is the same Abner Doubleday who, years after his death, was publicly anointed as inventor of baseball in Cooperstown, New York, despite having had absolutely nothing to do with the game. That was a joke of another kind played on the American public.)

At the height of the bombardment, Lincoln's relief flotilla from New York appeared but wisely chose to remain offshore and out of range of the rebel guns. In the afternoon of April 13, following 34 hours of shelling, Anderson finally surrendered Fort Sumter to General Beauregard. Among Beauregard's aides was Arthur M. Manigault, formerly a captain in the South Carolina militia and brother of Gabriel Manigault, the colonel who had arrayed the artillery to bombard Sumter. Arthur Manigault later became a brigadier general in the Confederate Army and commanded troops in Tennessee and Georgia. Fort Sumter lay in ruins, but despite some 3,000 cannonballs fired from Gabriel Manigault's 19 coastal batteries and countless rounds from the fort, not a single soldier had been killed on either side. Some defenders had been hurt by flying concrete or mortar fragments, however.

The Union troops abandoned the fort the following day with an artillery salute Beauregard permitted them to make to the United States flag before it was lowered. The ceremony was marred when a cannon fired prematurely, killing one soldier instantly and leaving another with fatal wounds. The two Union soldiers became the first of an estimated 620,000 fighters to die in the Civil War.

Afterward, the *Charleston Mercury* complained about the "brutal fanatics" in Washington who sought war, but held out hope that hostilities could be avoided, declaring, "We did not believe that a war between the North and the South would be the result of a dissolution of the Union by the secession of the Southern States. With the sound of our cannon still ringing in our ears, we are of the same opinion still."[30] The paper would soon be proven wrong. Within days, Lincoln called for 75,000 volunteers across the North willing to enlist for three months of service in what was expected to be a short conflict with the rebelling states. In response, and appalled that Lincoln would consider killing his fellow Americans, the border states of Virginia, North Carolina, and Tennessee joined the Confederacy, swelling its membership to 10 member states.

Lincoln's secretary of state Seward was fully aware of Britain's reliance on King Cotton. Shortly after the fall of Fort Sumter, a motion was introduced in Britain's House of Commons to recognize the Confederacy, but Foreign Secretary Lord John Russell managed to delay the vote, fearing official American reaction. Meanwhile, Seward learned that British troops had been sent to Canada, which already harboured Southern ships at ports like Halifax, and that British Prime Minister Lord Palmerston was sending three more regiments to Canada, all armed with the latest artillery. A garrison was also relocated from China to Canada, and Queen Victoria issued a statement declaring that "it is of great importance that we should be strong in Canada."[31]

On May 13, the Queen and the British cabinet announced that Britain would remain neutral. But they declared the Confederate States of America as a belligerent party, a move that permitted the Confederacy to arrange loans from foreign governments. At the same time, legislation from 1819 was invoked to prevent British subjects from volunteering for a foreign cause or encouraging others to do so.[32] The neutrality declaration meant the Confederacy could obtain fuel and supplies in foreign ports, including those in Canada. Several other countries followed suit with similar declarations of neutrality.

Seward was outraged at the declarations, which fell just short of official recognition, and again urged the annexing of Canada. Palmerston sent still more troops to defend Canada in the event that Seward managed to get the ear of the new American president. In all, the British prime minister wanted at least 10,000 well-equipped soldiers posted in Canada.

Seward's antagonism toward Britain and its colonies in North America was well known. About the same time as the first shots were fired at Fort Sumter, Seward received cabinet approval to send former Massachusetts congressman George Ashmun to Canada to lobby for support for the North and act as a secret agent, reporting his findings to Washington.

Ashmun knew Canada well and was on good terms with Governor General Edmund Head, having represented the Grand Trunk Railway in its dealings with government officials. But on April 17, the *New York Herald* revealed on its front page that Ashmun was sent north to act as "a confidential agent of the administration."[33] The secret was out. In Washington, Britain's top representative Lord Lyons complained to Seward about sending a secret agent to Canada, a step he found insulting. Lyons said British-American relations were being undermined and he demanded Ashmun be recalled. Seward agreed and assured Lyons there were no other agents operating in Canada. But because of poor communications, Ashmun didn't receive his call to return home for some time and continued gathering information and meeting government officials including Head and others.[34] This delay did not displease Seward.

But there was more. Not long afterward, Seward demanded that Head block the sale of the steamer *Peerless*, which was lying in Toronto harbour, to Southern interests. The North believed it was being retrofitted with armaments to become a runner of the blockades Lincoln had ordered outside Confederate ports on April 19. Seward wanted the ship seized, along with documents outlining its mission, and a report sent to him. If Canada wouldn't act, he vowed, Americans would seize it.[35] That would have been a clear violation of sovereignty, the sort of act that started wars.

Seward learned that envoys from the South had met Lord John Russell, Britain's secretary of state for foreign affairs, so he penned an incendiary letter intended for Russell in which he threatened war if Britain dealt with the Confederacy or any of its envoys. Advisers suggested to Lincoln that the letter be toned down, and he complied. But word of the inflammatory and provocative nature of Seward's initial draft reached the ears of statesmen in Washington, including Lord Lyons.[36]

Threatening war, dispatching a secret agent to gather information on a clandestine basis, and talking of crossing the border to seize the *Peerless* did little to reduce the widespread distrust of Seward and his aggressive expansionist notions. He won no friends in Canada or Britain for the Northern cause.

John A. Macdonald, the attorney general for the Canadas, wasn't particularly worried about the threats of invasion or annexation, but said they demonstrated the need for a stronger union among all the colonies, including Nova Scotia, New Brunswick, and Prince Edward Island. He wanted them bound together by a strong federal government, unlike the United States, where each state was considered sovereign. He believed strong states and a weak federal government contributed to the Civil War. Macdonald shared his thoughts with the legislature soon after the fall of Fort Sumter, knowing an election in Canada was imminent.[37] He'd win re-election on July 1, and his tireless determination to federate the colonies would lead to his becoming Canada's first prime minister six years later. It didn't hurt that while on the campaign trail Macdonald carefully painted the opposition Grits as sympathetic to the United States — and even toward annexation.

In the aftermath of Fort Sumter, Head in Canada West and Lord Lyons in Washington monitored unfolding developments with wary eyes, fearful the North would quickly vanquish the South, then unleash its forces to annex Canada. Rumours abounded. Despite sharing Northern sentiment against the practice of slavery, Britain's colonies were no ally for that part of the American republic lying immediately adjacent. During the next four years, as the Civil War raged in America, the Canadian colonies would become far more than mere spectators.

CHAPTER SIX

CANADIANS IN UNION BLUE AND REBEL GREY

July 21, 1861, was a memorable day for three Canadian brothers who joined the Union war effort, the same day a bloody battle was fought at Manassas Junction, Virginia, that ended any hope in the North that rebel states could be brought back into line quickly.

The Wolverton boys were attending school in Cleveland, where they also acted as agents for their father's lumber mill back in their hometown in Oxford County, which still bears the family name. One of the mill's customers for its lumber and shingles in Cleveland was Thatcher, Burt & Company, which built nearly all the first railway bridges, depots, and engine houses in Ohio.

The father of the boys, Enos Wolverton, was born in Cayuga County, New York, and came to Canada with his father, Robert, in 1826. His sons were part way through their high school studies in Cleveland by the spring of 1861, reliant on financial support from their widowed father. They proved to be diligent in their studies, but Alfred, 23, Jasper, 17, and Newton, 15, didn't hesitate to respond to Abraham Lincoln's call for 75,000 volunteers to help put down the rebellion by southern states. Recruiters in Cleveland were looking to hire teamsters to serve the Union Army. Soldiers were paid $13 a month, but teamsters earned $30 and wagon masters $40, so rather than enlist as soldiers, the Wolvertons decided to cash in on their familiarity with horses, which they'd learned in the family business.

Jasper explained their decision in a letter to his sister Rose:

> You will no doubt think it strange that we should go
> off south but we think it the best we can do at present.
> If we should remain here [Wolverton] . . . it is probable
> that we could not get into any business here until times
> get better and by going now we can, if not unfortu-
> nate, clear $500 or $600 a year and be enabled to go to
> school on our return. Where we are going we shall in all
> probability be in no danger at all . . .[1]

The boys felt that by pooling at least $90 a month, they could help their father as his business struggled in a slumping economy. Aside from a slowdown in business, Enos also faced a potentially ruinous lawsuit. The Wolverton brothers figured they'd earn enough to finish building their home in Cleveland, then perhaps sell it for $3,000. The pay for teamsters was considered good money at a time when the average working man earned about $300 a year.

The Wolvertons were among 38 men assigned to the 50th New York Infantry. They were sent to Washington, where they were posted to the United States Quartermaster's Department and put to work building bridges, repairing roads, and undertaking other projects in the capital.[2] Alfred, the eldest, was placed in charge of more than 100 six-horse teams, while the youngest, Newton, was assigned 25 six-horse transport wagons. Horses and wagons were vital to the war effort, being responsible for hauling ammunition to the front lines, a potentially hazardous job. Following their rushed delivery of two hundred tons of ammunition to Virginia in September, the exhausted Wolvertons returned to Washington, where Jasper fell ill. He was taken to hospital and died of typhoid fever on October 12, not yet 18 years of age. Alfred arranged a furlough so he could take Jasper's body home to Canada for burial in Wolverton Cemetery on October 20.

Jasper Wolverton was among the first of many Canadian casualties in America's Civil War. Also attending the funeral was another Wolverton brother, Alonzo, 20, who had rented out the just-completed house in West Cleveland and returned to Canada to help save his father's troubled sawmill operation.[3] Once Jasper was interred, Alonzo accompanied Alfred back to Washington where he, too, signed up as a teamster and was assigned to the Quartermaster's Office. Alonzo suffered a bayonet wound during the Battle of Antietam in September 1862, and after recovering served for a time in Kentucky and then in Tennessee, where he was captured and spent more than a year in prison. He escaped just in time to join a regiment commanded by General William Tecumseh Sherman for his march through Georgia in late 1864. Alonzo was discharged in August of 1865 and returned home.

During their time in the service, the brothers corresponded regularly with their father and sister Rose back in Canada. Hundreds of letters survived, and years later many were relied upon for a book written by Alonzo's granddaughter Lois E. Darroch, *Four Men Went West to the Civil War*. Before the war ended, death claimed another brother, a sad development duly captured in those letters sent home. Alfred died of smallpox in Washington on April 23, 1863, the second of the four brothers to die away from the field of combat.[4]

Jasper Wolverton was one of the first Canadian-born casualties in the Civil War. He and his three brothers, from the Oxford County community that bears the family name, enlisted as teamsters for the Union early in the war. Another brother, Alfred, died of smallpox contracted while in the service. Jasper lies in a small cemetery overlooking the river valley above the village of Wolverton. (PHOTO BY CHIP MARTIN)

By 1862, friction was growing between the United States and Great Britain, placing the Wolvertons, and all Canadians serving south of the border, in a difficult spot. As British subjects, they grew alarmed when American politicians and newspapers began suggesting the time had come for war with Britain. A small committee of Canadians serving in Washington met and decided to make a direct appeal to President Abraham Lincoln, urging him to avoid war and reminding him of the contributions to the North being made by Canadians.

Newton Wolverton, still only 16, was a leader of the group and was asked to speak on its behalf. He had been an excellent student and was well-spoken, so his choice as spokesman made sense despite his tender years. At the time, Lincoln was still accepting walk-in visitors at the White House, and the young Canadian teamster secured a meeting with him through contacts in the Quartermaster's Office. "We are here to help in the war against slavery," Wolverton reportedly said, then explained the quandary of all Canadians aligned with Lincoln. There was no appetite to fight against Canada or Britain, he said, seeking assurances the president had no intention to fight either. The reply was reassuring. "We are happy to have you Canadians helping the Northern cause and want you to stay," Lincoln said. "I am not in favour of war with either Britain or Canada. As long as I am president, there will be no such war, you may be sure of that. Good day, sir, and thank you for speaking up."[5]

Along with his ability with words, Newton Wolverton had a good eye that made him an excellent shot. He served for a time under General Ulysses S. Grant and became known, unofficially, as "Captain of Sharpshooters." After the second of his brothers died, Newton fought the Treasury Department to obtain back pay owing to both Jasper and Alfred. His father Enos joined him in Washington to help make the case, and they chanced to meet Lincoln one day as they left the Comptroller's Office after an unsuccessful visit. Newton stopped the president and introduced his father and explained their quest, which had accomplished little. Lincoln led the Wolvertons back into the office they had just left and demanded the claims be processed. By the end of day, the money was paid.

At the end of June 1863, his contract expired so Newton and his father, who was still in Washington, returned to Canada.[6] Back home, Newton joined the militia in response to renewed concerns of a rift between Britain and the United States. As a lieutenant, he was sent to command troops along the border between Canada East and Vermont to fend off Fenian raids launched by Irish expatriates angry at Britain. After the war, Newton became a Baptist preacher and renowned educator, dying in 1932. The following year his proud son, Alfred Newton Wolverton, wrote Newton's biography with a subtitle calling him "one of the most colourful characters in Canadian History." Given the source, the overstatement is completely understandable.

Overall, the Wolverton brothers were not unique, as confirmed by more independent sources, including military writer Geoff Tyrell. He said their story was typical of Canadians who were living in the United States and sought adventure and money from recruiting bonuses and military pay. And thousands more crossed the border for the same reasons.

⌐∽⌐

The ink was barely dry on the contracts signed by the Wolvertons when the bloodiest conflict of the war to date erupted a bit more than 20 miles southwest of Washington. There, near Manassas Junction, Union and Confederate forces met in what Northerners fully expected to be a speedy rout of poorly trained and hastily assembled Southerners. Known as the First Battle of Bull Run by the North, which named battles after rivers, or as First Manassas by the South, which preferred to use the names of communities, it was the first land battle between the two sides.

Five days earlier, 35,000 Union troops left Washington under the command of General Irvin McDowell, who had been ordered by President Lincoln to confront the Confederates. Lincoln was under intense political pressure to act against the South. The Union had won some recent skirmishes in western Virginia, and the president wanted an offensive that would open the road to the Confederate capital of Richmond, bringing the war to a quick and decisive end. McDowell's tired men confronted 20,000 Confederate troops under the command of General P.G.T. Beauregard, the "hero" of Fort Sumter in the eyes of Southerners. Beauregard's men were camped near Manassas Junction, about 90 miles north of Richmond. Southern spies in Washington had relayed details of the Union march south, and 11,000 more Confederate troops under the command of General Joseph E. Johnston were not far away. In the early going, the Union forces pushed back the rebel forces, but the tide turned as reinforcements arrived by train to boost Confederate numbers.

The battle was watched from nearby vantage points by members of Congress and hundreds of civilians, who brought picnic lunches from Washington to witness what they expected to be an easy rout by Union troops. Women with parasols were in their Sunday-best finery while men wore formal attire with silk hats, despite the heat that day. Journalist Benjamin Perley Poore looked on, noting the throng of spectators had gathered "as they would have gone to see a horse-race or to witness a Fourth of July procession."[7]

By the afternoon, an intense battle was underway on Henry House Hill and the Confederates prevailed, prompting Union generals to order a retreat about 4 p.m. Frightened federal soldiers fled for their lives, as did civilians, clogging bridges and roads heading north. Not far from the fighting, United States senators were having lunch and were startled to see Northern soldiers run past them, some of them crying, while others jammed roads with their northbound horses and wagons. Senator Benjamin Wade of Ohio picked up a discarded rifle and threatened to shoot soldiers in mid-flight, while his fellow lawmakers joined the chaotic exodus and later delivered eyewitness accounts personally to the president. One member of Congress who was in the crowd that afternoon actually achieved Lincoln's aim of getting to Richmond: New York Representative Alfred Ely was captured and taken there as a prisoner of war.

Among the Confederate generals engaged in battle that day was

Thomas J. Jackson, whose troops held important high ground at Henry House Hill. He sat prominently in the saddle despite the obvious danger from enemy fire, causing another officer to marvel at his courage and liken him to "a stone wall." From that time on, he was known as Stonewall Jackson.[8]

The Confederates had been victorious in battle but were too disorganized to capitalize on it and march on Washington. Bull Run demonstrated there would be no quick end to the war, which would drag on for four years. It was anything but a "picnic" for anyone. The Union suffered 480 deaths that day and 1,000 wounded, with another 1,000 missing (likely having deserted), while the South had 390 dead, 1,600 wounded, and only about a dozen men missing. Following the debacle, Lincoln relieved McDowell of command and called for 500,000 volunteers to join the Union cause, and then another 500,000, all for three-year commitments. Congress passed legislation to significantly increase the size of the army and on August 5 voted to reorganize the military entirely.

A week after Bull Run, Kentucky Senator John C. Breckinridge, the former Democratic vice-president, took to the Senate floor to oppose any move to declare that a state of insurrection existed in the United States. He warned of tragic consequences from the call to arms. "Here we have been hurling gallant fellows on to death, and the blood of Americans has been shed — for what?" he asked. "Nothing but ruin, utter ruin, to the North, to the South, to the East, to the West, will follow the prosecution of this conflict," he lamented. Oregon Senator Edward Dickinson Baker rose to his feet, clad in military dress, to challenge Breckinridge: "It is our duty to advance, if we can, to suppress insurrection; to put down rebellion; to scatter the enemy . . ." He acknowledged there would be a price to pay in blood but it would be worth it. Baker drew applause from spectators in the gallery.[9]

———

About 40,000 Canadians and Maritimers served in the Civil War, with as many as 14,000 losing their lives. Some had already moved to the United States in recent years to pursue jobs and other opportunities. Most served on the Union side: overall, Canadians joined 250 Union regiments and 50 in the Confederacy.[10] Some sources suggest as few as 5,000 Canadians died, but many thousands more returned home missing legs or arms or with other serious injuries, so they were considered casualties.[11] Canadians were in the thick of things on both sides, such as the military surgeons who found themselves in opposing camps during the Battle of Gettysburg. Four Canadians became generals and 29 won the Congressional Medal of Honor, the highest military citation that can be bestowed in the United States.[12]

Many notable Canadians enlisted to fight for the Union. Among them was Calixa Lavallee from the Montreal suburb of Vercheres, composer of "O Canada," the future national anthem. His family had moved to Rhode Island in 1857, but he ran off to join a minstrel show in New Orleans. In September of 1861 he signed on as a "musician, first class" and became a trumpeter with the Fourth Rhode Island Regiment. By the middle of 1862 he was transferred to combat duty; after being wounded in the leg during the Battle of Antietam, he was discharged in October.

About the same time Lavallee enlisted, a man born near Sherbrooke in Canada East, but then living in the Chicago area, joined the Eighth Regiment, Illinois Volunteer Cavalry. John Franklin Farnsworth was a lawyer and had been a Republican member of the United States Congress. Despite a complete lack of military experience, he was named a colonel, likely because of his friendship with fellow Illinois Republican Abraham Lincoln. Farnsworth advanced quickly and became one of several Canadians who attained the rank of general in the Civil War, despite his short stint in service. He fought under General George McClellan in the Peninsular Campaign, which failed to capture Richmond, and at Antietam, where the Union claimed victory. Re-elected to Congress late in 1862, Farnsworth was forced to end his military career early the next year, not for reason of his election to public office, but because of serious war injuries he suffered. Farnsworth never returned to Canada.[13]

One of the more intriguing characters to cast his lot with the Americans was a 50-year-old politician from Windsor named Arthur Rankin. The son of Irish immigrants, Rankin wore many hats during a varied and interesting career. He became a surveyor in 1837, and because he was eager to see action during the rebellion of Upper Canada in 1837 and 1838, joined the Essex militia, where he became an ensign. He helped repel the pro-republican, American-based Hunter's Lodges during the Battle of Windsor and five years later, upon his discharge, organized a group of nine Ojibway First Nations people from a reserve along the St. Clair River into a "Wild West" show that toured the British Isles. It proved wildly successful, and at Windsor Castle his troupe gave a special performance for Queen Victoria.

Rankin sold the successful show and returned to Canada, where he invested the proceeds in copper mine exploration and development, and in railways. He was back in Windsor by 1849 and pondering a career in politics. After a false start, in 1856 he was elected Member of Parliament for Essex in the legislature of the province of Canada, the same year he was appointed colonel and commander of the Ninth Military District. He'd written British officials with an offer to raise a battalion of Canadian volunteers to fight alongside Britain in the Crimean War, but his idea was declined. During his term of office, Rankin was implicated in a railway scandal and was defeated in the next election, but returned as the MP for Essex in July of 1861.[14] A man who loved the spotlight, he also acted in theatrical productions in Windsor. By the outbreak of the Civil War, Rankin was known widely throughout Canada West, but he had visions of success far beyond the province. While waiting for the legislature to convene, he came up with a plan to offer his militia expertise to the country just across the Detroit River.

Rankin met prominent supporters of the Union cause in Detroit and some Michigan government officials, offering to raise a regiment of cavalry to be known as the First Michigan Regiment of Lancers. It would consist of 1,600 men led by Canadian officers with experience in the British Army. The recruits would be volunteers from Canada.

Rankin so impressed his listeners that in late August they took him to Washington to present the idea directly to President Lincoln and Secretary of State Seward. Rankin was at his persuasive best, outlining his plan to a president desperate for fighting men and, on September 11, a warrant was issued to create the regiment.

Word of his offer to fight alongside Americans proved controversial in Canada, however. The *Montreal Gazette* was sharply critical: "There are not many men in Canada better known for his somewhat Quixotic eccentricities than Arthur Rankin."[15] The paper called him a "reckless soldier of fortune," arguing he should be arrested and deprived of both his military rank and his seat in the legislature. The *Detroit Free Press* praised Rankin's sympathy for the Union cause and his military experience, predicting the ranks of his Lancers would soon be filled. Rankin sought a six-month leave of absence from his command of the Ninth Military District in Canada, but Governor General Edmund Head knew what Rankin was up to and denied the request, reminding the MP about the Queen's proclamation of neutrality. That proclamation, Head stressed, included invocation of the Foreign Enlistment Act of 1819, which forbade any British subject from serving in a foreign army or encouraging other subjects to do so.[16]

Rankin continued with his plans despite the warning, and by early October of 1861 more than 500 men, mostly Canadians, were Lancers. The volunteers were paid $13 a month, with additional money for travelling expenses and if they owned a horse. Rankin sought more men with recruiting posters across Canada West and as far away as Montreal. On October 6, however, Rankin was arrested in Toronto for breaching the Foreign Enlistment Act, and it was soon learned the charge was based on a complaint filed by the editor of the pro-South *Toronto Leader* newspaper. Its editor, George Sheppard, was an expatriate Southerner and an outspoken proponent of slavery.[17] After a three-day trial, the judge declined to rule in the case and referred it to a higher court. On October 15, the governor general relieved Rankin of his militia command. The Crown eventually dropped the case against him and Rankin continued to recruit Lancers, but events far away soon stopped him dead in his tracks.

On November 8, in international waters off Cuba, the Union ship USS *San Jacinto* intercepted the RMS *Trent*, a British merchant ship and mail packet on its way to Britain. Two officials from the Confederacy were found aboard and arrested. One, James Mason, was a former U.S. senator from Virginia known as the "father" of the Fugitive Slave Act, while the other was John Slidell, a former senator from Louisiana. Mason was on his way to meet top government officials in London, while Slidell was headed to Paris for similar talks with the French. Both men were emissaries of the Confederacy seeking to enlist moral and other support for the South.

San Jacinto Captain Charles Wilkes took the men ashore as the incident drew headlines and condemnation from Britain, which threatened to declare war on the United States if the men were not released with an apology. Meanwhile, additional British troops were sent to Canada and the Maritimes as tensions increased.[18] Lincoln was advised to declare war on Britain, but steadfastly refused to do so, arguing his hands were already full with one adversary and he didn't need another. In the end, the Confederate emissaries were released and Captain Wilkes was blamed for acting without authority. An apology never came and the crisis eventually passed, but there was lingering damage to British-American relations. And to public attitudes.

The *Trent* Affair was a watershed moment for many Canadians and those in the Maritimes who initially favoured the North in the conflict, largely because of its stance on the slavery issue. Now the North was seen as a potential enemy, an aggressive bully. Sympathy grew for the South, which did brisk trade with the Maritimes in particular.

Arthur Rankin suddenly realized if war broke out he'd be horribly conflicted as head of a regiment in the Union while also a British subject and member of Canada's Parliament. On December 28, the *Detroit Free Press* published a letter from Rankin announcing he was severing his ties with the Lancers.

> I feel constrained from a sense of duty, not only as a British
> subject but as a member of the Canadian Parliament, to
> withdraw from the Service of the United States and return

to Canada, my native land, determined to share the fate of my countrymen, whatever their destiny may be . . . under no circumstance could I be induced to occupy an attitude of hostility to my own country.[19]

Within a few months the Lancers were disbanded and under scrutiny for their spending. The *Free Press* complained that the $117,200 in expenses they incurred seemed "exorbitant" and alleged that fraud was involved in raising money to finance the regiment. Rankin was not named, but the newspaper called for a complete and thorough investigation into this "unfortunate regiment" and how funds were spent.[20] Back in Canada, Rankin became an eloquent proponent of nationhood during parliamentary debates leading to Confederation in 1867, warning if Canada and the Maritimes failed to unite, the alternative was assimilation by the Americans. He was passed over as a delegate to the vital conferences that led to Confederation, however, most likely because his reputation as a showman and attention-seeker, along with his ill-advised foray in Detroit, were held against him.[21]

———

Beginning just two weeks before the *Trent* crisis, five young men named Boucher were among the first Canadians to enlist in the Confederate Army. All were from the same extended family at Amherstburg, just south of Windsor, and they travelled nearly 800 miles to an enlistment centre in Arkansas. Charles, J.W., Samuel, James, and G.L. Boucher may have been cousins and it remains a mystery why they decided to fight for the South and travelled so far to enlist. Perhaps they had family connections in Arkansas, or they could reach a Confederate recruiting centre in that state without crossing more densely populated areas in the North where they might be challenged.

The Bouchers became privates in Company E of the 16th Arkansas Infantry Regiment, which soon reorganized in Mississippi and consolidated with other regiments. The regiment surrendered in Louisiana during July of 1863 and its men were paroled the same month, but its officers were sent to the Union Army prison at Johnson's Island in Lake Erie near Sandusky, Ohio. James and J.W. died in battle during 1862, while G.L. and Samuel were discharged before the war's end. Charles was injured, captured, then involved in a prisoner exchange and returned to service until hostilities ceased in 1865.[22]

Also joining the Confederate cause was Canadian medical doctor Solomon Secord, who had practised in Kincardine, along the shore of Lake Huron. Shortly before the war he moved to South Carolina, thinking the warmer climate would be good for his health. But the political climate soon heated up far beyond his wildest expectations. Born near Hamilton in 1834, he was a grand nephew of Laura Secord, the heroine of the War of 1812 for walking nearly 20 miles through bush and swamp to alert British troops of American plans to attack them that she had overheard.

With the outbreak of the Civil War, Solomon Secord joined the 20th Regiment, Georgia Volunteer Infantry, and by September 1862 was regimental surgeon. In early 1863, he was officially appointed surgeon, a rank rivalling that of major, in Beauregard's corps, Army of North Virginia. Secord was wounded and captured at the Battle of Gettysburg, July 1–3, while treating patients. He was imprisoned for several months at Fort McHenry in Baltimore harbour but escaped on October 10.[23] Secord returned to the 20th Regiment and was posted to hospitals in Georgia and Virginia, resigning late in 1864.[24]

After the war Secord returned to Kincardine, where he married, raised a family, and practised medicine until his death in 1910. He was highly esteemed there, and after his death Kincardine residents raised the funds to erect a monument to their beloved doctor. Its inscription reads:

> To Solomon Secord, 1834–1910. Our family physician for fifty years. This memorial was erected by his loving friends. Served as surgeon with Southern Army during American Civil War. All that he lived he loved, and without regard for fee or reward, he did his work for love of his work and for love of his fellows.

The monument in downtown Kincardine remains the only monument in Canada dedicated to someone who fought for the South during the Civil War. An effort in recent years to remove it failed, despite the movement to topple statues of Confederate war figures across the South.[25] The town firmly rejected the plea, insisting that Secord's monument was paid for by personal friends, that he was a non-combatant physician, and that the monument does not celebrate the Civil War in any way.

Kincardine Doctor Solomon Secord had just moved to South Carolina before the Civil War for the good of his health. He didn't hesitate to sign up as surgeon for the Confederates, becoming one of many Canadians who served in the Southern army. After the war, Secord returned to Kincardine, a picturesque town on the shore of Lake Huron. Upon his death in 1910 his friends raised the funds to erect this monument to the beloved doctor. It is the only monument to a Confederate in Canada, but it salutes the man, not the Southern cause, and remains to this day, despite an effort to remove it.
(PHOTO BY CHIP MARTIN)

Like Secord, Francis Wafer was exactly the sort of medical recruit the armies of both the South and North wanted, given their critical shortage of doctors, or even near-doctors. Wafer interrupted his medical studies at Queen's University in early 1863 to apply his newfound skills and knowledge in the Union Army, joining the 108th New York Regiment. By the time Wafer signed on, the regiment was considered a veteran unit in the Army of the Potomac. In May, Wafer and his regiment appeared at the federal defeat at Chancellorsville, which left the Union Army scrambling to defend Washington from Confederate General Robert E. Lee. Less than two months later, Wafer found himself at Gettysburg, the decisive battle that halted further incursions by Southern armies into the North. About 3,000 Canadians saw action there, primarily on the Union side, including Wafer. Wafer continued serving in Union blue at several more battles and was likely at Appomattox Court House in Virginia on April 9, 1865, when Lee surrendered his armies to Union General Ulysses S. Grant, ending hostilities. Afterward, Wafer returned to Queen's to complete his medical studies and become a doctor, but he was plagued by chronic ill health attributed to his Civil War service and died in 1876.[26]

In 1861, Anderson Abbott received a licence to practise from the Medical Board of Upper Canada, becoming the first Canadian-born Black doctor. He was the son of wealthy and prominent parents who had fled Alabama after the family's successful grocery store in Mobile was ransacked by white people. The Abbotts moved first to New Orleans, then New York State, before settling in Toronto.[27] Early in 1863 Abbott applied for a commission as an assistant surgeon in the Union Army, but was rejected. Not long afterward he was hired as a "medical cadet" in a Black regiment. For more than two years Abbott served in hospitals in Washington and was placed in charge of one across the Potomac River in Arlington, Virginia. Abbott was part of a small group that stood vigil over President Lincoln as he lay dying from the wounds inflicted by assassin John Wilkes Booth. In April of 1866, Abbott resigned and returned to Toronto. He chose to practise medicine in a number of communities, including Chatham, near which he had studied for a time as a boy at Reverend William King's school at Buxton. He became president of both the Chatham Medical Society and the Chatham Literary and Debating Society. Abbott relocated to the Hamilton and Toronto areas and for a time was head surgeon at a hospital in Chicago before again returning to Toronto, where he wrote extensively about the Civil War, Black history, and other subjects. He died in 1913.[28]

Another Black doctor came from Canada but followed a completely different path. Alexander T. Augusta was born free in Norfolk, Virginia, in 1825 and had a burning desire to become a doctor. Barred from medical school there because of racial discrimination, he applied to Trinity Medical College, affiliated with the University of Toronto, becoming the first Black medical student in Canada West. Augusta received his Bachelor of Medicine degree in 1860 and practised for several years in Toronto. He became a leader of the Black community, provided books and school supplies to their children, and was active in anti-slavery activity on both sides of the border. Less than a week after the Emancipation Proclamation authorized Black military service, Augusta wrote President Lincoln asking for an appointment as a physician in one of the newly created "colored regiments." In April 1863, Augusta was given the rank of major, becoming the first Black commissioned as a medical officer in the United States Army, one of 13 Black surgeons in the Civil War. By 1865 Augusta was a lieutenant colonel, the highest-ranking Black officer in the army. After mustering out in 1866, he spent the rest of his career in Washington, working at local hospitals, in private practice, and teaching at Howard University Medical College. He died in Washington in 1890.[29]

Other Black people born north of the border decided to enlist to join the fight against slavery. It has been said at least 835 Black soldiers and 352 Black sailors born under the British flag fought for the Union, and they were joined by an equal number of American-born Black men who had been living in the British colonies.[30]

A few were tricked. In early 1864, the *Chatham Planet* related the story of two Black men from the Buxton area who decided to act as recruiting agents for a Colonel Barnes of the Colored Regiment of Detroit. Willis Hosey and Isaac Washington were charged with enticing an area boy to become a soldier in Barnes's regiment. They were accused of deceiving 15-year-old Mordacai Morris, the only son of Emilene Crose, a widow from the Buxton area. The *Planet* said the boy was promised a good-paying job on a farm in Michigan. But once across the border, Morris was enlisted, leaving his mother and family without support. The two men eventually offered the boy's mother $120, but she declined, saying she only wanted her son back. Both men were fined, but the boy's fate is not known. Later that same year Hosey was back in court, charged with trying to enlist a Chatham shoemaker.[31] It is clear Hosey, like most recruiting agents, was not dissuaded from his activities: a fine was simply considered a cost of doing business, devious as that business was.

The overwhelming majority of Black Canadians who enlisted did so of their own free will. Having fled the United States, they welcomed the opportunity to return and take up arms against the South in its desperate bid to retain slavery. The First Michigan Colored Regiment attracted many men from Essex and Elgin counties just across the border, while the 54th Colored Regiment of Massachusetts attracted many who had settled in Nova Scotia and New Brunswick.[32]

———

One of the more intriguing stories of a Canadian who served in the Civil War began in the spring of 1861, when a 19-year-old Canadian named Franklin Thompson appeared at the Union Army recruiting centre in Detroit. After a medical examination that did little more than test Thompson's eyesight, hearing, and firmness of handshake, the new recruit was assigned to the Second Michigan Volunteer Regiment. Had the examination been more thorough, it would have revealed that Franklin was a woman, Sarah Emma Edmonds.

The slight recruit was born near Fredericton into a large farming family and at a young age became an accomplished rider and crack shot. Edmonds dreamed of adventure beyond the drudgery of farm life, inspired by a book she received at age nine that described the adventures of Fanny Campbell, a teenaged girl who disguised herself as a man to sail off in search of her sweetheart and then pry him from the clutches of pirates.[33] When her abusive father tried to force 15-year-old Edmonds to marry a man twice her age, she fled home. To avoid detection by him, Edmonds began disguising herself as a man and took the name Frank Thompson, wearing men's clothing, cutting her hair short, and darkening her fair complexion with dye. She made her way to the city of Saint John, New Brunswick, where she found work as a travelling Bible salesman and was quite successful. Still as Thompson, she moved to the United States to sell Bibles in Boston and then to Flint, Michigan.

When she heard a newsboy shouting at a train station in Michigan that Fort Sumter had fallen, she decided to fight for the country she had so recently adopted, hoping to help as a nurse. She explained her decision this way in a book she would later publish: "It is true I am not an American — I was not obliged to remain here during this terrible strife . . . But the great question was, what can I do? What part was I to act in this great drama?" She explained she decided to step forward "in this hour of my adopted country's need to express a tithe of the gratitude which I feel toward the people of the Northern

Canadian Sarah Edmonds passed herself off as a man to enlist as a nurse in the Civil War for the Union side. Incredibly, she kept her secret throughout her time of service. She was one of a handful of women who took part in the war. Edmonds became a spy and later wrote a book about her exploits, but chose not to mention her successful deception. (AMERICAN BATTLEFIELD TRUST)

States."[34] Edmonds had been taught home remedies and how to treat injuries and illnesses by her mother, skills she felt could be put to use in the army. She was able to persuade the recruiter about her knowledge of basic treatments and Private Frank Thompson was made field nurse for F Company.[35]

At the time, military nurses were almost exclusively men, despite the success and influence of Florence Nightingale and her fellow caregivers in British field hospitals during the Crimean War. Acceptance of women as nurses had just begun in America when the Civil War began, but there was a lingering feeling that women should not be exposed to the gore and blood of battle, which were deemed to be beyond their emotional and physical abilities.[36]

After two months of training, Edmonds and her company were sent to Washington where they were inspected by President Lincoln. The Michigan regiment was deployed in the First Battle of Bull Run, where Edmonds helped convert a small stone church into a field hospital. The church soon was filled with bodies and the wounded, with stacks of amputated limbs nearby as blood pooled on the floor and spattered the walls. Edmonds helped comfort the dying and helped restrain unsedated patients while doctors sawed off mangled arms and legs. After the Confederates prevailed on the battlefield, she managed to escape under cover of darkness and found her way back to Washington, where she reunited with F Company. There, she immediately went to work tending to the wounded and sick in a makeshift hospital.

Edmonds eventually became a postmaster and later a spy for the Union, passing herself off at various times as an enslaved Black woman or Irish immigrant woman and appearing at battles, including Antietam. At one point, she became "Charles Mayberry" to help break up a Confederate spy ring in Union-occupied Louisville. In 1863, she explained later, she contracted malaria after the Union victory at Vicksburg while serving in a military hospital. Weakened and feverish, she couldn't continue her duties and was quietly discharged from service with a certificate of disability that kept her deception secret.[37] In another version of her departure, it was said she refused treatment for malaria at Vicksburg, fearing her identity would be revealed to her fellow soldiers, so without permission she travelled to Pittsburgh, where she changed into a dress and entered a hospital there. The story continued that upon her release, she learned that Frank Thompson was sought as a deserter, an offence punishable by death, so she decided to discard that identity forever.[38]

Regardless, in both versions of events, she eventually made her way to Washington to recover further, never again donning a uniform. As she recovered, Edmonds visited area hospitals, then moved back to New Brunswick where she penned her memoirs, released in 1865, titled *Nurse and Spy in the Union Army: The Adventures and Experiences of a Woman in Hospitals, Camps, and Battle-fields*. Inexplicably, she made no reference to her deception as Frank Thompson. The only illustration of her in the bestselling book depicts a woman in full skirt standing beside a horse. She donated all her book proceeds to the U.S. War Relief Fund. In New Brunswick, she married Linus Seelye, a carpenter with whom she had three sons, and moved to La Porte, Texas. In 1884, by which time her deception as Frank Thompson had been revealed, she was granted an honourable discharge from the U.S. Army by Congress for "a splendid record as a soldier." Edmonds was provided a modest cash bonus and pension, the first military pension ever awarded a woman. She died of malaria in 1898.[39]

While her exploits were extraordinary, Edmonds was not the only woman to disguise herself as a man to enlist. It has been estimated as many as 250 women did so to join Confederate forces and another 400 to join the Union, although some sources suggest the combined total was closer to 550.[40] It is not known how many Canadian women passed themselves off as men among the estimated 40,000 Canadians and Maritimers who joined the war effort. Women played a prominent role during the Civil War, without resorting to any disguise, acting as cooks, laundresses, couriers, flag-bearers, and a growing number as nurses. When necessary, women shouldered arms to fight the enemy, and as many as 60 of them were killed in battle.[41]

After the First Battle of Bull Run it became clear the fight between North and South would be prolonged. Both Lincoln and Confederate President Jefferson Davis acknowledged that grim reality and began to call for more volunteers, trying to find them wherever they could and eventually resorting to conscription. The two presidents would have been surprised at the number of volunteers they attracted from Canada and the Maritimes who were willing to take up arms in a fight in which they had so little at stake.

The motives were varied for Canadians who left their safe perch in America's attic to join a war from which 14,000 of them never returned. Some like Secord, Farnsworth, and Abbott sought the opportunity to develop their medical skills and help their fellow man, regardless of the side or cause for which they fought. Likewise, the Wolverton brothers cashed in on their skills as horsemen in a bid to help their father and improve their family fortunes. Lavallee filled the air with music while others filled it with lead, and like all musicians he appreciated a gig with steady pay. Some may have enlisted in the North to help fight slavery, at least in part. The five Bouchers may have been seeking adventure or financial rewards at a time when the economy in Essex County was not strong. Or, possibly, they simply wanted to fight alongside distant members of their family. For Sarah Edmonds, it was the lure of adventure along with a determination to prove herself by helping the ill and wounded. And then there was Arthur Rankin, a man who never missed an opportunity to promote himself and his schemes, having parlayed that ability into personal encounters with Queen Victoria before the war and then early in the conflict with President Abraham Lincoln. In the end, despite his grand talk, Rankin was among the least successful of the Canadians or Maritimers who committed themselves to a titanic struggle raging just a few miles from their homes.

CHAPTER SEVEN

SKEDADDLING, CRIMPING, AND DESERTING

By 1862 it was abundantly clear the struggle between North and South would be a prolonged one. One battle led to another, with neither side establishing its superiority, and the number of casualties (dead and wounded) continued to mount. Armies on both sides needed more men.

During the entire war, nearly two million served in the Union Army, while from 750,000 to one million others took up arms for the Confederacy. Men who signed up were paid "bounties" of $200 or $300 to as much as $1,000, raised from a variety of sources including public donations. The names of donors and the amounts they contributed regularly appeared in newspapers such as the *Detroit Free Press*. Meanwhile, the majority of those who enlisted were farmers and for some of them the bounty paid was an additional motivation, given their poor economic situation. Some men who were drafted avoided military service by legal means, such as hiring substitutes or paying a commutation fee of $300 (equivalent to the annual wage of an ordinary worker). Those provisions led to complaints that the wealthy could buy their way out of military service in what amounted to a "rich man's war but a poor man's fight." Commutation fees were repealed by the North in March of 1864, but substitution continued and by late in the war the cost to hire substitutes had risen substantially, compelling even some wealthier men to become evaders.[1] In the North, the substitution fee was capped at $299, but the South, where from 50,000 to 150,000 substitutes had been hired, abolished the practice entirely late in 1863.[2]

It has been estimated more than 160,000 men illegally avoided service after the North adopted conscription in March of 1863. They became known as "skedaddlers." Another 40,000 to 50,000 skedaddled to escape state drafts in 1861 and 1862.[3] It is unknown how many chose Canada as a refuge. Draft evading increased during the four drafts conducted by the Union. For the first, in July of 1863, 13.5 percent of men failed to report to their local draft boards, a figure that more than doubled to 28.5 percent in the final draft during July of 1864. Areas with the greatest evasion tended to be non-Republican in politics, with more Catholics and foreign-born residents. Proximity to Canada was important when the decision was made to evade the draft.[4]

The fear that wartime fugitives would take their work was a sentiment among the lowest-paid workers on both sides of the border. Once the Emancipation Proclamation took effect on January 1, 1863, the same sort of resistance Canadians and Maritimers had to American fugitives taking their jobs began to take root in two northern cities where new Black arrivals were seen as a threat to workingmen. Some Black Canadians returned to northern states and joined other Black people who had migrated there to take jobs previously denied them. On March 6, a race riot in Detroit was sparked by the criminal conviction of a Black man accused of raping a young white girl, but the underlying motivation was fear among working-class white people that newly freed Black people would take their jobs. Two died in the clash between the races, many were wounded, countless Black people were beaten, and 35 buildings burned to the ground. The *Detroit Free Press*, a Democratic paper with a large white working-class readership, helped fuel fears about white workers losing jobs to Black people, saying emancipation undermined white labourers.[5] It was Detroit's first race riot. It wouldn't be the last in that city.

Some Americans were motivated to enlist by love of country or to demonstrate bravery, while others had no interest in dying for either side. For Northerners among the latter group, the Canadian border at Detroit and Buffalo provided an opportunity to escape the growing pressure to enlist before being drafted. And the pressure was increasing for good reason. In February, the Union victory at Fort Donelson claimed 2,691 Union casualties and 13,846 for the Confederacy. In April, at the Battle of Shiloh, the Union again won, but suffered 13,047 casualties to the Confederacy's 10,699, making it the bloodiest battle fought until that time. On May 31, another 5,739 Union casualties were recorded at the inconclusive Battle of Seven Pines, while 7,997 men were lost by the South. In late June, 6,800 Union soldiers were casualties at the Battle of Gaines' Mill, a Confederate victory that cost it 8,700 men.

Casualties were felt more acutely in the less-populated South, whose pool of military-age men was less than one-third that of the North. The Confederate Army risked disintegration if it couldn't attract more men, most of whom had enrolled for only 12 months. In response, on March 29, 1862, Confederate President Jefferson Davis called for conscription of all men between the ages of 18 and 35.[6] Terms of service were extended from 12 months to three years, or until the war ended.

In response to pressure to increase enlistment, Republican President Lincoln set quotas of men the Union required from each state. If voluntary enlistment fell short, a draft of randomly selected men would follow. The pressure to enlist and the fear of being drafted prompted eligible young men to flee to Canada in increasing numbers.

Hundreds of skedaddlers had already crossed the border by August 8 when Lincoln issued an order prohibiting any citizen subject to military duty from going to a foreign country without permission.[7] Such permission could be obtained from various government officials and often included the requirement for a bond. Not surprisingly, his order triggered a new flow of skedaddlers. Within days, about 400 American men defied Lincoln and crossed into Canada West at Niagara Falls during a 24-hour stretch. By 1865, an estimated 10,000 to 15,000 or more skedaddlers had fled to the Canadas and the Maritimes.[8] Some American historians suggest there were even more. They followed a trail similar to that blazed during the previous three decades by other Americans — freedom seekers and free Black people.

The *Toronto Globe* commented in 1862 on the "extraordinary" flight from the United States and Lincoln's response to it. "So great has been the exodus, that the Washington Government has been induced to issue an absurd and tyrannical order, designed to prevent the escape from the country of persons liable to be drafted." The *Globe* said towns and cities in Canada West had become "crowded with motley groups of fugitives from the draft . . ." The newspaper, which was pro-North in outlook, labelled as "ludicrous" the posting of American officers at the border to dissuade other would-be fugitives. The *Globe* said that while tavern keepers might benefit from the new arrivals from south of the border, it predicted their eventual departure would "excite no regret" among Canadians.[9]

During that August, barely a day went by when the newspapers in Buffalo and Detroit didn't carry stories of skedaddlers, whose capture they applauded. Those who made the crossing into Canada safely were damned as traitors and cowards.

The day after Lincoln banned foreign travel without special permission, the *Buffalo Evening Post* carried this story:

> THE STAMPEDE TO CANADA — We hear that this forenoon quite a number of persons were stopped at Suspension Bridge, and also at Lewiston, on the way to Her Majesty's dominions. They were required to show cause, but on making the proper explanations and the necessary affidavits, some were allowed to proceed, while others were compelled to take backward steps much crest fallen.[10]

A couple of days later, the *Detroit Free Press* carried this report:

> THE RUSH FOR CANADA — The stampede for Canada is not so large as many have placed it. Some three hundred and fifty have passed over the Great Western

Road, taking up their line of march for the promised land where drafts are not expected to reach them. The large majority of these have little or no money, and will scarcely prove a very desirable addition, in a pecuniary point of view, to the Canadas. Already complaints have reached this side of robberies being committed in various places, which are directly traceable to these sneaking vagabonds.[11]

Occasionally, skedaddlers were confronted at the border by armed American troops, with dire consequences. The *Buffalo Commercial* related one such story:

MAN SHOT AT NIAGARA FALLS — We learn that a man who tried to run the guard at Niagara Falls yesterday, to get into Canada, was shot by one of the soldiers doing guard duty. He was ordered to halt, but paying no attention to the order, the sentry shot him, inflicting a severe wound. We were unable to ascertain whether the wound was considered dangerous or not. It will undoubtedly prove a lesson to others. We understand the guard at the Bridge was reinforced yesterday morning, by a squad of soldiers from Camp Church, at Lockport.[12]

The shooting of men who tried to evade military service was endorsed by the *Detroit Free Press* in an August 12 editorial entitled "Cowards Running." It noted that "quite a large number of persons have arrived here over the Detroit and Milwaukee, the Michigan Central and the Detroit and Toledo Railroads, for the purpose of making their way to Canada, for the purpose of avoiding the laws regulating drafting for the army." The editorial writer took some solace from the fact that few of the deserters were Michiganders, but insisted any man whose name was called in the draft "cannot escape the consequences. He must appear or be disgraced — and perhaps shot."[13]

The same Detroit paper noted that some Southerners had joined evaders from the North and together they were having a fine time "living on the most amicable terms" just across the river in Windsor at the Hirons Hotel.[14]

The influx of Americans in Toronto, a city of 45,000, was noted by the pro-South *Toronto Leader*, which never missed an opportunity to embarrass and ridicule Lincoln and the North. In Buffalo, population 81,000, the *Buffalo Courier* quoted a "patronizing" account published earlier in the *Leader* that the Toronto paper said was culled from various American newspapers:

> THE EXODUS FROM THE NORTH — From these extracts it will be inferred that an enormous depopulation is taking place in the North. Judging from the constant arrivals, by every train and steamboat coming into Toronto, thousands must have left their homes on Saturday and are now scattered over all parts of Canada. All trades and professions appear to be represented . . . It is to be supposed that they are all able and willing to work, and can earn their living honestly. Indeed several Northerners obtained employment in Toronto.[15]

The *Buffalo Commercial* couldn't help notice the brisk business enjoyed by hotels on the Canadian side of Niagara Falls and highlighted the arrest of a man trying to flee to Canada across the Niagara River.[16] Some skedaddlers were so determined to flee that they risked swimming across the fast-flowing and dangerous Niagara. Some likely failed in the attempt. On August 16, the story of three successful swimmers appeared in the *Buffalo Courier*:

> LATEST FROM THE SNEAKS — We are credibly informed that three men swam the river night before last to evade the draft. They had their clothes on and carried life preservers. Our information came through a gentleman at whose house on the Canada side they

presented themselves to get their limp and cowardly carcasses dried. Such enterprise almost deserves success.[17]

Nerve was abundant among most fugitives and some demonstrated real flair, as noted by the *Buffalo Evening Post:*

> On Wednesday last, two gentlemen who were stopping at the International Hotel, Niagara Falls, wishing to visit the Canadian side, took a carriage and rode across the bridge, having first provided themselves with a note from the proprietor of the house, Mr. Coleman, stating that they were travelers, and were riding for pleasure. On this the U.S. Marshal at the bridge, passed them across. As our informant states, no sooner had they reached Canadian soil, than they leaped from the carriage, gave three cheers for Jeff Davis, and sent the vehicle and driver back with the intimation that they didn't care a d—n for their baggage, as they were now where they wished to be.[18]

In Detroit, so many of its 46,000 residents pestered Acting Mayor Frank B. Phelin for passes to Canada that he felt compelled to announce in the *Free Press* he had been granted no such authority and couldn't help them.[19]

Back east along the busy Niagara frontier, gunfire erupted during an August 19 escape attempt by a trio in a boat at the river's edge, reported the *Buffalo Weekly Express.* Two armed officers whose job it was to stop fugitives "during the drafting season" persuaded the men to return to the American side and, when they scampered off, wounded one with gunfire.[20]

Immediately below that item appeared another, about a police attempt to "prevent a number of plug-uglies from Baltimore" from crossing the Suspension Bridge to Canada that same Sunday. The military was called in to assist, and during the incident a soldier was shot.

Shortly after regulations were issued for a draft of men in Michigan, a large number of what the *Detroit Free Press* called "poltroons" [cowards] were arrested trying to flee to Windsor. It added: "Strict guard is still kept up at this point and all skulkers, from whatever part of the country they may come, may rely upon their being subjected to a scrutiny which it will be difficult to evade."[21]

On August 11, 1862, the *London Free Press* reported that flight to Canada had increased "almost to a stampede" and many Americans had taken up residence in London, population 12,000, and lying 150 miles from both Detroit and Buffalo. The *Chatham Planet* also noted the constant stream of American fugitives arriving by rail and by boat along the Thames River.

Evaders continued to cross the border at Detroit in large numbers, spurred further when the United States Congress passed the Conscription Act the following March. Within days, the *Detroit Advertiser* reported the number of skedaddlers bound for Windsor was climbing on a daily basis, with many of them travelling from Illinois, Indiana, Wisconsin, and Iowa. The newspaper estimated as many as 400 evaders were then in Windsor, population 2,000, but local inhabitants put the number at as high as 1,000, making for a significant impact on a community of that size. Some escapees had already moved to Amherstburg, Chatham, and other communities not far from the border. In Windsor, the Detroit newspaper continued, many of the newcomers were eating cold meals and sleeping on floors, and offering to work for as little as 50 cents a day and board. The *Advertiser* said a Canadian source insisted that between 4,000 and 5,000 runaways had crossed the border the previous month. "As a general thing they are orderly," the Canadian man told the paper, "and the Windsor people have no reason to complain, so long as their guests are in funds and pay their board bills promptly." The Detroit paper concluded its report by reminding its readers the runaways were cowards and claimed that Canadians despise them as much as Americans.[22]

A similar influx of Americans was occurring in Canada East and in the Maritimes. So many skedaddlers crossed from Maine into New Brunswick that a small settlement of escapees, established northeast of Hartland, was named Skedaddle Ridge. And on the colony's Atlantic Coast at Montebello Island, the busy arrival point for such newcomers was known as Skedaddler's Reach.[23]

For the most part, the new arrivals were welcomed, although unskilled local workers began to resent them for depressing wages, a trend accurately predicted by the newspaper in Chatham, Ontario. Draft dodgers and deserters from the military were willing to work on farms for $10 a month, well below the going rate paid local men. This proved a bonanza for farmers, who were already reaping profits by supplying both sides in the Civil War. Prices rose dramatically for their crops and produce as unemployment grew among local workers. Resentment of the Americans grew among the lowest-paid workers and it spread to the wider community when some of the newcomers engaged in petty thievery rather than pursue any work at all.[24]

———

As the Civil War dragged on, the numbers of dead and seriously wounded continued to rise. The Second Battle of Bull Run in August 1862 claimed 25,251 casualties in total, Antietam another 23,000, Fredericksburg 17,900, Murfreesboro 23,514, Chancellorsville 30,051, Gettysburg 51,000, Vicksburg 50,000, Chickamauga Creek 34,444, the Battles of the Wilderness 54,000, and on, and on, with no end in sight. State recruiting offices constantly needed more men, despite the implementation of conscription, because so many potential recruits availed themselves of exemptions available to them. Quakers, for instance, were pacifists and refused to serve in the military because of their religious beliefs, while certain occupations were deemed essential and their workers excused. Meanwhile skedaddlers kept skedaddling and their ranks included deserters from the Union Army. Tinkering with conscription requirements to generate more candidates continued on both sides, such as expanding the age of men subject to it. But the need for manpower continued and bounties increased. Many Canadians jumped at the lure of those bounties or the money to substitute for wealthy Americans. Some Canadians joined military regiments in Michigan and New York, although numbers are hard to pin down. Regiments in Michigan were filled with hundreds of men drawn from the neighbouring Canadian counties of Essex, Lambton, and Elgin. One estimate put the total number of British- or Canadian-born Michigan troops at 19,341, a figure that is considered high and which included British Army deserters.[25] By 1864 in Maine, it was reported that fully 1,043 Union soldiers from that state were Canadian-born.[26]

While Americans were fleeing to British North America to avoid the war between the states, attempts were being made to fill the void they left behind. Enter the "crimps." Recruiting Canadians became a lucrative activity for American agents known as crimps, or crimpers, referring to the encouragement of someone to enter military service. The practice was not illegal, provided that no deception, threats, force, or violence is used. Crimps reaped financial rewards for signing up Canadians for the Union Army by alerting potential recruits to either the bounties offered or the opportunity to earn even more money by becoming a substitute. Successful crimps, like the men who enlisted, received bounties for their work.

Given the substantial money they could earn, however, crimps began to use methods that were often questionable when they crossed the border to find warm bodies. Under British law, no American could recruit a Canadian or Maritimer into the U.S. Army, and Britain's Foreign Enlistment Act forbade British subjects from joining of their own accord. But the laws on both sides were seldom enforced and crimpers took advantage to profit, some overseeing networks of crimps as "brokers." With money to be made, the practice continued until the end of the war, and recruiting offices across the North didn't care how Canadians came to enlist because they had quotas to meet. Questions were left unasked and the United States government took little or no action to prevent aggressive crimping, despite repeated complaints by British colonial authorities.

To get their men, crimps and their associates often resorted to plying young Canadians or British soldiers with drink, or drugging them, then spiriting them across the border to recruiting offices or military bases. Kidnapping was not uncommon. Sometimes prostitutes used their charms along with alcohol served in "crimping houses" to lure unsuspecting young men and hand them over to crimps. Sometimes the targets were British soldiers or sailors, other times simply the naive, who would regain consciousness on the American side of the border only to discover they had enlisted. Sometimes recruits were cheated out of the bounties they had been promised by crimpers.

To combat crimping, rewards of $50 were paid for catching a crimp in Canada, an amount that rose to $200 by 1864 as the practice continued unabated. But few crimps were apprehended.[27] To avoid the long arm of the law, particularly devious crimps would target a potential recruit, advance him some money and provide clothing, then accompany him to the United States to enlist. There, the crimp would receive a fee of $15 to $25 and as much of the bounty owing the recruit as he could swindle from him. The practice of crimping was yet another irritant that festered between Britain, its colonies, and Washington. When the American War Department tried to curb crimping in the New York City area during 1864, police refused to co-operate so the effort went nowhere.[28]

Oftentimes crimps lured men in the colonies with the promise of lucrative jobs south of the border. In Toronto, the pro-South *Toronto Leader* drew attention to misleading posters, such as those that appeared in July of 1862 describing the need for large numbers of men to work on a Pennsylvania railroad. The *Leader* blasted such deception by "agents of the United States," and labelled it "recruiting under false pretences."[29] About the same time in Windsor, a man named Marx was supposedly seeking men to work at a cotton mill and took 25 men to Detroit, where 15 of them belatedly realized he was a crimp and escaped back across the river. The others were plied with drink and shipped south.

At the village of Port Burwell on Lake Erie, a poster was found at a local inn late in 1863 announcing, "Splendid Chance to Make Money, Recruits Wanted." It was recruiting for the U.S. Army and offered bounty money of $302 and regular pay that totalled a further $468 in each of three years. It urged interested parties to contact an "authorized recruiting agent" in Tonawanda, New York, a town near Buffalo. The poster was forwarded to Governor General Lord Charles Stanley Monck, who was already well aware of aggressive efforts by the Americans to enlist young men in the colony.[30] Monck complained to the British Colonial Office that recruiting by Americans continued despite repeated requests it cease.

Monck learned aggressive crimps were using an increasing number of ruses as the war ground on relentlessly. In one case, crimps posed as Canadian police constables to recruit men in Windsor. William Fisher and Thomas Miller were arrested by said "officers" in July of 1864 while they were patching a boat and were taken across the river to Detroit. Fisher and Miller appeared before a magistrate there who said he would drop the unspecified "charges" if the pair agreed to join a regiment in Michigan. After some time spent behind bars and considering their limited options, the two Canadians finally enlisted. Their case enraged their friends, family, and colonial authorities alike, and a formal complaint found its way to United States Secretary of State William Seward. Upon investigating, Seward discovered the police officers and the magistrates were all frauds and directed the Canadians be released from duty. Miller was located months later and granted a discharge, but by then Fisher had already deserted.[31]

In 1862, United States Secretary of War Edwin Stanton authorized the creation of "colored regiments" in the Union Army. Black soldiers were called upon to help the North in its constant quest for able-bodied men and were offered an opportunity to join the fight against slavery. They responded well and by war's end about 180,000 of them had joined the ranks of the Union Army.[32]

In their first effort to combat illegal crimping, the provinces of Canada, Nova Scotia, and New Brunswick adopted measures in 1862 making it easier to arrest and convict crimpers and impose recently increased fines and jail terms. But this had little impact. Two years later, policing was beefed up in border areas, where 20 new magistrates were also assigned to hear cases of crimping. Early in 1864, a circular was sent to all Crown attorneys in the colonies advising them of the need to combat the growing scourge. "You will not fail to initiate proceedings, and to aid the efforts of the officers of Her Majesty's service," read the directive from John A. Macdonald. Rewards as high as $200 were offered to anyone who turned in a crimp.[33] Despite the new penalties, only 91 convictions were registered in Canada against crimps during 1864 and 1865, and crimps continued to ply their trade indiscriminately.[34] A 15-year-old white boy, John Bland Allinson, was snatched off the street of his hometown of Niagara on July 5, 1864. Allinson was accosted and rendered unconscious by a man he didn't know and taken aboard a train. When he came to his senses, the boy found himself aboard the USS *Michigan*, a United States Navy ship in Lake Erie. Allinson was eventually rescued through the intervention of Dennis Donohoe, the British consul posted to Buffalo.[35] Coercion and kidnapping of foreigners, including Canadians, to get them into the American military has been described by at least one Civil War historian as "the worst scandal of the war period, and, indeed it remains one of the darkest blots on the history of the United States."[36]

Alarmed at the activity of American "crimps" who often used trickery to enlist Canadians to fight in the Civil War, Attorney General John A. Macdonald imposed fines in a bid to halt the practice. They had little impact.
(LIBRARY OF CONGRESS)

British soldiers were particularly attractive recruits for the Union Army, having already been trained, and some had battle experience in the Crimean War. They were ripe for the picking because desertion was already a problem for the British Army in North America. Pay was poor, as were pensions, and discipline was harsh. Many were bored because of a lack of military action and being confined to their barracks with endless drills. Besides, with high bounties and pay offered to do a similar job in another army nearby, the lure was tantalizing. Sometimes word of an upcoming posting to the tropics, where prospects of survival by British soldiers were not good, led to the decision to desert.[37]

Crimps knew that Irishmen within the British ranks were particularly amenable to desertion because of their prejudice against England. James Miller, a crimp operating in Kingston, made this simple pitch to three Irishmen posted there: "You are all Irishmen, why did you all enlist in the bloody English service? Come along, I will take the whole lot of you."[38] The lure of money was particularly strong, given that non-commissioned British officers and even sergeants earned less than a dollar a day, whereas American bounties were $300 or more in a lump sum and the annual pay was well above that of the average wage earner.

As early as the spring of 1861, British authorities worried about the threat of desertion as they drew up plans to defend the border and strategic waterways across the colonies from possible American attack. In an April 29 letter to Governor General Sir Edmund Head, the British commander in Canada, Lieutenant General Sir William Fenwick addressed the problem. "Your excellency knows as well as I do, that these locations will afford peculiar facility for desertion, and therefore, that it is desirable to send hither only men who are perfectly trustworthy," Fenwick wrote.[39]

During the summer of 1862, crimps targeted British soldiers posted to Toronto. Late in July several disappeared "suddenly and mysteriously," according to a July 28 letter in the *Toronto Leader*. Soon afterward, another 27 men deserted from the same regiment, prompting special guards to watch the barracks overnight following careful head counts. Deserters were apprehended and punished, and some had a

"D" tattooed on their chests to further shame them. But desertions continued, and by January of 1863 all British troops in Canada were advised to be extra vigilant to detect "villains" who enticed their fellow soldiers to desert. Ten months later, military authorities offered rewards of $50 for help finding anyone who encouraged desertion.[40] At the Windsor-Detroit border crossing, British commanders were extra vigilant, posting guards along the border and arresting any soldier found more than a mile from his base. In Kingston, the commander of Fort Henry ordered an extra shot fired at curfew each day to mark every man who deserted that same day in a bid to shame remaining soldiers out of the practice and encourage their continued loyalty to the Queen and Empire.[41]

Some British soldiers went to extraordinary lengths to desert. One was Michael Benson, a private stationed in London with the 63rd Regiment of Foot. A 28-year-old Irishman, he had served in Crimea and was apparently bored with life in the barracks in the middle of nowhere. He was described by the *Detroit Free Press*, which chronicled his flight, as an "eccentric and ingenious individual." On the night of December 26, 1862, Benson donned women's clothing and slipped out of London heading west to the border at Detroit, about 150 miles distant. Like other British soldiers, he was not allowed to own civilian clothes, another of the measures that had been imposed to discourage desertion.

Where Benson obtained a dress is not known. He walked along the main east–west stagecoach route known as Longwoods Road, finding abandoned farmhouses along the way where he slept at night. He made it to the halfway point at Chatham undetected, where he switched to the railway track to continue his westward trek. Near Belle River, Benson met a man who queried him about his appearance and destination. Benson revealed his true gender, which prompted the stranger to suspect he was a deserter. The smooth-talking Benson assured him he was not and that he had married a woman in London against the wishes of his father. His wife, he said, had fled to Detroit and awaited him there. Benson admitted he had stolen $1,000 from his father and adopted the disguise to avoid detection. The story seemed to satisfy the man, who agreed to take Benson across the Detroit River for $20, and they travelled to the river near Windsor where they found a boatman to ferry them across. On the American side, the accomplice demanded his money, but Benson stalled, saying his wife had it. Realizing he had been scammed, the man from Belle River seized the woman's shawl Benson was wearing in a bid to get something of value for his troubles. With that, and still dressed in the remainder of his feminine attire, Benson strode into the recruiting office for the 28th Michigan Regiment and enlisted with a startled Captain Lee. The *Free Press* obviously enjoyed sharing the story on its front page, and predicted the bold and crafty Benson "will make an excellent soldier." It also took the opportunity to ridicule the British Army "look outs" on the Canadian side of the border who had failed to intercept their man/woman.[42]

Despite the colonial government's best efforts to stop desertions, they continued until the end of the Civil War. Attorney General Macdonald wrote to local Crown attorneys asking them to aggressively prosecute soldiers who were apprehended. In August of 1864, the death sentence was imposed on two deserters, but that penalty was eventually commuted and the men spent six months in prison. The situation so concerned Lord Lyons, the British minister in Washington, that by September he said it was clear a system was successfully luring soldiers and other British subjects from Canada and included "kidnapping them and carrying them across the border."[43]

Just as Canada and the Maritimes provided a safe haven, an attic of sorts, for Americans anxious to escape the rigours and danger of war, some colonial inhabitants, civilian and military alike, helped both the North and South wage war. The door to the attic, the border, was a two-way street. A busy one. Thousands of Canadian men and boys (and the occasional woman) willingly went south in search of adventure and profit. So, too, did British soldiers. Some colonists were hoodwinked by crimps and never returned home, dying on distant battlefields. Meanwhile, American skedaddlers continued to flood north in ever-increasing numbers as blood continued to flow back home. The steady flight in both directions ended only when the Civil War did.

CHAPTER EIGHT

BUYERS, PLOTTERS, AND SPIES

The highlight of the social scene of 1860 in London, Canada West, was the visit of the Prince of Wales during his well-received tour of the United States and the British colonies. The legislature of the Province of Canada had invited Queen Victoria to visit her colonies in North America in a bid to show support for the British monarchy and to express their appreciation of self-government and the freedoms colonists enjoyed under her reign. And they hoped to show how they had prospered in recent years. Victoria declined to make the trip herself and sent her eldest son, Albert Edward, 18, popularly known as Bertie. Once they learned the Prince of Wales was travelling to Canada, American officials extended an invitation to include stops in the republic, and it was accepted.[1] Wherever he went, Bertie created a sensation.

The royal tour began in Newfoundland, then proceeded through the Maritimes, Canada East, and Canada West. The prince dedicated the new Victoria railway bridge across the St. Lawrence River in Montreal and was present for the laying of the cornerstone for the new Canadian Parliament buildings in Ottawa. He then continued west to Chicago and St. Louis and circled back to Washington, New York, and Boston before heading home from Portland, Maine. Everywhere, the press was abuzz with excitement about the young royal, and politicians were determined to show off their communities and their citizens in the best possible light, freely spending public funds to do so.

Like Toronto, Montreal, and other cities, London was no exception in its excitement and desire to put on a good show for the royal visitor. Public money was spent to complete the Tecumseh House Hotel, which had languished incomplete for a couple of years. The colonial government leased the hotel and finished it just in time for the royal visitor. A grand reception and ball went off well, attracting about 600 guests at $10 a couple. Master of ceremonies was prominent local lawyer H.C.R. Becher, who oversaw the list of dancing partners selected for the prince by ball organizers from among ladies of the city elite. It proved to be an unexpectedly daunting task, and Becher related some of the troubles he encountered in his diary. "One old friend is nearly ready to eat me up & wants to fight a duel with me because his wife does not dance with the Prince soon enough," he complained.[2] Jockeying for position among the ladies occurred despite his best efforts to maintain the order agreed upon, and some of those on the list lost their dances entirely. One woman cleverly bypassed the list by having General Sir Fenwick Williams, the commander of all British forces in North America, introduce her to the guest of honour, and then she lingered long enough to get a dance at the expense of a woman on the official list. "Another lady displeased and all my fault," Becher lamented. He even managed to run afoul of Governor General Sir Edmund Head, who "complains to me of the age of the partners selected for the Prince . . ."

Other guests anxious for a dance accused Becher of selecting members of his own family and organizers of the gala while ignoring available young maidens Bertie might have liked. Things got ugly, according to a later newspaper account: "Judge James E. Small of Middlesex, threatened to assault him and stop the ball unless his wife was introduced to the future monarch. She danced with the Prince and a fight was thus averted."[3] While the city elite fawned over the guest of honour that evening, vied to get his attention, and squabbled about his dance card, burglars seized the opportunity to ransack their homes and made off with $1,200 worth of their property, a sizeable amount in the day.[4]

Within the hotel, other nefarious activities were going on. Guests who filled the Tecumseh House rooms during the Prince of Wales's visit included spies, buyers of horses, beef cattle and farm produce from both the North and South, some wealthy Southerners anxious to escape the war, and others who hatched plots and conspiracies from the comfort and safety of a grand hotel. The Civil War would be good business for the Tecumseh House, for London, and for all of British North America, given the proximity to the American border and Britain's declaration of neutrality.

———

London had profited over the years because of its role as a garrison town for the British Army, and Tecumseh House symbolized that growth. Following the rebellion of 1837–38, when dissatisfied colonists clashed with the colonial elites who governed them in Upper and Lower Canada, London became a base for the British military. The uprisings were put down with the help of the army and militia, and the garrison remained until 1852, when Britain began withdrawing troops from North America to deal with troubles in Europe and Crimea. In 1855, the barracks were converted to a refugee camp for 700 of the formerly enslaved.[5]

The community had grown from a village of about 1,000 into a bustling town of more than 10,000. Officers and enlisted men, some of whom were from aristocratic families back home, brought culture to the settlement freshly hacked out of the bush, which became known as the Forest City. The army hosted social occasions like balls, band concerts, theatrical productions, steeplechases, greyhound races, and cricket matches, all of which were among the highlights of the social scene. Some soldiers married local girls and took them back to the British Isles.

The economic impact of the military was great as local merchants supplied produce, flour, wood, hay, and other supplies needed by the garrison. Only Toronto, Ottawa, Hamilton, and Kingston were larger cities in the colony, which had grown from a population of 952,000 in 1851 to 1.4 million by 1861. London was surrounded by some of the best agricultural land north of the American border, and it shipped wheat and other crops to the United States and Europe. The city had several flour mills and ready access to the world because of new railways. The city's small manufacturers produced agricultural and other implements along with railway equipment, heavy machinery, harnesses, and carriages. Foundries and stove companies prospered along with those making consumer products ranging from biscuits to sewing machines.[6]

London was a bustling city before, during, and after the Civil War, selling agricultural products, horses, and other items to both sides in the conflict. New arrivals included not only buyers but spies for both sides, most of whom likely arrived at the Grand Trunk Railway station. (IMAGE COURTESY OF JOE O'NEIL)

The Crimean War, 1854–1856, had been a boon to local farmers when Britain replaced wheat it previously purchased from Russia with that grown in Canada West. The Reciprocity Treaty of 1854 had opened the doors to markets in the United States and more than doubled American trade with the British colonies. Business was booming in London, and late in 1855, when it was formally designated a city, its population reached 16,000. Several city boosters, including prominent businessmen and future mayors, were optimistic about the future and decided the city needed a fine new hotel. That was the Tecumseh House, a 160-room, four-storey brick hotel immediately west of the Great Western rail station, just south of downtown. It was named after the famed Shawnee chief who fought alongside British General Isaac Brock in the War of 1812 and who was slain the next year alongside the Thames River about 40 miles southwest of London. The Tecumseh House was the biggest and finest hotel west of Toronto and featured its own modern steam-heating plant. Backers had no trouble raising about $100,000 to begin construction in 1855. But some skeptics derided building such a grand hotel for a city the size of London as "folly."

The following year the end of hostilities in Crimea led to a depression. Investors retrenched, construction was halted, and the hotel sold at public auction for far less than had been invested to that point. By 1858, new investors appeared and completed the basement and first two floors. In all, about 100 rooms were available to the public.[7] Backers of the hotel continued to struggle with the economic collapse of 1857, triggered by the failure of the largest insurance company in the United States, then bank failures, factory closures, and business bankruptcies. The downturn spread to Canada and Great Britain. The recession lasted into 1859, by which time it was estimated three-quarters of all London businesses had gone bankrupt, and some people who couldn't pay their debts simply fled the city.[8] Aside from the economic woes, local agriculture was beset by unseasonable frosts and widespread crop failures. By 1859, the population of London had dropped to 11,000.

The only bright spot in the economic gloom was the city's newfound role as an oil-refining centre, the first in the world. In early 1858, crude oil was discovered in gum beds at Oil Springs, about fifty miles west of London. Even more was found at nearby Petrolia and soon crude oil was shipped east by train to London for refining into kerosene, the illuminating oil used in lamps in the days before light bulbs and electricity. The discovery at Oil Springs predated the more famous and celebrated discovery of sweet crude oil at Titusville, Pennsylvania, by a full year.[9] For two decades, London remained a leading centre for oil refining until producers left town and built refineries closer to the source.

The new Tecumseh House Hotel was the premier hotel in London, and many Southerners stayed there, some families for protracted periods. Union buyers and spies preferred the less opulent Arkell's Hotel for its vast stables where horses could be quartered before being shipped by rail to nearby states.
(ILLUSTRATED HISTORICAL ATLAS OF THE COUNTY OF MIDDLESEX, 1878)

London became a hotbed of intrigue during the war. Aside from filling its hotels, the Civil War increased demand for locally grown crops like wheat, although sales fell below expectations because newly settled areas like Kansas began adding to the supply. The demand for beef to feed Union armies was strong and many farmers adjusted their operations accordingly, becoming beef barons. Exports of all livestock were significant during the war years, horses in particular, along with cattle. Wool and flax were in great demand because both were used to make uniforms. The fledgling co-operative cheese industry found ready markets south of the border. To process farm output that became more diversified, new flour mills, linseed-oil mills, flax-scutching mills, cheese factories, and meatpacking houses were established. Buyers from the North and South sought not only horses but wagons and a wide variety of manufactured goods.[10] By the end of the conflict, London businesses and manufacturers had become prosperous.

The *Trent* Affair late in 1861 prompted fears that Britain and the United States might go to war. In Canada West, London lawyer H.C.R. Becher made this diary entry in December: "There is great excitement & we seem to feel war is almost inevitable & if it comes Canada will be the principal battlefield." About two weeks later, Becher wrote, "It is expected this Trent matter will lead to war."[11] Britain increased its troops in Canada, including the Maritimes, from 4,488 to 11,529 men. About 1,400 soldiers were posted to London, occupying the old barracks and erecting new ones. The return of the British military was welcomed, along with their theatrical productions, horse racing, and colourful inspections at Parade Square.[12]

Some clashes occurred between local officials and the military in London, however. The most notorious one came at a glittering social function, held at the Tecumseh House Hotel, between the mayor and the officer who was second-in-command at the British garrison in 1863. The garrison organized a ball that was intended to honour the marriage of the Prince of Wales to the Princess Alexandra of Denmark at the same venue where Prince Bertie had been feted nearly three years earlier. The ball took place March 10 to coincide with the royal nuptials in England. The day had been declared a public holiday by Mayor Frank Cornish and celebrations included the firing of a military salute, processions and parades through the streets, and the lighting of bonfires in the evening. The Tecumseh House ball was the highlight of festivities. The official host for the garrison was Major Vere H. Bowles of the 63rd Regiment of Foot.

Otherwise well attended and successful, the gala was marred by a fistfight about 2 a.m. between Cornish and Bowles. Rumours had been circulating that linked Bowles to Cornish's wife, Victorine. Cornish, who had a reputation for feistiness, suddenly confronted the major and they exchanged a flurry of blows, after which Cornish kicked Bowles in the butt. Two senior officers intervened as Cornish ripped off Bowles's decorative medals and threw them in his face, ending the incident almost as soon as it began. In police court the following morning, Cornish was convicted of unprovoked assault and fined six dollars. He told the judge he'd been antagonized when he was denied admission to the hotel's new ballroom and found the major was needlessly abrupt and rude. For his part, Bowles testified the altercation began when he was stopped at the entrance to the room "by a civilian whom I at first took for a cabman, but afterwards recognized as the mayor of the City of London." Insulting the mayor this way did not go over well with city council, which adamantly refused to issue an official apology demanded by the British Army. That wasn't the end of it. General Sir Fenwick Williams threatened to withdraw troops from London if an apology wasn't forthcoming.[13]

Months later, some soldiers from London were relocated elsewhere, but that likely reflected the growing realization that the Union Army was no longer expected to invade Canada. Cornish, whose antics embarrassed the city elite on more than one occasion, remained mayor until 1865. A few years later he moved to Manitoba, leaving his wife behind in London. He became active politically in Winnipeg: he was elected first mayor of the city and led his fellow Orangemen in bigoted anti-French and anti-Catholic campaigns during his one term as mayor and several as an alderman. Cornish also won a seat in the Manitoba legislature.[14]

During the war, the streets of London were filled with draft dodgers, Union spies and buyers, Confederate spies and buyers, British spies, Pinkerton detectives, and others. Some Southern families and operatives for the Confederacy took up residence in the Tecumseh House Hotel. Years later, an elderly mixed-race woman named Hardin told respected historian Fred Landon she had fled Kentucky with her sister in 1855 and had made their way to London. Landon related her experience:

> A few years later, while the Civil War was raging and when London was a home for many southern families, Mrs. Hardin found her services much in demand as cook for the Southerners far from their home and longing for the dishes so common in Dixie.
>
> Mrs. Hardin says that two and three times a week she would fill a basket with real southern dishes and take it to the rooms of some family at the Tecumseh House who would then call in other southern families for the meal. She also did sewing and washing for them . . . [15]

Buying agents and spies for the North favoured the nearby Arkell's Hotel. While less opulent than the Tecumseh, Arkell's featured large stables which buyers for the Union kept full with their purchases. So many horses were sold to both sides in the conflict that the supply was depleted across the entire region. Northern agents shipped horses to Buffalo, Detroit, and Cleveland, but Southern buyers had to be devious. Horses and cattle bound for the Confederacy were shipped to Montreal or Quebec City, where paperwork indicated they were bound for England or Europe. Once at sea, boats filled with the four-legged Confederate purchases were rerouted south, where the ships tried to outrun the Northern blockade of Southern ports.[16]

On the streets of London there was plenty of intrigue and foreigners snooping into each other's business, not unlike other cities in Canada and the Maritimes during the war. From his base in Toronto, Confederate Jacob Thompson oversaw a network of about 2,000 spies, soldiers, and Confederate sympathizers operating in Canada West. He found it particularly difficult to discuss plots against the North because wherever he went the city walls and streets all seemed to have ears. Thompson complained bitterly to his superior about the difficulty of operating in such an environment: "The bane and curse of carrying out anything in this country is the surveillance under which we act. Detectives, or those ready to give information, stand on every street corner. Two or three cannot interchange ideas without a reporter."[17] With so much happening on the streets of Canada West and in colonial hotels and taverns, clandestine and otherwise, residents became acutely aware their city had become a hive of activity for some and a safe haven for others. Years later, stories were still being related about those memorable days.

In London, for instance, cabinet maker John Hislop shared a vivid recollection with Edmund Carty, a newspaperman and member of the London and Middlesex Historical Society. Hislop said he was working one day in his furniture shop when he was visited by two "handsome young women" dressed in finery that suggested they were well off. Hislop recalled that these customers were hard to please. They were polite, however, and at one point asked about a type of short decorative hanging for shelf tops or the tops of window casings. Hislop responded: "Oh, the tastes of you Yankees are different to those of Canadians." His visitors immediately took offence, the older one retorting: "Sir, we would have you understand we are not Yankees. We are Southerners. My father is General Beauregard of the Southern Confederacy." The young ladies eventually found what they wanted and directed Hislop to send their purchase to the Tecumseh House, where it was believed members of the Beauregard family occupied a suite of three or four rooms.[18]

Biographies of Pierre Gustave Toutant-Beauregard make no mention of any member of his family spending time in Canada during the Civil War, however. So it was either an incredibly well-kept secret or the invention of gossipy Londoners — understandable perhaps, given all the strangers in their midst. Beauregard did have a daughter, Laure, who was born in 1850, but from 1861 to 1865 he didn't see her while she was reported living with the family of her late mother at their Louisiana plantation.[19]

As the war dragged on and the Confederacy lost important battles, sympathy for the South grew across all the British colonies. An incident late in 1863 in the waters off New Brunswick demonstrated the depth of feeling. That December, a small group of Confederates and their supporters in the Maritimes captured the *Chesapeake*, a Union steamship out of New York, in the waters off Cape Cod and diverted it to Saint John, New Brunswick, where they planned to refuel with coal. The captain was wounded and the engineer killed in the incident. The pirates planned to sail the ship to Bermuda and offer it to the Confederate navy there.

Two Union warships, the USS *Ella Mae* and USS *Dacotah*, pursued and caught the *Chesapeake* near Halifax, along with a Canadian ship that was attempting to refuel her there. Canadians John Wade and William Henry, and other Canadians on the refuelling ship, were placed in irons by the Americans and the *Chesapeake* was towed to Halifax by the Union vessels. Colonial officials insisted the *Dacotah* release the *Chesapeake* and the prisoners because its captain had violated international law by seizing the vessels in Canadian waters. The Americans wanted the ship turned over to Canadian authorities but made no mention of prisoners Wade and Henry. A crowd of pro-South Haligonians gathered at the harbour and helped Wade and Henry escape. Meanwhile, John Braine, leader of the Confederate pirates, was hailed as a hero in the city. At the pier, guns were drawn during the standoff and Lieutenant Governor Charles Tupper threatened to fire upon the *Dacotah* from army batteries if the ship didn't release the *Chesapeake* and the prisoners. To defuse the situation, American officials took a page from the *Trent* Affair by insisting the captain of the *Dacotah* had acted without authority, and within three months the *Chesapeake* was repatriated. During subsequent trials it was learned that local brewer Alexander Keith was involved in the episode and had purchased 12,000 muskets for the Confederacy that he planned to send south.[20]

The *Chesapeake* incident occurred not long after Confederate President Jefferson Davis approved a plan to establish what amounted to a second front based in Canada. The idea was to create trouble along the border and provoke a war with Canada, forcing the Union to negotiate a three-way peace that would let the South continue as a distinct entity within the United States. Davis and the Confederacy were growing desperate after having trouble finding enough recruits and losing too many battles and men. Besides, money was running short. Despite the scarcity of funds, Davis committed $600,000 to operations in Canada of the $1 million the Confederate Congress approved for clandestine activities.

On April 7, 1864, Davis sent a message to Confederate Army Colonel Jacob Thompson, who had just returned to his plantation in Mississippi following the Battle of Vicksburg, one of the Union Army's most successful campaigns of the entire Civil War. Thompson, a former member of the United States Congress, had served in the cabinet of former president James Buchanan as Secretary of the Interior and had known Davis for decades. "If your engagements will permit you to accept service abroad for six months, please come here immediately," the Confederate president wrote. Thompson didn't hesitate and made his way to Richmond, where Davis appointed him "Commissioner for Special Service in Canada."[21] Thompson's assignment was to fan anti-North sentiment in the colonies in a bid to undermine British-American relations. He was expected to manufacture some sort of crisis that might help the South, which was losing its war for survival on the traditional battlefield.

Thompson established his headquarters at the luxurious Queen's Hotel in Toronto, located directly across from the main train station. The hotel carried the latest American newspapers and had a telegraph office on the main floor where Thompson could contact his agents and emissaries and receive reports from them. Thompson was placed in the charge of Captain Thomas Hines, a Confederate already in Canada who was busily spreading anti-North propaganda. Hines was organizing a bid to encourage residents in several states then known as the Northwest to mount armed resistance against the Lincoln administration and a war they had grown to oppose. Hines was working with a secret, pro-South society known as the Knights of the Golden Circle and an affiliated group, the Sons of Liberty.

Hines believed many thousands of disaffected Northwesterners in the states of Illinois, Indiana, Ohio, and Missouri could be encouraged to revolt, creating a second secession movement that would help preserve the Confederacy as a distinct entity. Creation of a Northwestern Confederacy would see the partition of the United States into three distinct parts.[22] Judah P. Benjamin, the Confederate secretary of state, felt Thompson was just the man for the new assignment with the approach of the November presidential election in the North. He shared the news with the South's diplomat in Paris, John Slidell (of the *Trent* Affair): "We have sent Jacob Thompson of Mississippi and Clement C. Clay of Alabama to Canada on secret service in the hope of aiding the disruption between the Eastern and Western States in the approaching election . . ."[23]

The head of Confederate spy operations in Toronto was Jacob Thompson, a North Carolinian, who lived at the Queen's Hotel opposite the main rail station. The Queen's catered to Southerners and even offered mint juleps to its guests. Thompson had trouble with leaks of various Confederate-backed plans to the enemy and he complained bitterly that everyone in Canada seemed to be a spy.
(LIBRARY OF CONGRESS)

Thompson didn't get along with his assistant Clay, who was based at St. Lawrence Hall in Montreal, a city of more than 90,000, twice the size of Toronto. Thompson encouraged the Knights of the Golden Circle (known as "Copperheads") and the Sons of Liberty, who claimed to represent thousands upon thousands of discontented Northwesterners who were prepared to revolt, given enough support and a suitable crisis. The two organizations readily accepted financial encouragement from Thompson, but he soon discovered they were poorly organized. Thompson tended to be too trusting of others and freely dispensed Confederate money without adequate oversight. Thompson encouraged the holding of secret peace talks between emissaries of the South and the North from July 16 to 20 on the Canadian side of Niagara Falls. His initiative ended in failure when the South learned Lincoln would accept nothing less than full restoration of the United States in any peace agreement.[24] With the collapse of talks, Thompson embarked on acts of cross-border sabotage, hoping to provoke the Union to attack Canada and provide some hope of survival for the Confederacy.

That same month, Confederate Army Captain Charles Cole was on his way to Canada to hide out with other Confederates after escaping from a Union prison. He stopped at Sandusky, Ohio, where he came up with a daring plan once he saw Johnson's Island prison just offshore, guarded by the aging Union steamer USS *Michigan*, a 582-ton ship with 15 guns. Cole wanted to capture the *Michigan* and use its weapons to free the 2,700 Confederates imprisoned on the island, many of them officers. They could then cross to Canada to launch raids on neighbouring states and afterward fight their way to Virginia, wreaking havoc along the way. The *Michigan*, the only warship on the Great Lakes, would then cruise unmolested along Lake Erie with Confederates at the helm and turn its guns on Detroit, Buffalo, Cleveland, and Sandusky. Thompson approved Cole's plan and found 20 Canadian-based Confederates who were willing to participate.[25]

Representatives of the Confederacy met in London, Canada West, on August 7 for a secret conference believed to include Cole,

Thompson, and Clement Vallandigham, who had been elected supreme commander of the Sons of Liberty in February while living in exile in the city. A preliminary meeting had been held in Windsor in June.[26] The attendees in London likely considered plans to free Confederate prisoners held in Union camps in Illinois and at Johnson's Island, returning many of them to the South to continue the fight. In a town where it was hard to keep secrets, word of the Copperhead-Confederate gathering somehow leaked out.[27]

Vallandigham, a friend of Thompson, was a leader of the Democratic Party in Ohio and had served three terms in the United States House of Representatives. He was an outspoken opponent of President Abraham Lincoln and of the Civil War. He became a leading Peace Democrat and was arrested by military authorities in May of 1863 for speaking against the war in defiance of a wartime order that muzzled free speech. A military tribunal sentenced him to prison for the remainder of the war, but Lincoln feared his incarceration would further inflame Peace Democrats, so he commuted Vallandigham's sentence to exile in the Confederacy. Vallandigham remained in the South only a few weeks before travelling north to Windsor and later to London, where he took up quarters at the Tecumseh House Hotel. From London, he campaigned for and won the Democratic Party nomination for governor of Ohio, but lost the subsequent election on October 13 to Union Party candidate John Brough. As newly elected governor, Brough dispatched spies to assess rumours that Confederate sympathizers were planning to free prisoners at Johnson's Island and at Camp Chase in Columbus, the state capital.

The secret meetings in Canada West likely involved Captain Thomas Hines, a Kentuckian, who would lead the attacks on the prisons. An uprising was planned to coincide with the Democratic National Convention in Chicago from August 29 to 31. Armed with money, firearms, and ammunition, the Confederate conspirators travelled in small groups to Chicago, where they took a suite of rooms as the "Missouri Delegation" and rendezvoused with the Sons of Liberty. The scheme was to attack nearby Camp Douglas and free its 5,500 prisoners while some of the Confederates would travel 200 miles west to Rock Island Barracks and liberate the 9,000 Southern prisoners held there.

The Sons of Liberty seemed disorganized, admitting that problems had arisen and no orders to mobilize had been sent to the thousands of members they claimed to have in Illinois and Ohio. Besides, the Copperheads complained that spies and newspapers had learned of their mission and extra federal troops had been dispatched to protect Fort Douglas. Hines was enraged, quickly realized the Chicago plot was doomed, and ordered his men to scatter.[28] Vallandigham had been little help, busy hobnobbing at the convention with his fellow Peace Democrats and promoting the official Democratic Party platform he had helped write that called for a negotiated peace with the South.

———

The Confederates were angry at the turn of events and came up with a revised plan to attack the Rock Island Barracks. After storming the barracks and freeing men there, they'd commandeer a train and head south 200 miles to capture Illinois's state capital, Springfield. But when they learned they had perhaps only 25 men available to pull off the daring raid, Hines reluctantly agreed to postpone the mission to November 8, federal election day. Back in Canada, Thompson branded the Copperheads as cowards and was disgusted at Hines for giving up so quickly. Thompson became bitter and vengeful, accusing the Confederates who returned to Canada of being "deserters." To add to his black mood, Thompson had just learned Union troops had burned his plantation in Mississippi and assaulted his wife.[29]

Shortly after the aborted mission in Chicago, the siege of Atlanta ended with the burning of the city by Union troops commanded by General William Tecumseh Sherman, who then began his March to the Sea, looting and plundering along the way. The pressure increased on Thompson to divert Union attention to its northern border.

Undaunted by the fiasco of Chicago, and still hoping for success, Thompson focused on the upcoming attack of the Johnson's Island prison on Lake Erie. There, Captain Cole had spent a month wining and dining the officers of the *Michigan* under the guise of a wealthy Philadelphia banker as he sought to gain their trust and gather information for the raid slated for September 19. Cole also visited some of the prisoners at Johnson's Island to prepare them for the ship hijacking and jailbreak. But by the date picked for the raid, Cole was exposed and arrested while the ship was full of Union sailors and marines fully expecting an attack.

Cole's comrades had captured the passenger steamer *Philo Parsons* at Detroit and headed south to meet the *Michigan*, where they expected to find its crew had been sedated by Cole and his operatives. When a signal they expected to come from their colleagues aboard the *Michigan* didn't materialize, they realized something was amiss and sailed the *Philo Parsons* across Lake Erie, flying a Confederate naval ensign, before scuttling her. It marked the first time that a Confederate flag was flown on the Great Lakes. And the last. In Toronto, the *Globe* described the "piracy on Lake Erie" and complained about desperadoes doing their dirty work from bases on Canadian soil. Even the pro-Southern *Leader* viewed the episode as a serious violation of Canadian neutrality.[30]

Although it failed miserably, the Lake Erie raid generated concerns about security along the American frontier, so federal troops were posted to Buffalo, Sandusky, and Detroit. In Buffalo, Mayor William Fargo established an intelligence network to act as an early-warning system and the Union increased its fleet on the Great Lakes. Meanwhile, American newspapers used the botched raid as another excuse to unleash anti-British and anti-Canadian sentiments.

It turned out that Cole had been betrayed by the operator of a hotel in Windsor where 60 Confederate expatriates had been living. Cole spent some time there as he finalized his plans. Word of his intentions was relayed to military authorities in Detroit and then to the *Michigan*.[31] His rooms were searched and correspondence was found linking him to spymaster Thompson in Toronto. Cole was arrested and joined the very prisoners on Johnson's Island he'd hoped to liberate.

The following month, Union troops were deployed to defend the cities of Buffalo and Detroit and guns were installed on five tugboats. And money was also allocated to create a fleet of armed cutters.[32] While the Lake Erie raid was a bust, it did produce a diversion of Union men and money that would otherwise have been used in the Southern campaign. The Confederate mission to open another front was succeeding, at least to a limited degree.

As they grew more desperate to help the Confederacy, agents operating from the convenient refuge of Canada continued to devise other plots, some deadly, some far-fetched, in a bid to draw Union attention, money, soldiers, and resources to America's northern frontier.

CHAPTER NINE

RAIDERS, BRIGANDS, AND ASSASSINS

On October 19, 1864, at precisely 3 p.m., a 21-year-old from Kentucky, Lieutenant Bennett Young, emerged from the American Hotel in St. Albans, Vermont, 20 miles south of the Canadian border. He was dressed in the grey uniform of the Confederate Army. Young stood on the porch of the hotel, brandishing a Navy Colt revolver, which he fired once into the air, and loudly proclaimed: "In the name of the Confederate States, I take possession of St. Albans." With that, some of his 17 accomplices appeared and herded startled townspeople onto the town commons while others robbed the town's three banks and stole horses from nearby livery stables for their getaway. At the First National Bank, one of the armed robbers announced: "We represent the Confederate States of America, and we come here to retaliate for acts committed against our people by General Sherman."[1] The raiders made off with more than $200,000 and rode out of town, tossing bottles of "Greek fire" at buildings in a bid to set St. Albans ablaze. The highly flammable concoction was a mixture of sulphur, naphtha, quick lime, and water. Some residents shot at the raiders from nearby buildings and the Confederates returned fire, killing one man and wounding another.

They were followed out of town by a posse led by Union Captain George Conger, who happened to be in town on leave. Young and his fellow Confederates made it across the border, but Conger and his men ignored the international boundary completely and captured

Young and several other Southerners who had let down their guard, thinking they were safe in Canada. Young was being beaten by the Americans when a red-coated British Army officer appeared on the scene and warned Conger and his men that they were violating British neutrality. He took custody of Young with the promise the Confederate would be jailed. In all, 14 of the Confederate raiders were in custody by October 23, awaiting an extradition hearing sought by the Americans.

The governor of Vermont was concerned St. Albans marked the beginning of a border campaign by the Confederates and dispatched 1,300 men to guard the frontier. The St. Albans raid successfully stirred up fear in the area and rumours spread that similar attacks were planned for Ogdensburg, Plattsburgh, and Malone in neighbouring New York. To prevent any sort of disruption on election day, November 8, troops were placed at polling stations.

When General John A. Dix, Commander of the Military District of the East, learned of the St. Albans raid, he directed his men to pursue the perpetrators across the border and "destroy" them. He decided to violate British neutrality without consulting his higher-ups. Word of his order was hailed in Richmond, where a clerk in the Confederate War Department wrote: "A war with England would be our peace." The feeling was not universal, however. General Robert E. Lee wrote to Jefferson Davis complaining that the St. Albans adventure was illegal and ill-advised at a time when the operatives in Canada would be better deployed in battle or assigned to protect southern cities.[2]

United States Secretary of State William Seward protested the St. Albans incident, noting, pointedly, it was not his government that was "delinquent in the fulfillment of fraternal national obligations." Nevertheless, he countermanded the order by Dix to pursue the perpetrators across the border, which he considered a step too far.

The authorities were indignant about the Confederates abusing British neutrality to stage raids on the North, and public opinion turned against the South. Even the pro-South *Toronto Leader* and *Montreal Gazette* criticized the raid. Meanwhile, in Quebec City, leaders of the British colonies had already gathered to discuss Confederation to better deal with international episodes and band together to fend off potential American retaliation.

On the ground, it had been Spymaster Thompson's deputy in Montreal, Clement Clay, who had authorized the mission. He did so without Thompson's knowledge or permission, and Thompson was unimpressed with the mission, which he felt clearly violated British neutrality. However, the raid's legacy generated consternation on both sides of the border, an overarching goal shared by Thompson and Clay.

Alabama native Clement Clay led the Confederate spy operation based in Montreal. He was involved in planning the raid on St. Albans, Vermont, and likely the plan to spread yellow fever in the Union along with an early plot to kidnap President Abraham Lincoln. Clay and his colleague in Toronto, Jacob Thompson, had plenty of Confederate cash to fund their clandestine activities, but the two men had little respect for each other. (LIBRARY OF CONGRESS)

The extradition trial for the St. Albans raiders began November 5, 1864, in Montreal. Chief raider Bennett Young insisted he broke no Canadian or British laws and had been acting as a commissioned officer of the Confederate States Army waging war against the United States. In mid-December, the raiders were set free when a judge ruled he had no jurisdiction to consider the case. The Americans were livid. The raiders were arrested again by Canadian authorities and brought before another judge in February. On March 29, Justice James Smith ruled the raid was justified and released all accused, saying they were involved in an act of war and had broken no laws in Canada. To appease the Americans who were again incensed,

Governor General Charles Stanley Monck filed charges against the raiders of breaching the Neutrality Act. Not long afterward, however, the raiders were discharged, although Young was made to wait six months before his charge was dropped.[3]

———

The Confederates in Canada were not through with their plots. By early November 1864, they'd acquired a ship they planned to arm and let loose on the Great Lakes to shell lakefront American cities, creating as much terror as possible. They hoped to complete the earlier botched mission of capturing the USS *Michigan* at Sandusky and using it to free the prisoners at Johnson's Island.

Yet again, word of the scheme leaked out to both colonial and American authorities. The plan involved outfitting a ship named the *Georgian* with armaments that were being manufactured at a factory in Guelph. On November 21, the factory and warehouse were seized by Canadian officials along with the cannon and other arms that were made and stored there. More weapons produced in Guelph and intended for the ship were seized at Sarnia.[4] With that, the *Georgian* episode fizzled and its captain disappeared.

In early November, eight Toronto-based Confederates were in New York City with a Thompson-approved plan to take the city and spark a revolution in the war-weary metropolis that would lead states, including New York and New Jersey, to secede from the Union. Word of the plot soon leaked out and even the *New York Times* began reporting about Confederate activity in the city.

Meanwhile, to thwart any disruption, thousands of Union troops were moved into New York, forcing the conspirators to scale back their plans. The plotters decided instead to firebomb the metropolis in retaliation for the way Northern troops had callously torched southern cities. They calculated their inferno would frighten the populace and send a powerful message to Lincoln. On November 25, armed with bottles of Greek fire, the Confederates set fire to 19 hotels and several theatres. The conflagration would have been greater, but many of the fires extinguished themselves or simply smouldered.[5] The plotters returned to Toronto having succeeded in panicking America's largest city. It was learned later they'd been betrayed by Godfrey Hyams, an Englishman who'd settled in Arkansas but was now living in the Queen's Hotel, where the Confederates were headquartered. He was liked and trusted by a rather naive Jacob Thompson.[6]

Congressional politicians in the United States grew increasingly angry at what they felt was a tepid response from Britain to conspirators using Canada as a base of operations. They began to demand firm action. Talk began of abrogating the Rush-Bagot Agreement of 1817, which strictly limited Britain and the United States to only one armed ship on lakes Ontario and Champlain and two each on the Upper Great Lakes. Nothing came of that threat, however.

In December of 1864, newly re-elected President Abraham Lincoln issued an order that no one could enter the United States without a passport. His move was aimed at cross-border raiders but it produced collateral damage for Canadians and Maritimers, even though it was hard to enforce with such a long, undefended border that crossed many lakes and rivers. At formal border crossings, however, it impeded the flow of Canadians who lived in Windsor and worked in Detroit, for instance. And it created aggravation for Maritimers engaged in cross-border trade with New England. Even more problems arose when the Americans called for an end to the Reciprocity Treaty of 1854, the free trade deal under which Canada, in particular, had benefited. On January 12, 1865, the United States Senate voted overwhelmingly to abrogate the treaty, effective the following year.[7] Pressure built on the Canadian Parliament to do something substantial to curb Confederate plotters. In response, in February of 1865 it passed the Alien Act, which called for the expulsion from Canada of any foreign national suspected of engaging in or planning hostile acts against friendly nations. In Washington, Seward was pleased with the belated move and on March 11 rescinded the passport regulation.[8]

Clement Clay, the commissioner behind the St. Albans raid, used Confederate funds to pay legal fees of more than $80,000 incurred to defend the men. He worried he himself might be charged with violating

Canadian neutrality, which did nothing for his fragile health. The strain of the trial weighed heavily on Clay, and he left Montreal for his home in the South at the outset of December 1864, taking a circuitous route around the Union blockade and eventually reuniting with his family in Georgia. Clay soon learned a $50,000 reward had been offered for his arrest because of his activities in Canada. To underline his claim he was innocent of any wrongdoing, he turned himself in. Clay was held for a year at the Union Army's Fort Monroe at Hampton, Virginia, before his release was ordered by new American President Andrew Johnson.[9]

With Thompson's spotty record of success in Canada, Confederate Secretary of State Judah Benjamin decided to recall him. But Thompson wasn't ready to leave just yet and, desperate for success, argued he was working on other plots. Some were bizarre and some were deadly, with huge potential implications. He was allowed to remain.

One of his plots involved a plan to free Confederates held in Northern prisons, then create a "foraging" army with them and let them fight their way back to the South. He needed leaders, but many Confederate generals were locked up, many of them languishing at Johnson's Island. Thompson learned several of those generals were to be transferred to Fort Lafayette in New York shortly before Christmas. Four of them were rather well known: Major General Edward Johnson, Major General Isaac Trimble, Brigadier General John R. Jones, and General John Frazer. All were battle-hardened. Johnson had inherited Stonewall Jackson's brigade and fought at Gettysburg. Trimble was captured at the same battle during Pickett's Charge and lost a leg. Jones was wounded at the Second Battle of Bull Run and again at Antietam before finally being captured at Chancellorsville. Frazer was captured during a late 1863 raid in eastern Tennessee.

Thompson felt these men could provide the leadership he needed for his ambitious scheme. He assigned a team led by Colonel Robert Martin and Lieutenant John Headley to board an eastbound train at Erie, Pennsylvania, that was carrying the generals. Just southwest of Buffalo they would be joined by more men at a station, then derail the train, overpower any resistance, and quickly rescue the generals, who could cross the border and start planning their next steps. Money from the train's safe was to be given to the generals and the raiders were to scatter.

On the day picked for the operation, the generals were not on the train as expected, so Martin and his men went to the station in Buffalo, where they kept a close watch on all arrivals for a day. The plotters then relocated to the rail line west of Buffalo, where they placed an iron rail across the tracks. After striking the rail and sending it flying, the engineer stopped the train and sent his crew to investigate. But rather than swing into action, Martin's men simply scattered and raced back across the border. Three were captured, however, when they stopped for a bite to eat before leaving New York.[10]

Another plot was in the works when the free-the-generals plan fell apart. Sometime around February, Thompson came up with yet another plan as the prospects for the South grew ever more bleak, with desertions in the ranks and a lack of food, pay, and success on the battlefield. This one called for the Confederacy to evacuate Richmond at the same time General Robert E. Lee launched a massive counterattack on the Union. Lee's offensive would be combined with an uprising in the North led by the Sons of Liberty, in whom Thompson retained faith — for reasons unknown. He sent details of his "Hail Mary" plan with two trusted envoys, Martin and Headley, from the ill-fated train derailment scheme, to newly appointed Secretary of War John C. Breckinridge.[11] Nothing came of this far-fetched plan because Breckinridge had concluded the war was lost and argued the Confederacy "should surrender as a government," rather than army by army on a piecemeal basis. He was acutely aware the South had run out of money to pay its soldiers and was struggling to clothe and feed them.[12]

———

While these plots were being hatched, another was being discussed in Canada and in Boston. Thompson himself was likely involved in preliminary talks when he told some friends a dramatic move was needed to bring about a peace treaty the South might be willing to accept. He suggested that President Lincoln and some of his top lieutenants should be "put out of the way" to start that process.[13]

During this time, Thompson was splitting his time between Toronto and Montreal. In October, shortly before the St. Albans raid, a handsome young American actor and ardent racist named John Wilkes Booth checked into St. Lawrence Hall in Montreal, while Clement Clay was still overseeing Confederate operations. Booth was in town to deliver readings from William Shakespeare's *Merchant of Venice* and British poet Lord Alfred Tennyson's *Charge of the Light Brigade* at Corby's Hall. The Maryland-born Booth was 26 and already a success on the stage, like his late father and two brothers, all of whom specialized in the works of Shakespeare. Booth was devoted to the South and hated Lincoln, suggesting he should be kidnapped, then taken to Virginia and used as a bargaining chip with the North. In exchange for Lincoln's release, he said, the North would be forced to release enough Confederate prisoners to help the South win the war.[14]

During Booth's nine-day stay at St. Lawrence Hall, an establishment filled with Southerners and advertising "the best mint juleps in the city," the actor spoke openly about his disdain for Lincoln. Before leaving Montreal, he visited a photographic studio and opened an account at the Ontario Bank, the same institution used by Thompson to hold funds from the Confederacy. Booth also spoke to Patrick Charles Martin, a man described by the Union War Department as "an uncompromising rebel." Martin, another native of Maryland, revealed he had been asked by some southern planters to kidnap the president, so he and Booth decided to work together. They were joined by another Lincoln hater, George Sanders, a charming Kentuckian and avowed revolutionary.

Six months later a courtroom would learn of a conversation carried on by Booth and his associates around the hotel pool table in which the upcoming American election was the topic. "It makes little difference head or tail," a well-lubricated Booth was recalled as saying. "Abe's contract is near up and whether re-elected or not, he will get his goose cooked." He added: "I can bag the biggest game . . ."[15] Something was afoot. In November, Booth visited Toronto, where he stayed a few days at the Queen's Hotel, the other gathering place favoured by Confederates in Canada, before leaving for Washington.

———

Things continued to deteriorate for the Confederacy. In mid-December, Union Major General George H. Thomas defeated the Army of the Tennessee under Lieutenant General John Bell Hood at Nashville, virtually ending its fighting abilities. On December 21, Union General William T. Sherman's army completed its devastating March to the Sea from Atlanta to Savannah, leaving a wide swath of destruction in its wake, with property damage estimated at more than $100 million.[16] In February 1865, Sherman turned his troops north to sack and burn Columbia, the capital of South Carolina, and then east to bombard Charleston on the coast. In Virginia in late March, Union General Ulysses S. Grant launched a major offensive west of Richmond. On April 1 at Five Forks, a key crossroads, Union forces overwhelmed the Confederates protecting that vital access route to Richmond, and the following day the Confederate capital was evacuated.

Among the first Union troops to enter Richmond on April 3 were Black soldiers of the Fifth Massachusetts Cavalry. The city's Black residents were overjoyed and, in the words of one observer, "completely crazed, they danced and shouted, men hugged each other, and women kissed."[17] Meanwhile, Confederate President Jefferson Davis hurriedly moved the seat of government south to Danville, while Lee's forces began to dissolve. Unpaid and unfed, many of his men were deserting as the end of the conflict approached. Lee surrendered his Army of Northern Virginia on April 9 at Appomattox Court House, Virginia, without authorization by Confederate president Davis. Lee had about 13,000 troops left, compared to more than 115,000 for Grant. Surrender of the remaining Confederate armies on other fronts would follow in coming days.

The United States House of Representatives had passed the 13th Amendment to the Constitution at the end of January, 1865, abolishing slavery in the United States. Lincoln felt it would bolster his chances at re-election and ensure emancipation would last beyond the end of the war. Black people everywhere rejoiced, including in Canada, with the assurance their freedom would not end with the coming of peace. Some had already begun drifting back home following Lincoln's Emancipation Proclamation.

Jefferson Davis, Secretary of War John C. Breckinridge, Secretary of the Treasury George Trenholm, and Secretary of State Judah Benjamin stayed in Danville only a brief time while remaining Confederate armies collapsed. Following the surrender of Lee and his Army of Northern Virginia, the war was effectively over but Davis and his cabinet continued to meet, moving south to Greensboro, North Carolina, and then to Charlotte. Davis stubbornly refused to surrender and maintained hope of somehow reuniting Confederate forces still fighting in North Carolina and west of the Mississippi, and then governing in exile from Mexico. There was a $100,000 bounty on his head as Davis and his entourage headed west toward Texas, taking with them $288,022 in gold and silver coins.[18] On May 4, Davis and his retinue, including his wife, Varina, were captured by the Fourth Michigan Cavalry near Irwinville, Georgia. In a bid to humiliate him even more, a story was concocted that he tried to escape arrest by wearing women's clothing.

In Washington, Abraham Lincoln and his cabinet began discussing terms for readmitting to the Union the states that had seceded. Lincoln favoured clemency for the South, believing retribution against its political and military leaders would make reconciliation even more difficult than it was bound to be. Gideon Welles, his secretary of the navy, recalled the president didn't want to inflict any more death. "None need expect he would take any part in hanging or killing those men, even the worst of them," Welles wrote in his diary. Lincoln wanted to "frighten them out of the country, open the gates, let down the bars, scare them off," insisting, "Enough lives have been sacrificed. We must extinguish our resentments if we expect harmony and union."[19]

Secretary of War Edwin Stanton was told Jacob Thompson was en route to Portland, Maine, where he planned to board a ship for England. Stanton wanted to arrest the Confederacy's commissioner in Canada, but Lincoln disagreed. "I think not," the president said.

"When you have got an elephant by the hind leg, and he's trying to run away, it's best to let him run."[20] Thompson sailed for Europe, supposedly taking some of the Confederate funds entrusted to him and settling in the Lake District of northern England. Sometime later, Thompson returned to Canada to hide out until the American government announced an amnesty for former high-ranking Confederate officials. The Commissioner for Special Service in Canada was never prosecuted for any crime despite his masterminding the Confederacy's efforts to spread terror across the North from a convenient sanctuary.

On April 12 a bombshell dropped when it was learned that a desperate Confederacy had gone so far as to attempt bioterrorism against its enemy. That day, Godfrey Hyams appeared at the Toronto office of United States consul David Thurston and provided a lengthy statement about a plot in which he had played a role. Hyams, a native of England, lived nine years in the South before showing up in Toronto, where he befriended Thompson and became a courier for him.[21] Hyams now needed money because work for Thompson had dried up, and he sought to profit from what he knew. This wasn't the first time he'd switched sides for money. The previous September, he alerted American authorities to the planned attack on the USS *Michigan* and the attempt to free the prisoners held at Johnson's Island.[22]

Hyams told the consul about a plot led by Doctor Luke Blackburn to spread yellow fever in northern cities and even to President Lincoln. (Unmentioned, or possibly unknown by Hyams, was that Blackburn had also considered poisoning the water supply of New York City.) Blackburn, a Kentuckian and proud Southerner, was well known for his work with victims of the fever that had ravaged populations in New Orleans and elsewhere. He spent some time dealing with an outbreak in 1864 in Bermuda where he devised a scheme to transmit the disease to Union cities.

Yellow fever was characterized by a "black vomit" in its terminal stage, when the stomachs of its victims hemorrhage. In Bermuda,

Blackburn collected soiled bedding and clothing from infected patients and packed them into trunks along with new shirts and coats in a bid to contaminate the new attire destined for unsuspecting Northerners. Blackburn failed to understand that the fever is transmitted by mosquitoes, not by physical contact. Regardless, he shipped a number of trunks to Halifax, where Hyams took charge of them.

Thompson, the overseer of Confederate operations, was aware of the yellow fever plot and provided some funds to Hyams at one point on behalf of Blackburn, Hyams later testified. Blackburn directed Hyams to smuggle the trunks into Washington and other cities in the North.[23] Included was a valise containing supposedly contaminated fancy dress shirts, intended as a gift for Lincoln. Blackburn promised the impoverished Hyams a fee of $100,000 upon completing his assignment by having the clothing auctioned off or sold.

Hyams said he took some of the trunks to Washington and turned them over to a merchant who sold them at auction, while he gave others to a man headed for Union-controlled North Carolina where he promised to sell them on commission. With that accomplished, Hyams returned to Canada, after refusing to deliver the valise intended for Lincoln.[24] He waited for payment from Blackburn, who demanded proof the goods had been sold. The doctor then went to Bermuda where yellow fever broke out again early in 1865. Hyams was still awaiting a receipt from the merchant in Washington when Blackburn left without paying him the money promised. Desperate for funds and realizing the North had won the war, Hyams grew tired of waiting and offered his shocking story to the American consul for cash.

Blackburn was arrested on May 25 after returning to Montreal and charged with violating Canada's neutrality law. During his trial in Toronto, Hyams testified against the doctor, but Blackburn was acquitted for lack of sufficient proof the trunks had been in Canada. Blackburn remained for a time in the colony and, despite a murder charge facing him in the United States, returned to the South in 1867 to treat yellow fever victims during an outbreak in New Orleans. He was never arrested for his hideous plot and returned to his hometown of Louisville, where he was celebrated as a hero. Such was his

Dr. Luke Blackburn came up with a plan to spread yellow fever in northern cities and even to Abraham Lincoln. The Kentucky doctor's efforts failed because of poor execution of his effort and the even more pressing problem that yellow fever could not be spread by contact with the contaminated clothing he distributed. (HOUSE DIVIDED PROJECT, DICKINSON COLLEGE)

popularity that Blackburn was elected governor of Kentucky in 1879, a post he held for four years. He died in 1887. His headstone in Frankfort includes a bas relief image of "The Good Samaritan" and an inscription that says of Blackburn, "his life consecrated to charity is an example of heroism and fidelity."[25] Never mind the attempted bioterrorism.

⸻

Two days after Hyams exposed Blackburn, an event occurred that would prove to be a historic date in America for two reasons — one symbolic, the other tragic. On Good Friday, April 14, 1865, at the remnants of Fort Sumter in Charleston harbour, the same American flag that had been lowered by departing Union troops exactly four years earlier was raised in a formal ceremony before more than 3,000 guests. Major Robert Anderson, who was the last Union commander of the fort and had ordered the flag lowered when his men surrendered to the Confederates, personally raised the flag, which snapped smartly in the springtime breeze. He had come out of retirement to return Old Glory to its place. Also on hand was Major Abner Doubleday, who as a captain and Anderson's second-in-command had finally seen the "trifling difference of opinion" settled "between us and our neighbours opposite." Several senators, generals, admirals, and officers from the navy, marines, and army were among the attendees.

Anderson thanked Secretary of War Edwin Stanton for the opportunity "to fulfill the cherished wish of my heart though four long years of bloody war — to restore to its proper place this very flag which floated here during peace before the first act of this cruel rebellion — I thank God I have lived to see this day." When the Stars and Stripes reached the top of the mast it was saluted by 100 guns from the fort, echoed by salutes from other forts in the harbour area as naval vessels decorated in bunting and flags bobbed on the adjacent waters. "National airs were also played by the band, which was followed by the Star-Spangled Banner with an effect that was thrilling," reported the New York Times.[26] Prayers were also offered by prominent preacher Henry Ward Beecher on this particular Good Friday, which was starting out as a very good day.

That night at Ford's Theatre in Washington, John Wilkes Booth fatally shot President Abraham Lincoln shortly after 10 p.m. while he and the First Lady watched the comedy Our American Cousin. Booth and his associates had abandoned their scheme to kidnap Lincoln, which no longer made sense with the war over, so they came up with a deadly alternative.

The killing of Lincoln was one of three deaths Booth and his associates hoped to accomplish that night. While Booth was preoccupied with Lincoln, Lewis Powell went to the home of ailing Secretary of State William Seward about 10 p.m., claiming he had brought medicine from the doctor. Seward had been injured April 5 in a carriage accident and was bedridden. A servant took Powell to the third floor where Seward lay, but Seward's son Frederick grew suspicious of the visitor and refused to allow him into his father's room. Confronted, Powell tried to shoot Frederick, but the gun failed to discharge so he used the weapon to beat the young man unconscious. When a male nurse tending to Seward opened the door to investigate the commotion, Powell burst in and began stabbing Seward in the head and neck with a bowie knife. Another son and a State Department messenger who arrived on the scene were also stabbed by Powell before he ran off.

Meanwhile, fellow plotter George Atzerodt, who was assigned to kill Vice President Andrew Johnson, got cold feet and spent his time at a bar that night.

Lincoln died shortly after seven o'clock the following morning. Seward was in bad shape and drifted in and out of consciousness for several days, but would recover. His throat had been slashed and his right cheek nearly sliced off; he didn't learn for several days that Lincoln was dead and that Johnson had been sworn in as his successor. Seward's sons were badly injured, but they, too, recovered.[27]

In Canada, news of Lincoln's death evoked widespread sympathy. Nearly every city passed resolutions of condolence, many businesses closed, and special church services were held. In the Windsor area, Canadians streamed across the border into Detroit to attend services of mourning. Every newspaper except the *Toronto Leader* expressed regret at the passing of the American president. At the Queens Hotel, two participants in the St. Albans raid openly toasted John Wilkes Booth.[28]

Meanwhile, Booth himself was on the run, despite a broken leg he suffered when he leaped from Lincoln's box onto the stage at Ford's Theatre. About 12 days later he was discovered hiding in a barn in Virginia. When he refused to surrender, the barn was set alight to smoke him out. He was shot when it appeared he was preparing to fire on the troops who had him cornered, and he died the next morning. Booth's connection to Canada, where the plotting against Lincoln may have begun, soon came to light. In his Washington hotel room investigators found his Bank of Ontario passbook from Montreal, showing a balance of $455.[29] It was soon confirmed Booth was at St. Lawrence Hall in October for his performances in that city.

Charges were laid against eight persons in the assassination, including Lewis Powell and George Atzerodt. The trial for all of them began May 12 before a military commission of eight generals and a colonel at Washington's Old Arsenal Penitentiary. A War Department spy named Richard Montgomery, who had infiltrated the Canadian Confederates, was the first of 350 witnesses called to testify. He said that Jacob Thompson and others were planning to "take care" of Lincoln and that the Confederate spymaster had conferred with Booth during his time in Montreal. Montgomery insisted Thompson either directed or knew about all Confederate terrorist activities, including the St. Albans raid, the burning of New York, and Dr. Blackburn's yellow fever mission. The trial heard from other Union spies who had infiltrated the covert Canadian operation.

The connection to Canada was clear, although evidence from some witnesses about certain details was not, and it was later revealed some were paid to tell their stories while others perjured themselves to ensure convictions. The trial ended June 29, finding all eight accused guilty. Sentenced to hang were Powell and Atzerodt, along with Mary Surratt, who operated a boarding house where the plot was discussed, and David Herold, who helped Booth escape. Sam Arnold and Mike O'Laughlen, Booth's friends since childhood, were sentenced to hard labour for life as was Dr. Samuel Mudd, who tended to Booth's broken leg and had participated in the original planning for a kidnapping. Edmund Spangler, a stagehand at Ford's Theatre who had helped Booth escape, was given hard labour for six years. The four hangings, which included the first of a woman, took place July 7 in the prison courtyard.[30]

That same month *The Atlantic* magazine sought to make some sense of the assassination of the president. It saluted Lincoln's achievements in challenging times and said the real blame for his killing rested with those who started the Civil War. Booth committed a vile crime, it said, which made it "impossible for honourable men to sympathize with him." The publication made the Canadian connection clear. The lengthy article continued:

> Whether Booth was the agent of a band of conspirators, or was one of a few vile men who sought an odious immorality, it is impossible to say. We have the authority of a high Government official for the statement that

the President's murder was organized in Canada and approved at Richmond . . . there is nothing improbable in the supposition that the assassination plot was formed in Canada, as some of the vilest miscreants of the Secession side have been allowed to live in that country. We know that there were other plots formed in that country against us — plots that were to a certain extent carried into execution, and which led to loss of life . . . but it is not probable that British subjects had anything to do with any conspiracy of this kind. The Canadian error was in allowing the scum of Secession to abuse the "right of hospitality through the pursuit of hostile action against us from the territory of a neutral."[31]

If not complicit, Canadian provinces certainly were guilty of turning a blind eye to the Confederates operating in their midst, at least until the final stages of the Civil War when the visitors tried to drag their hosts into a war that Britain and the provinces sought to avoid. But the St. Albans raid had turned the tide of public sentiment against the South. For the longest time, the Southern guests were tolerated because they shared similar sentiments about Northern aggression, but when their cross-border terrorism threatened war, it was felt they had gone too far. Colonial authorities had used neutrality as a sort of shield and began to co-operate more fully with Americans, fearing retribution if they didn't. At the same time, colonial leaders were talking about banding together in Confederation to fend off an annexation that some politicians in Washington still wanted.

PART THREE

RECONSTRUCTING

CHAPTER TEN

THE LURE OF NIAGARA

Tourism in Niagara Falls dates back to the 1820s, when entrepreneurs began capitalizing on the natural wonder that straddles the international border. In 1822, William Forsyth erected the first grand hotel, the Pavilion, overlooking Table Rock and Horseshoe Falls. The three-storey hotel featured viewing galleries and an observatory on its roof. It burned down in 1839, by which time it had been supplanted by the handsome Clifton House Hotel, completed in 1835. The three-storey, 60-room Clifton House was the grandest hotel at the Falls for more than six decades and became the accommodation of choice for wealthy visitors. British novelist Charles Dickens stayed there for nine days during 1842 and was enchanted by the "tremendous spectacle" of nature. Soon after his visit, the *Maid of the Mist* sightseeing boat began taking tourists to the base of the Falls, and in 1848 the first bridge across the Niagara Gorge was opened, allowing for easier access by American tourists.[1]

That same year, fledgling Illinois politician Abraham Lincoln and his family took in the Falls and its surroundings. Among other cross-border visitors were those from wealthy families in the South, anxious to escape the summertime heat and humidity back home. During the Civil War, Confederates made good use of Niagara Falls and allied with some of its sympathetic residents. One of them, Thomas Barnett, operated the Niagara Falls Museum. A system developed whereby visiting Confederate agents or couriers would sign the guest register at the

museum, making it known they were in town to local agents who monitored the register. Meetings were then held, or messages swapped, based
on prearranged plans. Visiting and local agents often mingled among
the crowds at the museum to avoid detection. In 1864, the ill-fated
Niagara Falls peace talks between North and South promoted by *New
York Tribune* editor Horace Greeley ended as quickly as they began.[2]

With the end of the war, many Southerners were feeling threatened and displaced in their own land. Some recalled the Niagara
area from more carefree days and decided to move there. The town
of Niagara, where the Niagara River empties into Lake Ontario
14 miles north of the Falls, became a favourite destination. The
quiet community had been rebuilt after being sacked and burned
by retreating American troops during the War of 1812. Niagara
was busiest during the summer months when part-time residents,
including those from Toronto, 32 miles across Lake Ontario, swelled
the population. Just southeast of downtown lay Fort George, built by
the British between 1796 and 1799. Across the river was venerable
Fort Niagara, built by the French in 1726, captured by the British
and finally turned over to the United States.

Southerners began arriving in the town of Niagara just before
the war ended, when the outcome was becoming clear. Many
rented or bought homes, some staying only a matter of months,
others for years. Several divided their time between Toronto and
Niagara, while those of more modest means preferred to remain
in the smaller community with its less expensive housing. Exiles in
Niagara included at least four Confederate generals, two colonels,
one prominent clergyman, the Confederate commissioner to Britain,
and several members of Morgan's Raiders, who had launched
disruptive attacks in Indiana and Ohio during the summer of 1863.
The Southerners became a strong presence in the community, whose
permanent population was barely 1,500. Their arrival and activities
were noted by William Kirby, publisher of the *Niagara Mail* newspaper. Born in Yorkshire, Kirby immigrated to the United States
with his family in 1832, then moved to Canada seven years later.
He was deeply conservative politically, disliked America's liberal

democracy, and sympathized with the South during the Civil War. Kirby became acquainted with Confederate exiles and their friends who took up residence in the town, one of them eventually moving in next door to his home on Front Street.

———

One of the first prominent Southerners to arrive in Niagara was Reverend William T. Leacock, former rector of Christ (Episcopal) Church in New Orleans. He was a longtime friend of Jefferson Davis and distantly related to him. Leacock was unabashedly pro-Confederate and clashed with Union authorities in 1864 during their occupation of the city. He was banished from New Orleans by military governor General Benjamin Butler for refusing to pray for President Lincoln. Leacock and his family moved to Niagara that same year, finding a suitable house on King Street. During his time in the community Leacock preached at St. Mark's Anglican Church.

Captain William Sidney Winder, of the Confederate engineers, spent time in Niagara during 1865 before returning to his home in Baltimore the following year. An occasional visitor in 1865 was Confederate Brigadier General William Preston, a close friend of Major General John C. Breckinridge, a fellow Kentuckian who'd been vice-president of the United States just before the war. Preston returned to Kentucky late in 1866, the same year General Jubal Early appeared in Niagara and boarded in a home at Regent and Johnson streets.[3] Early, who participated in nearly every campaign of the Confederate Army of Northern Virginia and in 1864 reached the outskirts of Washington, D.C., also maintained a residence in Toronto. In that city he published *A Memoir of the Last Year of the War of Independence in the Confederate States of America*, detailing his campaign in the Shenandoah Valley.

Another newcomer was a former vice-president of the United States. To avoid capture by the Union after the war, Confederate Secretary of War Breckinridge made his way to Florida and joined several other men on a perilous trip by small boat to Cuba. He then

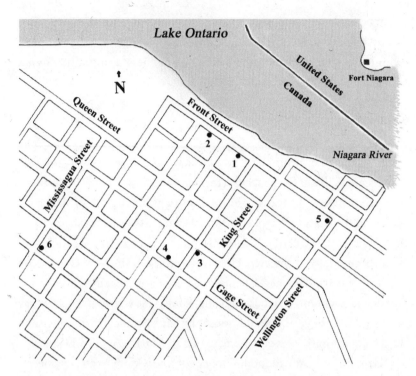

The town of Niagara, now Niagara-on-the-Lake, attracted several Confederate officials and generals after the Civil War. President Abraham Lincoln suggested that rather than try prominent Confederates as traitors and undermine efforts to reconnect with the South, they should be allowed to flee. Many did. Niagara, just across the border from New York, proved to be a popular place for the Southerners to live until things calmed down and they could return home. 1. Home of General John C. Breckinridge, 1866; 2. Breckinridge family, 1868–69; 3. General Jubal Early, 1866; 4. Confederate envoy James Mason, 1868–69; 5. Mason, 1867; 6. Major J.W. Avery, 1872–80. (MAP BY CHIP MARTIN)

went to England, where he spent time with James Mason, former Confederate commissioner to Britain. Both men had arranged for their families to move to Canada, where they would reunite. In late 1865, Breckinridge joined his family and found a place in Toronto after a brief stay at the Queen's Hotel. Toronto didn't provide Breckinridge the peace and quiet for which he longed and his wife Mary's health was poor. Her doctor suggested that a less busy environment would work wonders for her.

In early May, the Breckinridges moved to Niagara into a modest home at 80 Front Street.[4] Breckinridge, the last secretary of war for the Confederacy, vice-president under James Buchanan, and failed presidential candidate in 1860, was finally able to relax after a decade of intense pressure. He and has family enjoyed the scenic surroundings, the fresh fish that were brought to their door, the inexpensive accommodations, and the friends that surrounded them. From his new home, Breckinridge could clearly see the Stars and Stripes flying above Fort Niagara across the river "to refresh our patriotism," Breckinridge mused, tongue in cheek.[5] It was both a comfort and a taunt, as biographer William C. Davis wrote, reminding Breckinridge of the country the former vice president longed to return to, but could not.[6] It was said that when the wind blew from the east, Breckinridge could hear the bugle call at the American fort across the water. On Front Street, he played host to General John Bell Hood late in 1866 and the old soldiers no doubt swapped war stories with other exiled Confederates in town.

Breckinridge learned Mason had settled in Montreal with other expatriates such as General George Pickett and some displaced families. Breckinridge encouraged Mason to join the growing community of Southerners living in Niagara. He sang the praises of life there. Mason's daughter, Virginia, recalled many years later in her book about her father's life that Breckinridge's "description of its quiet seclusion and the great economy of its simple village life induced Mr. Mason to leave Montreal in July of the same year and spend the rest of the summer with the party of Confederates there assembled."[7] The Masons rented a home on Wellington Street that became a gathering place for visiting Confederates and those living nearby. They spent the winter in Toronto before returning to hospitable Niagara and finding a larger home on Gage Street for their extended family. "In Toronto, as in Montreal, indeed everywhere in Canada, the kind welcome extended to the Southern people contributed greatly to cheer and brighten the lives of these exiles," Virginia recalled. "Such was certainly the case with Mr. Mason's family, and the writer is glad to record their grateful appreciation of the kindness they received." Virginia, one of eight Mason children, said her father enjoyed tending the garden in Niagara and raising chickens and collecting eggs, a simple life compared to recent years. "He was never idle and he was habitually cheerful." Mason also read newspapers voraciously to stay abreast of postwar events in the United States, and he spent many hours corresponding with old friends and acquaintances.

The most prominent of the Confederate fugitives to take up residence in Niagara was General John C. Breckinridge, who had been vice-president of the United States from 1856 to 1860 under President James Buchanan. Breckinridge ran for president in 1860 as one of two Democratic Party candidates. By the end of the Civil War, Breckinridge was secretary of war for the Confederacy and made a harrowing escape to Cuba and then to England before making his way to Canada. (BRECKINRIDGE 1860 PRESIDENTIAL CAMPAIGN PENNANT, COURTESY OF BOB STRAWHORN)

The Breckinridges went to France in mid-1866, thinking the climate might help Mary's health, which remained poor. She and the children remained in France while Breckinridge toured England, the continent, and the Holy Land, reconnecting with former Confederates along the way. In Rome, he was granted an audience with Pope Pius IX and began pining to return to Niagara.[8] In June of 1868 the family returned to Canada and found a fine place at 120 Front Street in Niagara from which the old warrior could again keep an eye on the republic and its flag on the other side of the river he dared not cross. Their next-door neighbour was William Kirby, publisher of the *Niagara Mail*, who had been sympathetic to the Southern cause. Mary Breckinridge particularly enjoyed Niagara and was pleased at the family's return to what she described as a "piece of heaven."[9] When members of her family visited, they all took the short trip to Niagara Falls for photographs with the American Falls as the backdrop.

In 1866, John Porterfield, the financial agent to the Confederacy's former commissioners in Canada Jacob Thompson and Clement Clay, rented a home on Centre Street. Porterfield, a banker from Nashville, had worked under Secretary of State Judah P. Benjamin in a bid to undermine public trust in federal government finances. Operating out of Montreal, Porterfield had urged Southern sympathizers in the North to convert paper money into gold and began currency manipulation, buying gold with Confederate funds and exporting $2 million worth of it. His efforts failed to destabilize Union finances as intended and one of his partners was arrested.[10] Also living in Niagara during 1866 was Stuart Robinson, former minister of Second Presbyterian Church in Louisville, Kentucky. An ardent Confederate, he was outspoken in his effort to debunk charges following the war that Jefferson Davis, Clement Clay and other Southern agents in Canada were involved in the conspiracy to kidnap or kill President Lincoln.

Confederates continued flocking to Niagara in 1867, the year that Canada West, Canada East, Nova Scotia, and New Brunswick banded together in Confederation. Among the new arrivals was former Colonel Charles J. Helm, who had been special agent for the Confederate states in Havana, Cuba. After the war, Helm travelled to Europe like other Confederate officials, then to Canada to join his family. He lived in Toronto before settling in Niagara, where one of his sons was born. Helm died in 1868, the only prominent Confederate to pass away in Canada.

Nathaniel Beverley Tucker, a member of Jacob Thompson's mission in Canada, came to Niagara in 1867 before moving east to Drummondville, Quebec. Tucker returned to the Niagara area and purchased the Stephenson House Hotel in St. Catharines. He left for the United States in 1872. A dashing young Kentuckian also moved to Niagara in 1867 and stayed with the Breckinridge family. Lieutenant Bennett Young had led the Confederate raid on St. Albans, Vermont, in October of 1864 that prompted Canadians to re-evaluate their long-standing support for the South. Before that, he'd been a member of the daring band of soldiers known as Morgan's Raiders in 1863 and was captured, but escaped to Canada the next year and worked with Confederate commissioners Clement Clay and Jacob Thompson. While living with the Breckinridges, Young tutored one of their sons, Owen. Other members of Morgan's Raiders also settled in Niagara.

———

A highlight for Confederates in Canada came late in May 1867, when newly freed Jefferson Davis arrived in the colony. Two years earlier, on May 22, 1865, Davis had been imprisoned at Fort Monroe, 80 miles southeast of his former Confederate capital of Richmond. He joined one of the two commissioners he had posted to Canada, Clement Clay, who had turned himself in several months earlier and was still protesting his innocence. To humiliate Davis, the former Confederate president was originally placed in leg irons, but they were removed a few days later when a Philadelphia newspaper said he was manacled in a small damp room known as a casemate. He was not a well man, suffering from neuralgia, recurring bouts of yellow fever, and lingering pain from a wound suffered during the Mexican-American War. Davis was thin and haggard, but did not complain.

He'd been charged with treason and with conspiracy in the plot to kill Lincoln. The conspiracy charge was dropped for lack of evidence connecting him to Booth and his accomplices, but the treason charge remained alive. His trial was slated to take place in Richmond but was delayed until after military rule was lifted in Virginia.

The government of Andrew Johnson was locked in debate about whether to grant clemency to Davis and his political allies, a position espoused by Lincoln. General William T. Sherman recalled that Lincoln wished privately that they flee the country, but the president dared not say so in public.[11] Some of Johnson's cabinet members and advisers wanted him to ensure Confederate leaders were tried for treason, a conviction which carried the death penalty.

Early in May of 1867, Davis was released from prison on $100,000 bond and immediately travelled to New York City with Varina to reunite with son William, eight, and daughter Varina ("Winnie"), aged three. The family promptly went north to Montreal where their two other children, Jefferson Jr., 10, and Margaret, 12, had been living with Varina's mother, Margaret Howell, since August of 1865. One of Varina's sisters was also living in the city and other members of her family would follow.

Jefferson and William were studying at Bishop's College in Lennoxville, about 85 miles southeast of Montreal, where other Confederates had enrolled their children, while Margaret was enrolled in school at a Montreal convent. Davis visited St. Lawrence Hall, where he renewed acquaintances with former Confederates, including envoys James Mason and John Slidell, who had returned from Europe. Davis kept a low profile in Montreal before deciding to visit other Confederates in Toronto and at Niagara. Shortly after reuniting with his family in Montreal he'd been encouraged to visit Toronto and Niagara by Jubal Early and James Mason, among others, who were anxious to reconnect with their former leader.

His old comrades Mason and Helm went to Montreal to accompany Davis on the westward trip to Toronto, where a large crowd greeted him when his boat docked. Among the spectators was Lieutenant Colonel George T. Denison, commander of the Governor General's bodyguard, senior police magistrate, and member of Toronto city council. He was a stout defender of the Confederacy and had been the sole member of city council to vote against Toronto sending condolences to the United States following the assassination of President Lincoln. "I was a strong friend of the Southern refugees who were exiled in our country, and I treated them with the hospitality due to unfortunate strangers driven from their homes," Denison explained in his memoirs.[12] Early, Mason, and Helm were among regular guests at Denison's fine home and they became friends. He said he enjoyed discussing military matters with Early, with whom he became particularly close.

Denison learned of Davis coming just a couple of hours before his arrival aboard the steamer *Champion* on the morning of May 30. He quickly passed the word among associates to join him and others to provide Davis a rousing reception at the Lake Ontario dock near the base of Yonge Street. Denison recalled:

> By the time the vessel arrived a crowd of several thousand people filled the landing place. I got on a pile of coal with a number of friends to give the signal and start the crowd to cheer. As Mr. Davis appeared on the gangway with Messrs. Mason and Helm, I was so astonished at the emaciation and weakness of Mr. Davis who looked like a dying man, that I said to a friend near me, "They have killed him," and then I called for cheers which were most enthusiastically given, and nothing could have been more cordial and kindly than the welcome he got.[13]

An hour or two later, at a lunch hosted by Helm, Mason introduced Denison to Davis and invited him to join the party that was sailing at 2 p.m. for Niagara. He'd be with General Early, Mason, and others aboard the *Rothesay Castle* for the 32-mile trip. Denison found the arrival at Niagara memorable: "I remember as we were walking from the wharf at Niagara, up to Mr. Mason's house, Mr. Davis noticed a large United States flag on Fort Niagara just across the river and pointing it out he said to Mr. Mason, 'Look there Mason, there is the gridiron we have been fried on.'"[14]

Davis spent three days in Niagara reconnecting with other exiles from the South who were living there. He stayed with Mason and took part in games with his former envoy's grandchildren and helped them gather eggs that wandering chickens had laid in his garden. Davis made a brief speech from Mason's verandah after a local band serenaded him with "Dixie" and other tunes. They were the first public remarks in a very long time from the old politician, grateful for his warm reception in the small community just across the international border from his old adversary. Davis said:

> Gentlemen: I thank you sincerely for the honour you have shown to me; it shows that true British manhood to which misfortune is always attractive. May peace and prosperity be forever the blessing of Canada, for she has been the asylum for many of my friends, as she is now the asylum to myself. I hope that Canada may forever remain a part of the British Empire, and may God bless you all and the British flag never cease to wave over you.[15]

Davis attended an agricultural fair while in Niagara and found himself finally able to unwind after so many years of unrelenting stress. He was deeply touched by his reception at Niagara and elsewhere in Canada, confiding months later to Robert E. Lee that it came in stark contrast to the hooting and jeering he received in the northern states during his train trip to Montreal. Davis told Lee that for the first time in two years he was able to draw a full breath of free air. Lee recalled: "He said that he instantly felt better and told me earnestly that he believed it saved his life."[16]

After the community settled down with the departure of Davis, *Niagara Mail* publisher Kirby reflected on the visit of the high-profile visitor who played such a key role in events of recent times:

> It is a subject of pride to Canadians that they can offer the hospitality of the soil and the shelter of the British flag to so many worthy men who are proscribed and banished from their homes for no crime, but that which, according to all American principles, is no crime at all, *viz*, to assert the right of every people to choose their own form of government.[17]

The *New York Times* carried an article about Davis in Toronto and Niagara that was gleaned from the *Baltimore Gazette*, whose sympathies lay with the South. The *Times* headlined it as a "Rebel View" of the reception provided the former Confederate president. The New York paper, which still promoted annexing Canada, used italics to highlight the copy it found particularly objectionable in the *Gazette* account, which said a large crowd welcomed Davis to Niagara, augmented by spectators who came across the lake from Toronto. It continued:

> Thus he has been made to feel that, although in the land of strangers, he is in the midst of friends desirous to evince their respect for the man, and *their sympathy for the victim of suppression and tyranny* . . . If he remains in Canada he may spend it [his time] at this little town of Niagara, *where a pleasant Confederate society is springing up*, where bracing winds from the lake may go far to reinvigorate his enfeebled constitution, and where he will be accessible to friends from the South, and yet removed from the prying curiosity so character-istic of the Yankee.[18]

Davis returned to Toronto on June 3, his 59th birthday, and the following day attended the wedding of a friend from the South that was held at St. James Cathedral. Emerging from the church after-ward, Davis was cheered loudly by a large crowd that had gathered and he bowed his head in acknowledgment.[19] Three days later, Davis boarded a boat for the return trip to Montreal, having successfully touched base with many friends and followers living in Canada West.

Davis had little money and thought he would explore job pros-pects in Canada's most populous city and perhaps write his memoir. Friends helped the Davises move from a modest boarding house to a fine home at 247 Mountain Street, not far from McGill University, whose rent was covered by local Confederate sympathizers.

Back in Montreal, the Davis family witnessed the celebrations on July 1, when Canada became a federated nation of 2.6 million people within the British Empire. It marked the banding together of Canada

East and Canada West, to be called Quebec and Ontario, with Nova Scotia and New Brunswick. Confederation had been achieved in part because of the fear of attack or annexation by Davis's old enemy.

Davis lived quietly as he regained his health and turned down invitations to social events. He made an exception late in July when he attended Sheridan's play *The Rivals* at Theatre Royale, an event that was raising funds for the Southern Relief Association. When he was spotted in the crowd Davis drew cheers, applause, a standing ovation, and repeated choruses of "Dixie." The spontaneous eruption of support delayed the show for nearly a half hour. Unsmiling and somewhat uncomfortable at the recognition, Davis rose to his feet in acknowledgment.[20]

Earlier that same month, he and Varina had visited sons Jeff Jr. and William in Lennoxville, and during a train stop in nearby Sherbrooke they were greeted by a cheering crowd. In an impromptu speech he

During the time Confederate President Jefferson Davis and his family spent in Montreal upon his release from prison, Davis and his wife Varina found time to sit for formal portraits.
(MCCORD MUSEUM, MONTREAL)

told his admirers: "I thank you most kindly for this hearty British reception, which I take as a manifestation of your sympathy for one in misfortune." He and Varina soon moved to Lennoxville along with their two youngest children, taking up residence in a local hotel.[21]

The Davis family lived for a time in Montreal and Lennoxville, Quebec, where their two eldest sons attended school. This formal portrait of the Davis children was taken in Montreal in 1867. (MCCORD MUSEUM, MONTREAL)

As the weather turned cold in late November, his doctor advised Davis to return to the South. Upon arriving, Davis learned his two plantations in Mississippi lay in ruins and his friends were impoverished.[22] While there, he was ordered to Richmond when it appeared his much-delayed trial would finally get underway, but it was delayed again by the impeachment proceedings against President Johnson. By

March, Davis was back in Montreal. He couldn't bring himself to begin his memoir, however, telling Varina: "I cannot speak of my dead so soon."[23] He found no job prospects in Montreal and his financial situation was poor.

He and Varina moved to Lennoxville for a few months, where Davis fell down a flight of stairs, breaking three ribs. After his recovery, his doctor again suggested a change of scenery. The Davises joined friends named Rawson who were returning home to England, where Davis decided to look for employment. In July, the Davises sailed for Liverpool, where they were well received, but the employment situation in Britain was no better. The Davises funded their trip with money Davis earned from a small investment he'd been encouraged to make in copper mines near Montreal and Sherbrooke. On Christmas Day, 1868, President Johnson issued a general amnesty for most Confederate leaders and two months later the case against Davis was dropped. An intriguing question left unanswered by this turn of events was the perplexing one of whether seceding from the Union amounted to treason.[24] Meanwhile, the Davises toured the continent well into 1869 and sailed for New Orleans that October to take up residence in the South.

———

In 1868, General John S. Preston of South Carolina joined the Confederates in Niagara for several months and became a member of the tight circle of friends who often gathered for conversation at Mason's house or on the lawn under shade trees. Virginia Mason, who would have been about 37 at the time, years later described the scene, which was often repeated:

> The writer recalls very vividly the appearance of the group of Confederate officers as they were so frequently seen sitting together under the trees in front of Mr. Mason's house; sometimes looking grave and anxious when letters from home brought accounts of the devastation of the South, the destruction of its homes and the consequent

poverty and suffering of its people — or the newspapers reported the oppression and tyranny of the conquerors in the appointment to all the offices in the Southern States of only such men as were willing tools in the work reconstructing not only the system of State Government but the whole of their social and domestic organization.[25]

———

Jefferson Davis returned to Canada in 1881 following the release of his two-volume memoir, *The Rise and Fall of the Confederate Government*, which he wrote at a plantation he acquired near Biloxi, Mississippi.[26] The memoir received poor reviews and didn't sell well. In April, *The New York Times*, never a fan of the Confederate leader, was particularly critical of his literary effort:

> The country is at peace. The young and progressive men of all sections want to forget the past. They will not take kindly to Mr. Davis's book. For his own reputation it would have been much better had he never written it. He should not have thrust himself into public notice. This country has had quite enough of the man who led the lost cause.[27]

Canadians didn't share that sentiment, apparently. During his promotional visit to Montreal in late May Davis was feted at a reception at St. Lawrence Hall, the old Confederate headquarters in that city. It attracted a number of former Southerners who had decided to remain in Canada's metropolis.[28] Davis also travelled to Toronto, where he reconnected with some old friends who were still there before he returned to the South. He died in New Orleans in 1889 at the age of 81.

Jefferson Davis found Canada was the safe refuge he needed to escape the aftermath of a war his side lost and for which he was pilloried in many quarters — even by some Southerners upset at the extent of the carnage of war. More than 620,000 soldiers had died in the conflict (258,0000 of them Confederates), slavery had been abolished, the South lay in ruins, and a way of life had been destroyed. Many Southerners had fled to Canada by the time Davis and his family arrived. Some stayed only a matter of months, while others remained for years. A few never returned home. Life in America's attic, they found, like the thousands of Black people who preceded them north in the decades before the war, was far better than they expected.

At Christmas 1868, a general amnesty was proclaimed by President Andrew Johnson and many of the Confederates in Niagara and elsewhere in Canada began returning home to see what remained there for them. Years later, *Niagara Mail* publisher Kirby tried to summarize the Niagara-Confederate connection:

> Niagara was in some sense, from the residence of so many Southerners here, their headquarters in Canada. They were welcomed and kindly treated by the townspeople, and the best of relations subsisted until they finally, one after another, bade us adieu and returned to their ravaged homes and estates in the South.[29]

Among the last of the old Confederates to leave Niagara were the Breckinridges, Early, and the Masons during 1869. The departure of the Breckinridges came first, prompting journalist Kirby to lament the loss of his neighbour. "General Breckinridge and lady leave this town with the sincere respect and best wishes of all classes, which they have deservedly won, by the invariably kind and friendly manner in which they have lived among us," Kirby wrote.[30]

Breckinridge returned to Kentucky, where he resumed the practice of law and became counsel for some railways. Early returned to Virginia, where he practised law and wrote extensively about the Civil War, pioneering the "Lost Cause" school of historians who insisted the conflict was about states' rights and not about slavery at all. Mason returned to his native Virginia, resuming correspondence with friends and former comrades as his health began to fail.

When former United States vice-president John C. Breckinridge, the last secretary of war for the Confederacy, first moved to Niagara in 1866, he occupied this home at 80 Front Street, known as the Captain's House. Across the river he could see the American flag fluttering atop Fort Niagara. He knew that if he returned to the United States he could be tried as a traitor and possibly executed. (PHOTO BY CHIP MARTIN)

When the Breckinridge family returned from an extended visit to Europe in 1868, they rented this home at 120 Front Street. Their next-door neighbour was William Kirby, publisher of the Niagara Mail, who had welcomed Breckinridge and other Confederate leaders to town. (PHOTO BY CHIP MARTIN)

This home at 83 Gage Street in Niagara was the second of two homes occupied by James Mason, the Confederacy's envoy to Britain during the Civil War. It became a popular gathering spot for the former Confederate leaders as they awaited the day when they could safely return home. (PHOTO BY CHIP MARTIN)

He died in April of 1871, less than two years after leaving Niagara. Bennett Young returned home to Kentucky and became president of several railways, a founder of Central University in Richmond (later renamed Eastern Kentucky University), and of Louisville Presbyterian Theological Seminary. In later life, Young returned to visit Niagara. The daring leader of the St. Albans Raid died in 1919 at the age of 75.

Other Southerners remained for a time in Niagara after the Confederate officers left, while others continued to arrive, likely because of its reputation as a welcoming community or simply on the recommendation of their countrymen already there.

Among them in early 1872 was one of the most wanted men in the United States. Major J. W. Avery, a leader of the Ku Klux in South Carolina, had a reward of $60,000 for his capture. A fugitive from justice, he was implicated in murder and terrorizing Black people across the northern section of the state, contrary to laws enacted to eradicate the Ku Klux and its hate-fuelled racist attacks. This late arrival was carrying much more baggage than he could fit into suitcases. He would be welcomed like the other Southerners before him and would remain longer in Niagara than any of them.

CHAPTER ELEVEN

THE KU KLUX CONNECTION

W hite Southerners like Major J.W. Avery in South Carolina were bitter at the loss by the Confederacy, and of their way of life. The South lay in ruins. One in four white Southern men between the ages of 17 and 45 had been killed, with at least that many more left with debilitating injuries. Fully 80 percent of the country's wealth was in the North, while the South could rely only on cotton, tobacco, and rice after its small industrial base was destroyed. And now there was a shortage of manpower for its labour-intensive agriculture. The value of plantations, which relied so heavily on enslaved labour, had plunged to one-third of their prewar value, even those that were located nowhere near battlefields and had escaped destruction.[1] About 9,000 miles of railway tracks had been torn up by Union forces and most merchant shipping was gone. Southern banks had been emptied of coins and Confederate paper currency was worthless.

The total direct cost of the Civil War has been calculated at $6.6 billion in 1860 dollars, a figure that includes $1.5 billion of destruction wrought in the South. Overall, the total cost was split roughly in half between the combatants.[2] Slavery had underpinned the economy of the South, and by 1860, the four million enslaved people were valued at close to an estimated $3 billion. It was gone. In South Carolina, the first state to secede, the enslaved population stood at 57 percent of its 703,708 inhabitants in 1860, and white residents derived more than a third of their income from slavery.[3]

Neglect of plantations when some white men left for war, the damage they suffered, and the loss of enslaved labour left plantation owners with massive losses. Many were forced to break up their large landholdings and rent small parcels to newly freed Black people. Because few had money to pay rent, a system of sharecropping began in which the small farmer turned over to the landowner a significant amount of his produce or earnings from the fruits of his labour.[4] Financially, many Black people remained dependent on white people.

Avery and like-minded white people were unwilling to surrender power to anyone, Black people or the postwar officials appointed by the victorious North. White Southerners had relied heavily on slavery and sought to reinstate their old way of life, using terrorism and violence to achieve that goal, it soon became clear.[5] They became active in a new organization, the Ku Klux, that was determined to suppress voting by the Black majority.

Avery was a prominent retailer in downtown Yorkville, South Carolina, the county seat of York County, having purchased a successful dry goods and grocery business there in late 1868. He became a local leader of the Ku Klux and over the course of several years conducted secret initiation ceremonies in his businesses or those owned by other merchants. His efforts to suppress the Black majority would draw scrutiny and eventually legal troubles that would eventually lead him to escape to Canada, where other disaffected white Southerners had found refuge.

The Ku Klux was a secret paramilitary organization founded to oppose the Republican Party and restore white supremacy in the South. It was established by former Confederate General Nathan Bedford Forrest in 1866 in Tennessee and many of its members, like Avery, had military experience. Within two years, the organization had spread to every southern state because it successfully tapped into widespread resentment among the white population. White Democrats played a leading role in the new organization, which attacked, horse-whipped, and sometimes killed leaders of the Republicans, especially Black people. Fires were set to property by nighttime raiders to instill fear among the Black population. The attacks were often called "outrages" in the press, but many newspaper editors, despite decrying such activities publicly, were members or supporters of the new Ku Klux, to which "Klan" was occasionally appended in their reports.[6]

In the northern reaches of South Carolina including York County, as elsewhere, Ku Klux members often wore white robes and white cone-shaped hoods during their nighttime raids, terrorizing anyone who dared challenge white supremacy. Sometimes the wives and children of their targets were also beaten. One report was made to the federal Freedmen's Bureau, established to provide food to newly freed Black people and destitute white people, that said in the "upper country" of South Carolina, three Black men refused a "lifetime" contract offered by a planter. Angry, he drove the men away and then arranged for a band of armed white men to track them down. Two of the men were found and killed, while a woman accompanying them was carried back to the plantation.[7]

Members of the Ku Klux intimidated any Black people they felt were getting out of line and warned them against voting for Republican candidates. Their "reign of terror" drew particular attention to York County and it was said "the county received more national publicity and governmental attention than any other in the South."[8]

Sworn membership in the York County Ku Klux organization reached about 1,400 men, with three of its dens of 10 members apiece based in Yorkville. Dr. Rufus Bratton was a Klan Chief, or Grand Cyclops, as leader of one of those dens, while J. W. Avery was called Grand Giant as head of the county organization.[9]

The strongly Democratic *Yorkville Enquirer* was published by white supremacist Lewis M. Grist and was an influential paper across the northern part of South Carolina. In April of 1868 it carried an article headlined "The Ku Klux Klan — What is it?" in which Grist sought to downplay any connection to fires, beatings or murder. Its work, he assured readers, was political in nature and intended "to thwart Radicalism [and] arrest Negro domination in the South."[10]

In 1866, former Union Brigadier General Robert Kingston Scott had been appointed assistant commissioner of the Freedmen's Bureau in South Carolina. An Ohioan, Scott was dismayed by the cruelty that many white people displayed toward the formerly enslaved. A Republican, he was elected governor of South Carolina in 1868, heavily supported by Black people and largely despised by most white Democrats. That same year, white terror and violence held several upcountry counties, including York, in its grip. Dozens of white and Black Republicans were threatened, beaten, and killed. In response, Scott signed a bill to create a state militia which attracted mainly Black men anxious to restore law and order.

White men declined to join the militias established by a government they felt was corrupt and illegitimate, and besides, the militias were full of Black people. When Scott later authorized the arming of the militias, violence by white people increased and they added disarming of militia members to their activities. By 1871, President Ulysses S. Grant saw that Scott's move did little to quell the ongoing violence and dispatched federal troops to South Carolina. He also suspended the writ of habeas corpus — a legal guarantee that prohibits the detention of persons who have not been charged with an offence — to help authorities in nine counties, including York, round up and detain suspected white terrorists.[11]

Major Lewis Merrill was ordered to Yorkville with Company K of the Seventh Cavalry to help locals curb Ku Klux Klan violence, which was continuing unabated. Merrill had been a tenacious fighter of anti-government guerrillas who operated behind Union Army lines during the Civil War. When hostilities ceased, the Pennsylvanian was sent to New Mexico and then Kansas, and became embroiled in a personal dispute with General George Armstrong Custer. The night before Merrill's arrival in Yorkville on March 26, 1871, the town of 1,500 had been awakened by shouts and the sound of gunfire in its streets. A mob of 100 men, many of them in disguise, descended upon Rose's Hotel, a fine establishment on Congress Street in the centre of town. The hotel was located next door to the home of medical doctor Rufus Bratton, who had built the hotel with a partner in 1852 and later sold it.[12]

During the final days of the Civil War, Bratton had played host to Jefferson Davis as he and his cabinet fled through York on their way to Texas, where they hoped to regroup. While Davis stayed with Bratton April 28 and 29, 1865, some of the soldiers and other officials accompanying him lodged at the hotel.[13] During their stay, Secretary of War John C. Breckinridge delivered a speech to the assembled townsfolk from a second-floor balcony at the hotel, urging them to "keep the faith." The noisy mob that March night preceding Merrill's arrival was looking for Edward Rose, who lived in the hotel his family owned and maintained an office there. Rose was the York County treasurer, and a Republican. As the angry mob surged through the front door, intent on hanging Rose in the belief he had embezzled $12,000 in county funds, their target leaped out a back window to escape. His office and the hotel bar were ransacked and looted by the

In 1851, Yorkville doctor Rufus Bratton and a partner built Rose's Hotel in Yorkville, beside Bratton's home. When Confederate President Jefferson Davis fled westward from advancing Union troops in early 1865, he stayed at the doctor's house for one night. The rest of his men took rooms at the hotel next door, from whose balcony General John C. Breckinridge, the Confederate secretary of war, exhorted townsfolk to keep up the fight. A few days later Davis was captured, but Breckinridge escaped. (KMS PHOTOGRAPHY)

invaders, who made off with plenty of whisky to drown their sorrows after missing their quarry. They then set off in search of a Black county supervisor but couldn't find him, either. When some Black men fired at the passing mob from a nearby field, the mob scattered into the darkness. Rose was completely rattled by his close call and sought protection from Merrill's infantry before slipping out of town in an army uniform. He fled to the state capital of Columbia before finding refuge in Canada, where he remained for a year.[14] For Merrill, this was an eye-opening introduction to the turmoil in Yorkville. He established his office in Rose's Hotel and began studying recent reports of arson, beatings, and murder.

⌣

After Civil War guns fell silent, racial troubles grew in the South while political turmoil gripped Washington. Under what terms would the states that had seceded be accepted by a reunited country? How would Black people be treated under federal law? What should be done with the leaders of the Confederacy who had torn the country apart? The questions and challenges were many as the country's leaders sought to rebuild the republic.

Lincoln had barely turned his mind toward the challenge of how to reintegrate the South into the Union when he was assassinated. Historians have often wondered how the reconciliation process would have unfolded under Lincoln, a man determined to end slavery but also willing to show compassion for the defeated leaders of the Confederacy. His successor, Andrew Johnson, was no Lincoln and his efforts fell short in many ways. Johnson enslaved at least half a dozen people and had lobbied Lincoln to exclude Tennessee from the Emancipation Proclamation.[15] He wanted to preserve the Union, but also slavery. Lincoln had been willing to overlook that latter opinion, however, firmly believing he needed an ally from the South to help him win the 1864 election. He picked Johnson as his vice-presidential running mate.

As newly installed president, Johnson encouraged southern states to rejoin the Union as quickly as possible. He was stubborn, inflexible, deeply racist, and not good at compromise. He focused on the rights of individual states and felt they were best equipped to chart a new course forward without being forced to do so by Washington. Johnson decreed that if former Confederates simply took the oath of allegiance to the United States, he'd grant them pardons, but their military and civilian leaders would have to earn theirs. Johnson wanted southern states to elect new governments and let them determine issues like the rights of citizens and who could vote. Not surprisingly, many of the old leaders returned to public office following those elections and began enacting "Black Codes" that were intended to suppress and control newly freed Black people.

Many Republicans demanded strong efforts be made to implement measures like the 13th Amendment to the Constitution, which permanently abolished slavery. They became known as Radical Republicans because they wanted to rebuild the South in the image of the North. They saw Johnson as far too lenient and conciliatory. Soon the new president was also at loggerheads with the Republican-controlled Congress, to which even more Radical Republicans were added in the 1866 election. Earlier that same year, Johnson vetoed the Freedmen's Bureau Bill, legislation intended to continue the bureau's operations, and also the Civil Rights Bill, actions that drove a wedge between himself and his party. Then, in 1868, Johnson urged southern states not to ratify the 14th Amendment, which guaranteed citizenship rights to Black poeple and equal protection under the law. Southern states were required to ratify it before being allowed to rejoin the Union. Johnson's time in office was marked by the failure of his attempts to rebuild the country and the friction that developed within his own party and with Congress. Consequently, Johnson was impeached by the House of Representatives, but saved from removal from office by a single vote in the Senate. Often considered among the worst presidents in American history, Johnson decided against seeking a second term in the 1868 election. The United States had the misfortune having him at the helm of government during a pivotal time when his country needed one of its best presidents.

In 1868, Republicans chose Civil War hero Ulysses S. Grant as their party standard-bearer, and he swept to victory. Grant wanted to protect the rights of the formerly enslaved, which new Southern governments had been limiting with their Black Codes. In 1870, he signed the 15th Amendment, which guaranteed the right to vote regardless of race. The Republican-controlled Congress passed legislation against voter suppression in the South, permitting use of the military to protect newfound rights, and allowed the suspension of habeas corpus to detain persons who violated those rights. By 1870, all 11 Confederate states had been readmitted to the Union and some Black men had been elected to state legislatures and the United States Congress.[16] Grant was returned to office by a landslide, largely because of Black voters.

———

Rufus Bratton and J.W. Avery were friends and had served together as staff officers in the Fifth South Carolina Volunteers during the war. Bratton was among the community leaders that Major Merrill met upon his arrival in 1871 to explain his purpose and the pressing need to curb violence. At public meetings and in the *Enquirer*, Bratton and other prominent citizens had already been calling for an end to violence, which heartened Merrill. It took him a while, however, to learn about the activities of the KK in the area as he documented recent incidents.

Avery, the KK's Grand Giant for York County, wielded considerable influence in South Carolina. In February of 1871, when fear of arson and Black uprisings reached a peak in the county, Avery called for help from Klan members nearby in North Carolina. Almost 300 men from neighbouring Cleveland County arrived to support Avery and his men, but the crisis passed without further violence. After the lynching of a Black militia captain, many of the white men involved feared retaliation from angry Black people and sought protection from the Klan. Avery dispatched 15 or 20 men to keep a watchful eye on them. Another Black militia leader, saying he was afraid he could not control his angry men, approached Avery and asked him to take his men's guns, which had not yet been surrendered, and deliver them to the sheriff. Avery initially balked, but then delivered the 15 or 20 rifles as requested. Perhaps because of the surrender of weapons, or the ring of protection around suspected perpetrators, the lynching did not provoke the bloodbath many had feared.[17]

The Black population significantly outnumbered the white population in South Carolina, where society was in flux. The white population were mainly Democrats who hated Radical Republicans for pushing their liberal agenda on the conservative South. Black communities formed their own religious and political societies, such as Republican clubs and affiliated Union Leagues that pushed for Black rights, alarming and angering their former enslavers. Resentment was particularly strong in the town of Yorkville, located in the Piedmont region, 80 miles north of the state capital of Columbia.

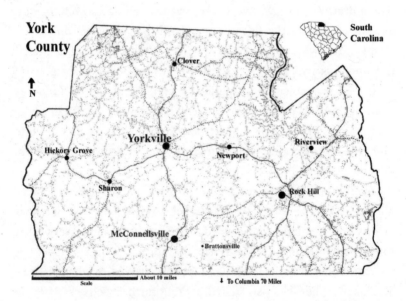

Yorkville was centrally located in York County, northern South Carolina. Following the Civil War it became a hotbed of activity by the new Ku Klux organization, whose members threatened newly freed Black people to keep them from exercising their newfound right to vote. This map depicts the county around the time of the Civil War. Today, Yorkville is known as York. (MAP BY CHIP MARTIN)

Bratton was among those who struggled to deal with the changes in the society he knew. A community leader, he practised medicine in Yorkville, and his family operated a large plantation in nearby Brattonsville. Over the years they had enslaved many people. In his diary, Bratton made this note about a change he found distasteful: "The man Bob and his family I sent away from the farm in 1868 on account of his radical politics."[18] Bratton and his fellow planters and farmers found they'd lost control of the men who toiled for them. He and other white men soon organized to use terror and violence in a bid to reassert their control over Black people and dissuade them from politics. Like Bratton, many joined the secretive Ku Klux.

Rufus Bratton's brother John joined him in Ku Klux activities, as did Avery's older brother, Edward Tillman Avery, a medical doctor who had served in the 17th South Carolina Volunteers and operated a plantation near Ebenezerville, about 12 miles east of Yorkville. Dr. Edward Avery was active in Democratic politics, and evidence at a later trial showed that he tried to suppress Black voters in the election of November 1868. The Klan was determined to elect Democrats that year and decided to "crowd off" voters likely to support Radical Republican candidates and Ulysses S. Grant for president. At the town of Rock Hill, near his home, Dr. Avery and other Ku Kluxers circled the polls and jostled Black men, telling them to vote Democrat. Others were simply pushed away and told they were not old enough to cast a ballot. The Democratic candidates prevailed in Rock Hill, but Congress later overturned the results upon learning about fraudulent or illegal activities.[19] On March 18, 1870, likely as retribution for his white supremacist activities, a barn on Avery's plantation outside of Ebenezerville was burned to the ground. Black people were beginning to fight fire with fire in York County. Literally. Avery said he lost 500 or 600 bushels of corn and a large amount of cattle feed. A Black man was charged with arson in the incident and carted off to the county jail.[20]

Edward Avery was a regular night rider with the Klan and an active leader of the organization, which continued terrorizing Black

Republicans into early 1871. One night in early March, he led six men on raids of two Black homes near Rock Hill. About 10 o'clock, Avery and his band broke into the home of Abram and Emeline Broomfield. As they approached the house, dogs started barking, Abram slipped out the back, and his wife was confronted by Avery, who was in disguise. She recognized him from his voice and his lame left hand, however. The intruders demanded to know whether Abram was president of the Union League and if he retained militia guns that had not been turned in. Emeline denied both claims. The men found Samuel Sturgis upstairs, dragged him down and began beating him. Sturgis, 61, would later recall he recognized Avery and all his associates, one of whom, a Black man named Howard White, placed a noose around Sturgis's neck and dragged him about the house. "After they had beat me, they made me swear never to vote the Radical ticket again," Sturgis said.[21] The Avery-led band then visited the home of Black minister Isaac Postle, known as "Isaac the Apostle." There, the minister's pregnant wife refused to reveal his hiding place, so Avery knocked her to the floor and pinned the baby she was holding with his foot while another white stepped on her. She adamantly refused to reveal her husband's whereabouts, prompting the men to beat her head against a wall and place a noose around her neck. Postle suddenly emerged, and the men took him outside and conducted a mock hanging of him before releasing the terrified man with a warning against voting Republican.

———

One of the most notorious lynchings was that of Black militia Captain Jim Williams three weeks before Major Merrill's arrival in Yorkville. Early in 1871, Governor Robert Kingston Scott disarmed and disbanded many state militias when it was clear they were not curbing violence and may have actually contributed to it because the Ku Klux was attacking militia members to disarm them. The York County militia was ordered disbanded in February, but Captain Williams, who was particularly militant and hated white people, refused to surrender his militia's guns despite the governor's order. Williams was feared and hated by white people across York County because he had threatened to form a Black Ku Klux organization. A Black man named William Bratton, who took his surname from the Bratton family plantation where he'd been enslaved, was a member of the militia and testified Williams told him in January: "I intend to rule this country. I'll Ku Klux [terrorize] white women and children, and if I can't manage things then, I'll kill from the cradle to the grave."[22] A witness for the prosecution of several men involved in the lynching, William Bratton said Williams was angry at the KK for "bothering colored people" and that he had the means to carry on a war with white people. Upon learning of his threats, leaders of the Ku Klux decided to eliminate Williams.

One of the local members later convicted in the killing was M.S. Carroll, who kept a journal about what happened on the night of the lynching. He recalled Williams sometime earlier delivering a speech at Rose's Hotel in which he "boasted that if ever the KKK came into his country very few, if any, of them would return to their homes." Carroll's Yorkville den, led by Rufus Bratton, went to Williams's home in nearby McConnellsville late one night. Carroll and the doctor went to Williams's door and found only the captain's wife home, along with an unknown Black man. His wife insisted she didn't know the whereabouts of Williams. Carroll continued:

> We made a thorough search of the house but did not find him. After a moment's reflection Dr. Bratton told someone to pull up some of the plank flooring. "He might be under there," he said. And sure enough, there was Jim crouched under the floor. We hauled him out and placed a rope around his neck and started back toward our horses. We had got back about half way to the horses when someone spied a large tree with a limb running about 10 or 12 feet from the ground and suggested that this was the place to finish the job. And we left Captain Williams dangling from the limb.[23]

For Bratton and other white supremacists the lynching of Jim Williams had the desired effect of spreading further fear among the Black population in York County.

⁓

Meanwhile, J.W. Avery continued to lead his fellow white supremacists and was often willing to get political in advertisements for his store that he placed in the local paper. His clientele doubtless knew about his KK activities, his dislike of Governor Scott, and his suppression of Black people. One of his advertisements in early April of 1871 mixed politics and business in a bid to generate sales. It read, in its entirety:

> GOVERNOR SCOTT'S MILITIA.
>
> The Governor having disarmed and disbanded his Militia, and removed the most objectionable of the Trial Justices, it is certainly the duty of every white man in the county, to do all in his power to preserve the peace and keep down all disturbances; so that every man, woman and child may come, in safety, and see my large and elegant stock of Goods, just purchased in the Northern markets, very low for cash, and to be sold at correspondingly low rates for the money and the money only. Absolutely no credit. J.W. Avery[24]

The federal government increased its troops in South Carolina to compensate for the disbanding of militias. But the total complement amounted to only 900 men, a force the Ku Klux could easily muster in a matter of hours, if necessary. Throughout March and April of 1871, violence and terrorism continued in South Carolina, particularly in the northern reaches of the state in the communities of Unionville, Spartanburg, and Yorkville.

This caught the attention of President Grant in Washington, who announced that curbing Southern violence had become a top priority for him. He justified federal intervention because "the power to correct these evils is beyond the control of State authorities . . ." On April 20, Congress passed the Third Enforcement Act, more commonly known as the Ku Klux Act. It targeted "unlawful bands" of persons who denied other citizens "equal protection of the laws." Federal power now existed to punish state crimes like murder for anyone engaged in "the deprivation of any rights, privileges and immunities secured by the Constitution." The president was free to suspend the writ of habeas corpus, a provision that would allow authorities to make mass arrests without being required to file charges in a timely manner. It also permitted prosecutors to keep the names of detainees secret so as not to alert others they were planning to apprehend.

The same day the new legislation was passed, Congress established the Joint Select Committee to Inquire into the Condition of Affairs in the Late Insurrectionary States. In May, the new committee heard witnesses in Washington and in June conducted a series of Southern hearings in South Carolina.[25] The *Yorkville Enquirer* lamented the new federal resolve to curb violence, calling it overreach. It objected to the denial of equal legal protection of persons suspected of engaging in acts of violence because of the suspension of habeas corpus. And trials would be held in distant Columbia, Charleston or Greenville with prohibitive costs for bail, defence lawyers and witnesses. "This [KK] act will be enforced, and rigidly enforced," it opined, "and unless our people at once determine that there must be no further acts of violence in the county, we will soon have occasion to observe the practical operations of the law in its utmost severity and with all its unpleasant consequences."[26]

The congressional subcommittee looking into violence in the South spent several days in South Carolina, which was considered the epicentre of the worst reign of terror by the Ku Klux. A wide range of witnesses was called to testify in Columbia, Spartanburg, Union, and Yorkville, including members of the Klan itself.

Several identified Major J.W. Avery as leader of the organization across York County. Carriage maker William Owens testified he was initiated into the organization by Avery in the back of Avery's dry goods store. "I think he was general chief of the Ku Klux over this upper portion of the county; I think all obeyed his will," Owens testified July 25 in Yorkville.[27] His testimony came immediately after that of Rufus Bratton, who stoutly insisted he was not involved with the organization in any way and anything he knew about it was gleaned from newspapers and rumour. Bratton said he doubted as many Black people had been whipped as had been claimed. He testified many of them dislike work and he didn't believe their testimony, adding, revealingly, he believed it was the duty of white men to teach the Black man to be "quiet and passive and attend to his duties." Bratton insisted most people he knew had a good opinion of Black people, but their race was not suited to politics or holding government positions in South Carolina because "the honest, intelligent white people are the only persons capable of ruling it."[28] In his subsequent testimony, Owens was asked about Bratton's

Dr. J. Rufus Bratton was a medical doctor in Yorkville and his large family owned plantations nearby. He became a leader in the local Ku Klux organization and was implicated in the murder of a Black militia leader. Rather than remain in Yorkville and face trial before what he felt would be a jury biased against him, Bratton fled to Canada in early 1872. (ARCHIVES AND SPECIAL COLLECTIONS, WESTERN UNIVERSITY, LONDON, ONTARIO)

involvement in Ku Klux affairs and the lynching of Black militia leader Jim Williams. Owens testified he was told by eyewitness Rufe McLain, leader of his Yorkville den, that Bratton and several other men took part in the killing of Williams.[29]

By October 1871, as violence continued across the South, President Grant suspended habeas corpus in nine counties in northern South Carolina, including York, and ordered federal troops and marshals to round up suspected perpetrators. His move was recommended by United States Attorney General Amos T. Akerman, who had assessed the situation in the South first-hand. Grant's move instilled fear of federal power in many places, especially among citizens who had tacitly supported the Ku Klux and its activities. Hundreds of accused men soon filled local jails to overflowing while the authorities prepared charges under the Ku Klux Act. The sweep effectively crippled the organization in York and the other eight counties, but convictions were few compared to the number of men detained. By November, nearly 500 accused were awaiting their trials in the state capital of Columbia. Given the number of men arrested, justice was not swift. By early 1872, only 54 men had been convicted of violating the Ku Klux Act and sentenced, of whom 49 had pleaded guilty and only five convicted at trial. Another 38 men were acquitted and 30 cases thrown out. By April 1872, about 400 persons still faced trial and arrests continued. The most severe punishment meted out was five years in jail, while most sentences ranged from six to 18 months and fines imposed were from $10 to $100.[30]

———

Rather than face justice, many South Carolinians who feared arrest and harsh penalties fled the state. Attorney General Akerman insisted that estimates of 500 flights from justice in York and Spartanburg counties were too high and insisted to the New York Times the number was much closer to 200. "Many of those who have left are known as prominently connected to the order," the Times reported on October 31.[31]

The Avery brothers and Rufus Bratton would soon join the exodus. In December, a grand jury found sufficient evidence to commit J.W. Avery and Bratton to trial on charges of planning and executing the murder of Jim Williams. Dr. Edward Avery and others were charged with conspiring to prevent Black men from voting and in particular with conspiring against Samuel Sturgis, Abram Broomfield, and Isaac Postle. At his trial in Columbia, J.W. Avery leaped from a courtroom window during a recess and hopped onto a saddled horse left for him by some friends who were pessimistic at his chance of acquittal. His escape prompted federal authorities to offer a reward of $60,000 for his capture.[32] Avery made his way to Canada, where he understood other former Confederates were then living. Within months, Bratton would also be in Canada.

Edward Avery's trial on four counts began on December 29. The prosecutor said he planned to prove the doctor was an active leader of the Ku Klux and had taken part in many of its violent nighttime raids intended to frighten Black men and suppress their vote. His lawyer argued Avery had absolutely no connection to the organization. The prosecution rested its case on the first count on January 2, and defence counsel F.W. McMaster had just begun addressing the jury when Judge Hugh L. Bond interrupted him, having noticed Dr. Avery was not present in court. Bond asked McMaster where his client was, but the lawyer refused to answer, notwithstanding threats of censure from the bench.[33] Avery, who had been freed on bond of $3,000 posted earlier by friends, had fled the jurisdiction and he, too, was soon in Canada. The bond was forfeited, his trial continued, and Avery was convicted *in absentia*.

Despite the number of suspects arrested and jailed, the rate of conviction remained low for members of the Ku Klux and those who rode with them. Federal government action is credited with accelerating the demise of the KK, but it was already in decline even before the first arrests were made under the presidential roundup order because white people had begun to back away when violence was getting out of control. Acclaimed Reconstruction historian Eric Foner contends that while Grant's draconian crackdown was a failure tactically and had little immediate impact, it did help to restore law and order, reinvigorate Southern Republicans, and enable Black people to enjoy their rights as citizens.[34] Another historian, Richard Zuczek, is more circumspect in his take:

> After a wave of political terrorism unprecedented in the history of the United States, a handful of low-ranking Ku Klux Klan members had been sentenced to a few years in jail. To be sure, hundreds had been arrested, indicted and now awaited trial. But many more avoided arrest, while a large proportion of those arrested were walking around free — and would never see the inside of a courtroom.[35]

Three of them, the Avery brothers and Bratton, were soon walking the streets in faraway Canada, where they were welcomed by others who had already fled South Carolina, including former planter families and enslavers named Manigault and Mazyck.

Once in Canada, J.W. Avery made his way north to London, where he knew some southern families had made their home. He would have known the prominent Manigault and Mazyck families of South Carolina, who settled there in 1869 after spending several years in Yorkville. They'd likely met Avery at his store or through his extracurricular activities leading the Ku Klux. The latter is plausible because we know from his later writings that family patriarch Gabriel Manigault was a white supremacist, although his name was not mentioned publicly in connection with Ku Klux terrorism in York County. The Manigaults and Mazycks put out the welcome mat for others from the South who fled justice being meted out by Northern-backed governments they distrusted and felt were illegitimate. They also helped other Southerners who suddenly felt alienated in their own land, having lost enslaved labour, plantations, and an entire way of life, and wanted to escape Reconstruction.

Avery found accommodation in London with the help of the Manigaults and Mazycks, as did his older brother Edward Avery who followed him north. But the Averys did not remain in the city for long and moved east to Niagara, which they knew had been the home of so many Confederate military and political exiles in recent years. Niagara was about the same size as Yorkville so that may have been part of its appeal, while London, with a population of 16,000, was one-third the size of Charleston, the metropolis of South Carolina.

During his absence, Edward Avery learned he had been pardoned. Apparently, several men convicted of Ku Klux crimes, including a man on his deathbed, swore affidavits that Avery was not present on the fateful night when Sturgis, Broomfield, and Postle had been confronted by white terrorists.[36] The doctor returned home in May of 1873, but was arrested late that same year before the exculpatory affidavits were presented to free him. He left behind in Niagara his brother, who was now calling himself John (instead of James) William Avery, perhaps to avoid detection by American authorities. While Edward Avery was out of the country his Ebenezer Place property was sold at auction by the United States marshal because he'd used the property as security for the bond he forfeited when he fled justice.[37]

Late in 1872, J.W. Avery penned a letter to the *Enquirer* back in Yorkville in response to claims by U.S. government officials that he'd been "the chief of an extensive conspiracy of a political character to overthrow Radical Grantism and prevent the freedmen from voting, and that in pursuance of this conspiracy, divers persons of color were killed, many whipped and innumerable schools broken up." Avery pulled no punches in denying the allegation:

> I never was a member or chief of any organizations, club or conspiracy for such purposes and objects, either *directly* or *indirectly*, and I *never* have *ordered, aided* or *abetted* the killing or whipping of any one, (black or

white) because of his politics, or *for any other reason whatsoever*. That I was a member of an organization in the winter and early spring of 1871, for self protection, especially against fire, is most true.[38]

He went on to recall the fears among the white population of violence from Black men and that Radical Republicans now controlled the government and the courts. "As to the so-called klux raids, I had nothing to do with them and am satisfied I did far more to suppress them than Major Merrill with all his troops . . ." Avery said he fled South Carolina because he feared he'd never get a fair trial before a Northern-appointed judge and a "Loyal League" (Black) jury. In his lengthy letter to the newspaper, Avery made no mention of his

Former Confederate Major J.W. Avery, a leader of the Ku Klux in South Carolina, was wanted for conspiring against Black people and for murder. He arrived in Niagara in 1872 and eventually settled into this house with his family at 392 Mississagua Street, which he purchased. The Averys held onto the property long after they returned to the South and kept it until seven years after Avery died in 1892. (PHOTO BY CHIP MARTIN)

whereabouts. Late in 1874, he purchased the house at 392 Mississagua Street in Niagara, which he and wife Laura had been renting and where they had been raising their eight children, aged from 4 to 19. Shortly before the family acquired the handsome home for $1,450, their eldest child, Jessie, married William McNair of Cheraw, South Carolina.[39] Avery kept a low profile in Niagara, where he swore an oath to the Queen and remained unmolested as memories of his Ku Klux activities began to fade back home.

———

Reconstruction came to an end in 1877 when white Democrats ousted the last Republican governor and took control of South Carolina's State House, senate, and supreme court. With many of its old leaders back in charge, South Carolina began to restrict the right of Black men to vote, turning back the clock to recreate the state they knew before the war.[40] The subjugation of the Black majority returned through legislation, known as Black Codes. In late 1876, United States President Grant pardoned all persons convicted under the Ku Klux Act and by 1877, Avery felt that the pardon and the change in the political climate made it safe for him to return home.

The *Yorkville Enquirer* reported he spent several days visiting old friends in Yorkville during November. The paper reminded its readers that Avery had been an "esteemed citizen and prosperous merchant of Yorkville" but now lived in Niagara. "Major Avery speaks in glowing terms of the place of his adoption, and is in fine health and spirits," it added.[41] In September of 1878, he enrolled his 18-year-old son, Ralph, at the Royal Military College at Kingston. Ralph became cadet number 50 in the new facility modelled on the United States Military Academy in West Point, New York. Upon graduating after four years, young Avery would be eligible for a commission in the British Army. But at the request of his parents, military college records show, he withdrew from the college after two years of study with a certificate of military qualification.[42] He never pursued a military career and died of typhoid fever in 1893 in Virginia.

After pulling their son from the Royal Military College, the Averys returned to the United States late in 1880 but kept the house in Niagara for a number of years, presumably for use during summer vacations. The family settled near Norfolk, Virginia, where they purchased a farm and lived quietly. The old Confederate warrior and chief of the Ku Klux Klan in South Carolina died there in 1892 without a will, and his former home in Niagara was not sold by his estate until 1899.

Their eight years in Canada made the Avery family's stay among the longest of the Southerners who chose to hide out until the postwar political and social climate changed enough that they could return to the South without fear of legal or other consequences. With the re-establishment of white supremacy, even those who had previously practised it in a savage way like Major J.W. Avery could feel comfortable going home. Refuge in Canada, the convenient attic, had served its purpose for Avery and his family as it had for so many others.

CHAPTER TWELVE

SOUTHERNERS CHOOSE LONDON

Niagara and Windsor were small communities just across the American border, so anyone wishing to escape social or political conditions in the republic needed to take only a few steps into Canada to find refuge. For some, however, those places were too tantalizingly close for bounty hunters or others pursuing them, so they moved farther away, often to Toronto or Montreal, which by the end of the Civil War had grown to about 50,000 and 100,000 inhabitants respectively. While it was easier to hide in a large city, the cost of living was often prohibitive for newcomers, especially those who found themselves in difficult circumstances.

London became a popular alternative. Located 150 miles west of Niagara and the same distance east of Windsor-Detroit, its population stood at about 15,000 by the end of a war from which its merchants, manufacturers, hotels, and area farmers had profited so handsomely. The identity of the first Southerners to arrive is not known, but the guest book at the Tecumseh House Hotel would have provided some clues. Word of mouth about London and its acceptance of newcomers likely played a role in making it an attractive destination, only a few hours by train from the border. The last British regiment departed in 1869, two years after Confederation, and London remained staunchly loyal to Queen Victoria. Its inhabitants remained wary about the neighbouring northern states, from which Fenian raids had been launched.

After 1863, London shifted from being a refuge for spies, agents, and buyers to a permanent home for Southerners. One of the first was Matthew W. Manville, a 21-year-old trooper who served in the 2,400-man Kentucky cavalry unit of Brigadier General John Hunt Morgan. The unit was known as Morgan's Raiders for their daring raids throughout Indiana and Ohio during the summer of 1863. On July 26, Morgan and 360 of his men were captured at Salineville, in northeast Ohio, marking the farthest incursion into Union territory ever made by Confederate troops. Their exploits were overshadowed, however, by the Confederate defeat at Gettysburg earlier that month.

Morgan and several of his officers, including Captain Thomas Hines, who later helped develop the Northwest Conspiracy from Canada, broke out of the Ohio State Penitentiary in Columbus in late November.[1] Manville, captured during an earlier raid, also managed to escape. For reasons unknown, he decided against returning to duty and found his way to London. Manville appeared one night at the door of a large-frame boarding house on King Street operated by Elizabeth Mountjoy. He was not the first American who sought lodging there and would not be the last. She took him in.[2]

Manville adjusted to London easily and established the firm of Manville and Brown Auctioneers, which also sold real estate and goods on commission. It proved to be successful venture and in 1867 he married local woman Frances Saunby; the couple had two children, Jenny and Clay.[3] Manville became active in the temperance movement and in 1877 was elected president of the London Temperance Club at a meeting that attracted 500 people, including two Michigan reformers who warned about the impact of alcohol on family life.[4] Manville declared that the sober man is "the noblest work of God," reflecting the evangelical fervour about temperance that was spreading quickly at the time. Manville's wife died of tuberculosis early in 1877 and in 1882 he married Carrie Strong, with whom he moved to his home state of Arkansas.

Another Southerner to take up residence in London and go into business was James Ladson Barnwell, who was 40 when he arrived in

1874 with his second wife, Elizabeth, and several children. His family was from Beaufort, South Carolina, and by 1858 he and his first wife Eliza were living in Charleston. Barnwell managed to avoid military service and after the war returned to Beaufort County, where his wife died in 1871. He soon remarried, but may have struggled financially because in 1873 the United States House of Representatives passed a bill providing him with relief, as it did for others in need.[5] The next year, likely hoping for a fresh start, Barnwell was in London working as a bookkeeper for the News Depot store of Ezra Taylor. Within a few years he acquired *The Echo*, a firm which published a weekly newspaper, advertising material, and undertook contract printing jobs. A son, Robert, was born in London. A daughter from his first wife Eliza, Hattie Wistar Barnwell, married the son of another South Carolina family living in London. Barnwell sold *The Echo* in 1887 to printer Alfred Talbot and returned to South Carolina.[6]

In about 1874, Henry Ragin Thomas, a South Carolinian who had been active in the Ku Klux organization in that state, also relocated to London. A native of Clarendon County, located between Charleston and the capital of Columbia, he was born in 1845. During the war he served briefly with the Fifth South Carolina Infantry, but was discharged when it was discovered he was underage. This was the same regiment in which Yorkville's J.W. Avery and Rufus Bratton were serving. When he turned 16, Thomas joined the Fifth Cavalry and enrolled in the South Carolina Military Academy. Upon graduating, he became a First Lieutenant in the 23rd South Carolina Infantry. After the war, Thomas studied civil engineering, but then took up farming in neighbouring Sumter County. There, he became involved in the Ku Klux and their attacks on the Black population.[7]

Thomas became a wanted man for his activities and began the process of changing his family's original surname of Ragin to Thomas, hoping it might help him avoid detection in his daily life. But that effort took time and the General Assembly of South Carolina didn't finalize it until June 8, 1877.[8] By then, Thomas had settled in London. While in the city, Thomas would have socialized with his fellow South Carolinians and likely visited Niagara to renew acquaintances with J.W. Avery as they awaited an opportunity to return home. He acted as a civil engineer and, following pardons issued for Ku Klux members at the end of Reconstruction in 1877, he returned to South Carolina where he married Anne Caldwell and fathered three children. There, while serving as a member of the South Carolina railroad commission, Thomas became embroiled in a nasty public dispute with an engineering expert about a rail bed near Sumter and its susceptibility to flooding. The expert went so far as to challenge the character of Thomas and allege he'd been a fugitive from justice. Thomas felt compelled to set the record straight in a lengthy letter to the *Watchman and Southron* newspaper in Sumter:

> As to my record, I am proud of it. I deny that I was
> ever a fugitive from justice. After the war I was accused
> of killing some negro soldiers who were terrorizing the
> women and children and old men about my old home at
> Summerton, Clarendon County. If there is any dishonor
> in the part I really did take just after the war in protecting
> the women and children of Confederate soldiers, then I
> am dishonored, for on that account alone I was a fugi-
> tive, with many of the best men of the country, from
> Radical persecution. I changed my name and sought
> the protection of the British flag sooner than be tried
> for my life before Radical Judges and negro juries . . .
> I then lived in London, Canada. My friends and asso-
> ciates were Dr. John R. Bratton, of Yorkville (a fugitive
> like myself), Mr. Jas. Barnwell, a brother-in-law of Mr.
> Jos. W. Barnwell, now living in Beaufort; Mr. Edward
> Manigault and Alexander Mazyck, of London Canada.[9]

Some of the Southerners who settled in London late in the Civil War and afterward were members of prominent families, notably the Mazycks and Manigaults, formerly of Charleston, South Carolina.

By the fall of 1866 Alexander Mazyck, 65, was residing in London, where on November 15 he received a letter from his brother Edward, 67, who was still in the South.[10] Within two years, Edward joined Alexander in London as the flight of plantation owners from the agricultural Santee area of South Carolina continued.

Neither of the Mazyck men married, so they were more mobile than other Southerners, many of whom had large families. Both steadfastly refused to live under a United States government they felt was illegitimate. President Andrew Johnson announced in 1865 he would pardon participants in the rebellion and restore their rights to vote, run for office, or obtain federal appointments, if Southerners were willing to swear an oath of allegiance.

Exempted from Johnson's pardon for the time being were high-ranking Confederate officers, political leaders, and persons who took part in raids launched from Canada, among others. Debate was still raging about what should be done with leading Confederates who many in the North considered as traitors. In the minds of most Southerners, it was bad enough the Confederacy had lost the war, but to swear allegiance to the North, which had exploited them for so many years, made it so much worse. For some, like the Mazycks, who had enjoyed comfortable lives because of slavery, it was the last straw. Why they chose London as a refuge is a matter of conjecture, but they must have known someone familiar with the city, most likely Southerners already living there. The Mazyck brothers played a key role in the subsequent decision by the large Manigault clan to join them early in 1869.

The Mazycks and Manigaults were descended from Huguenots, French Protestants from France. The Reformed Church to which they adhered was established there in the mid-1530s, influenced by the teachings of Martin Luther and later by John Calvin. Huguenots were persecuted for their beliefs by the dominant Roman Catholic Church. More than 400,000 Huguenots abandoned their homes in France and moved to England, Holland, Germany, and other countries where Protestantism flourished.[11]

As early as 1670, King Charles II of England sent two shiploads of French Huguenots to South Carolina to begin cultivating grapes, olives, and silkworms in its warm climate. In 1687, another 600 Huguenots arrived in the Americas, primarily in the Carolina area but also in Nova Scotia, Jamaica, Virginia, New York, and New England. In Carolina, the Huguenots generally settled in the vicinity of the Santee River and others in Charles Town (later Charleston). They tended to be merchants, tradesmen, artisans, and craftsmen, and many were well educated and had a strong entrepreneurial spirit. Some established agricultural plantations.

Among those who settled in the Goose Creek area north of Charles Town were prominent families, including those of Isaac and Paul Mazyck.

In 1793, brothers Isaac and William Mazyck acquired a tract of more than 1,000 acres in Berkeley County along the Santee River at Goose Creek, known as the Oaks Plantation. There they grew rice on the low-lying land.[12] Isaac's son, Paul, operated Springfield Plantation just to the east in Georgetown County, where he grew rice and other crops. The plantation was nearly 1,000 acres and at one point as many as 100 enslaved people worked it. The Mazyck family sold it in 1846.[13] In Charleston County along the Santee River at McClellanville, Alexander Mazyck owned the Montgomery Plantation, but like other Santee planters, he sold it after the Civil War.

Pierre and Gabriel Manigault were among the Huguenots who fled France and made their way to the Charleston area in the 1690s. Prominent landowners in France, they remained in England for a decade before selling their properties to finance a fresh start in Carolina, where they began acquiring land.[14] They joined others who farmed alongside the Santee River but then returned to the city, where Pierre established two brandy distilleries and operated several businesses. His son Gabriel, born in 1704, profited from the lucrative move to rice cultivation and greatly expanded his business interests, becoming one of the richest merchants in North America. He was so wealthy he was able to lend the government $220,000 to help it wage war against Britain during the American Revolution. His businesses exported lumber, rice, and naval supplies, while importing West Indies rum, sugar, and wine.

For years, Gabriel Manigault and his family dominated Charleston society and politics. It was said that upon his death in 1781, Gabriel's estate was valued at $500,000 in land, enslaved people, and bonds. His only son, Peter, was educated in England, practised law there, sat for 16 years in the House of Commons, and died there in 1773. Peter's sons, Gabriel and Joseph, inherited about 40,000 acres and 500 enslaved people when their grandfather Gabriel died. Young Gabriel served several terms in the legislature. He was a talented, self-taught architect who designed houses for himself and his brother, as well as the fine building that now serves as Charleston City Hall.[15] The Joseph Manigault House on Meeting Street, built in 1803, still stands and is a National Historic Landmark.

Gabriel Manigault was from a wealthy family of planters in the Charleston, South Carolina, area. Pictured is the Joseph Manigault House in that city, where Gabriel was born in 1808. It is now a museum in Charleston. Gabriel Manigault became a lawyer and a member of the South Carolina legislature, where he voted to secede from the Union late in 1860. (LIBRARY OF CONGRESS)

Joseph Manigault and his wife Charlotte Dayton had eight children, three of whom served with the Confederate States Army during the Civil War. His son Gabriel Edward Manigault, born in 1809, was an aide to South Carolina Governor Francis Pickens and a colonel in the Confederate ordinance department, where he helped array the guns across from Fort Sumter for General Pierre Gustave Toutant-Beauregard. His younger brothers Edward and Arthur held the ranks of major and brigadier general respectively. Edward was a staff officer in the Sixth and 26th South Carolina Infantry and commanded "Manigault's Volunteers" in a combined infantry, artillery and cavalry unit. Arthur became colonel of the 10th South Carolina Infantry and participated in the shelling of Fort Sumter.[16]

The Manigault and Mazyck families didn't raise cotton like many other planters. Because their vast landholdings were near the swampy coastline of the Atlantic in a broad fertile plain about 100 miles wide, they cultivated rice. Settlers in the late 1600s had little success in agriculture until they began planting rice imported from Asia across what was known as Carolina's Low Country. It was a success as a cash crop, and throughout the 1700s the economy of the region boomed. Rice fetched high prices in England and made South Carolina one of the richest colonies in North America. Charleston, its capital and principal port, became a wealthy and fashionable city. Initially, planters in South Carolina were unfamiliar with proper cultivation methods and began importing enslaved people from rice-growing areas of West Africa.[17] There were at least 100 rice plantations along the coastal rivers of the Low Country of South Carolina by the outbreak of the Civil War. Rice went into decline after the war when labour and capital became scarce and crops were wiped out by several severe storms. By the early 1900s, rice cultivation had disappeared completely.[18]

The Manigaults and Mazycks were among the wealthiest families in the state and profited handsomely from its slavery-based economy. They were linked by marriage in 1846 when lawyer Gabriel Manigault married Anne Porcher Mazyck and the couple began raising a family in Charleston.

When not in the city, the Manigaults lived at their Romney plantation in Charleston County. Gabriel was elected to the South Carolina state legislature, as was Alexander Mazyck, the brother of his wife's father. Mazyck was a prominent lawyer in Charleston and operated plantations in the area with his brother, Edward. Alexander was chairman of a railway company and was elected to the South Carolina Senate in 1848. Alexander Mazyck and Gabriel Manigault were among the delegates at the Charleston convention of December 1860, which unanimously approved the "Ordinance of Secession." Four months later, both attended a conference to approve the constitution of the Confederate States of America that had been drawn up in Montgomery, Alabama.

During the war, Gabriel Manigault commanded troops in the South Santee area and then focused his efforts on recruiting. By 1863, the tide was turning against the South and he had grown critical of Confederate leadership over their plans to defend Charleston. In mid-September, Manigault sent a letter to South Carolina Governor M.L. Bonham in which he suggested poor decision-making by Confederate generals had left Charleston vulnerable to attack.[19]

Manigault felt that his city and his landholdings were becoming vulnerable as the tide of war was turning against the South, and he felt compelled to speak out. He didn't win many friends in so doing.

───

By 1865, Manigault was making his home in Yorkville, to which he and his family had moved to escape the devastation inflicted on Charleston and his family's nearby plantations. Members of the Mazyck family may have joined the Manigaults for a time in Yorkville as well. Why the fugitives from Charleston chose Yorkville is not clear, although those from other parts of the state had flocked there late in the war, such as Ann Barnwell, of Beaufort, who later married into the Mazyck family.[20] All plantation owners would have understood acutely that the Confederacy's loss was their loss. They could no longer rely on enslaved labour to operate their plantations, some of which had been heavily damaged, especially those nearest Charleston. Like other families, the Manigaults and Mazycks may have feared retaliation from suddenly freed Black people anxious to settle scores with the white man after years of servitude. In addition, Gabriel Manigault and Alexander Mazyck had likely angered their fellow white men who had been ruined because both men helped trigger the war by voting to secede.

Gabriel and Anne Manigault had five children who survived, born between 1848 and 1859: Eliza, Edward, William, Mary, and Charlotte, all of whom were provided a good education. Eliza, about to turn 18, saw the need for a school in Yorkville and in early September of 1865 she placed a notice in the *Yorkville Enquirer* to announce she was opening a school for children aged 5 to 14 "in all branches of an English education."[21] Also joining Gabriel Manigault's family in Yorkville were three of his nieces, Julia, Josephine, and Emma, daughters born from 1829 to 1833 to his younger brother Charles and his wife, Emma Lynch Horry. Their mother died at age 29 in 1835, likely in childbirth, and Charles died three years later at age 33, so the girls were left without parents. Gabriel assumed responsibility for them and they joined his immediate family in Yorkville. Like their cousin Eliza, they also decided to teach.

A notice in the *Enquirer* in November of 1866 announced the reopening of Yorkville Female College, with Julia Manigault teaching "natural philosophy and astronomy, geography, physiology, and botany." Emma and Josephine would provide instruction in music and French. Courses would be taught in two terms, with a fee of $26 for the six-month first term, and $13 for the three-month second term. Board was $15 a month, payable in specie (coin, not paper money).[22]

The departure of the Manigault family in 1869 was lamented by the *Yorkville Enquirer* on May 6 that year:

> Tender social ties and links of friendship were sundered
> by the departure from our midst, on Tuesday last, of
> Mr. Gabriel Manigault and family, who leave us to seek
> a home in Canada. Mr. Manigault and his family came
> to our town as refugees from Charleston, about the time

Sherman was ravaging the lower part of the State with his fire-bummers [sic]. His fine property in Charleston and Georgetown, by the calamities of war, had become almost a total loss to him; and under the most unfavorable auspices, he became a resident of our community. Four years of residence with us had endeared him and his family to our people with something above the ordinary character of mere personal esteem.

Mr. Manigault is a descendant of the old Huguenot colonists of South Carolina, and his family have been identified with our State history for a long period of years. Mr. M. was for several sessions a member of the Legislature from Charleston, where he resided until the commencement of the war.

The genial and elevated character of himself and family, and the pleasant associations connected with their memory, will long be cherished by our people. He purposes to locate in New London, Canada, under the protection of the British Crown, and we congratulate the subjects of Her majesty in that locality upon their valuable acquisition.[23]

The same article appeared four days later in the *Charleston Daily Courier*, which felt compelled to inform its readers of the northward flight of such a prominent Charlestonian and his family.

———

The Mazyck brothers had settled into a home on Alma Street in north London and just west of the newly erected Hellmuth Boys College. Here they welcomed Gabriel Manigault and his family, who rented a home on Piccadilly Street several blocks to the south before finding larger quarters on nearby Waterloo Street.

Gabriel Manigault and his immediate family had left Yorkville before the establishment of the Ku Klux and the killings and arson that left both Black and white populations across York County living in fear. But Julia, Josephine, and Emma Manigault and their aunt, Ann Julia Horry, would have been acutely aware of the troubles, concerned for their safety and feeling compelled to leave. When they arrived in London, Julia was 43, Josephine, 40, and Emma, 39. When the nieces joined their extended family in London, they brought along their 72-year-old aunt, the spinster sister of their late mother. The women never married and lived together in a modest frame home; it is unclear whether they earned a livelihood or were supported by other family members. Their aunt passed away in 1878. The nieces lived on Wellington Street, a few doors away from a boarding house operated by widow Sarah Hill at 855 Wellington, which attracted Southerners and others.

Not long after reuniting with her extended family in Canada, Julia Manigault explained why they had forsaken South Carolina. At one point she wrote:

> My sisters and myself are natives of Charleston, S.C., where we lived the greater part of our lives. During the war between the Northern and Southern States, we were compelled to leave our home and, at length, settled in Yorkville, S.C., and lived there for six years and a half, ending April 14, 1872. We had extensive acquaintance among the people of Yorkville and surrounding country, and had good opportunities of knowing the condition of that part of the State. Within a year or two after the end of the war we heard frequently of the "Loyal League," a secret political society, organized by the radical party with a view to control the negro voters, and a source of anxiety to the white inhabitants of the town.[24]

The Mazycks and the Manigaults were within easy walking distance of each other as they put down roots in a foreign city about one-third the size of Charleston. Their sharing of accommodation

This is the modest home at 300 Piccadilly Street in London into which Gabriel Manigault and his family first moved after fleeing South Carolina and reuniting with the Mazyck brothers. (PHOTO BY CHIP MARTIN)

suggested they were careful with their money, and few of them sought or needed employment. Today, most of their homes remain standing.

In 1869, when London became home for the Manigaults, Eliza was 21, Mary, 15, and Charlotte, 10. Sons Edward and William turned 20 and 18 that year. In the 1871 census, Edward was listed as a clerk and William as a student. Edward took a position at Ezra Taylor, a stationery store that also sold school books and in 1886 he married Harriet "Hattie" Barnwell, daughter of fellow South Carolina expatriate James Ladson Barnwell, owner of *The Echo* publishing concern in London. The following year, Edward Middleton Manigault Jr. was born to the couple, joined three years later by Ann "Nancy" Mazyck Manigault. Edward Sr. became a bookkeeper and then accountant and acted for a short stint as manager of London Soap Company. He died in 1915.

Gabriel Manigault and his family moved to 808 Waterloo Street in London, not far from other members of his family and South Carolinian bachelors Edward and Alexander Mazyck. After Edward died Alexander moved in with the Manigaults. (PHOTO BY CHIP MARTIN)

This is the former boarding house at 843 Wellington Street operated by Sarah Hill where many Southerners were welcomed during and after the Civil War. Doctor Rufus Bratton had just moved in when he was abducted and taken back to the South Carolina to face charges under the Ku Klux Act, sparking an international incident. (PHOTO BY CHIP MARTIN)

Gabriel's son William found a job as a surveyor in the town of Strathroy, about 25 miles west of London, and lived at the Queen's Hotel there. In 1885 he married Isabella McIntyre, the widowed daughter of the hotel proprietor, who had a young son and daughter. William never returned to London to live and died in Strathroy in 1916, while Isabella lived until 1934.

Julia Manigault and her two sisters, all of them nieces of Gabriel Manigault, lived out their lives here in London, immediately north of Sarah Hill's boarding house on Wellington Street. (PHOTO BY CHIP MARTIN)

Edward Manigault Jr., William's older brother, was quite artistic, and at the age of 18 he was commissioned to create a series of ink drawings of prominent London buildings for postcards issued by the Red Star News Company. He enrolled at the New York School of Art with plans to become a pen-and-ink illustrator and travelled to Europe for inspiration. When the First World War broke out he volunteered as an ambulance driver for the British Army. Within months, however, Manigault was discharged, due to mental issues or because of exposure to mustard gas, depending on the source.

He settled in California and began to experiment with fasting in the belief it would help him see colours "not perceptible to the physical eye."[25] By late August of 1922, he had fasted so much that he was too weak to transfer his visions onto canvas and died at the age of 35.[26] Manigault's works survive at the Whitney Museum of American Art and at the John Paul Getty Collection. His sister, Ann "Nancy" Manigault, never married and died in London in 1989, a few months shy of her 100th birthday.

Gabriel's wife Anne passed away in 1881, the same year as Edward Mazyck. Alexander Mazyck died in 1894. Mary, Charlotte, and

Young Edward Manigault, one of two sons of Gabriel and Anne Manigault, pursued a career as an artist and in about 1905 was commissioned to create pen-and-ink renderings of London buildings for use on postcards. Here is his rendering of city hall. He later moved to California, where he starved himself to death in a misguided effort to see the world more vividly.
(COURTESY OF JOHN AITKEN)

Eliza Manigault lived until 1901, 1915, and 1919 respectively. The Manigault nieces remained in the same house on Wellington Street, where Emma taught music lessons. Julia died in 1890, followed by Josephine in 1901 and Emma in 1918.

Gabriel Manigault, the family patriarch, didn't seek employment during his years in London, but he wasn't idle. He took the time to reflect upon what had happened in the United States and put his thoughts on paper. In 1878, he released a book that was sharply critical of the federal government, defended the South and slavery, and demonstrated his white supremacist views. His effort was the cumbersomely titled *The United States Unmasked: A Search into the Causes of the Rise and Progress of These States*. He found London publisher J.H. Vivian for his 178-page treatise. The trained lawyer, a bitter man, carefully laid out his criticisms of the "monster republic" he had abandoned. He argued the country had become corrupt morally and "the forty millions of people in the United States are most strongly characterized by their unblushing political, social and financial corruption."[27]

He argued that races were distinctly different and each country should be occupied by only one race, one that is best suited to the climate of that country. Manigault insisted Black people were an inferior race best suited to hot countries and they "need to be controlled and directed like children," as had been practised in the southern states.[28] He went so far as to assert that with their newfound freedom following emancipation and without being under white control, Black people "were falling back from civilization and Christianity, into savagedom."[29] No wonder no American publisher would touch his hateful tome, which reflected Manigault's profound and deep-seated racism.

Six years later, Manigault found an American publisher for his 215-page *A Political Creed: Embracing Some Ascertained Truths in Sociology and Politics*. Manigault argued for as little government as possible, one that limits its impact on citizens to providing defence and a system of justice. He decried taxation and government spending: "The history of private expenditure is usually that of economy; that of public expenditure is, very largely, that of corruption and waste."[30] He argued the state should not fund education, charity, or the post office monopoly because of corruption. He spent less time demeaning Black people than in his earlier effort, but was critical of Jews, the Chinese, and the Roman Catholic Church. Not surprisingly, he insisted that plantation owners were more productive and better stewards of the land than smaller land-holders. It is not known how much Manigault may have earned from his books or how many were sold, but he likely found an audience among other bitter racists at a time when the South was actively curtailing the rights of Black people, including their right to vote.

Little is known about Manigault's reception among members of the elite in London, but the burial of his family members in "Millionaire's Row" in an Anglican cemetery suggests acceptance. Many of the city leaders and most prominent citizens were of that faith, had sympathized with the South, and doubtless held similar views on the matter of race. When Gabriel Manigault died in 1888, he, too, was buried within steps of leading London citizens.

The headstones for South Carolinians Gabriel and Anne Mazyck Manigault are among nine markers for members of their family in Woodland Cemetery in London, close to many notable local citizens. Their son William is buried in the nearby town of Strathroy to which he moved. Anne Manigault was a niece of bachelors Alexander and Edward Manigault, who settled in London shortly before the Manigaults.

(PHOTO BY CHIP MARTIN)

Alexander Mazyck joined fellow South Carolina legislator Gabriel Manigault in voting to secede in late 1860, making the Palmetto State the first to rebel. Mazyck and Manigault were related because Manigault married a niece of Mazyck. After the war, with the enslaved freed and plantations in ruins, the bachelor Mazyck brothers, Alexander and Edward, moved to London, Ontario, where they were soon joined by the Manigaults. The Mazycks are buried alongside the Manigaults in a section of Woodland Cemetery known as "Millionaire's Row" because of the number of wealthy and prominent citizens interred there. (PHOTO BY CHIP MARTIN)

At least 14 sons and daughters of South Carolina are buried in London, with one of their offspring in Strathroy and another in California. Other Southerners lie in Canadian graves elsewhere, some having changed their names when they fled north. Many have been forgotten and few are as well documented as the Mazyck brothers and the Manigaults of Charleston. For them, unlike other fugitives who sought only a place to hide out while the heat was on, Canada provided a home for eternity.

CHAPTER THIRTEEN

AN INTERNATIONAL INCIDENT

When it came to finding trouble, Joe Hester was adept. He was shamelessly opportunistic and a man without scruples who liked money. Often on the wrong side of the law during his life, he was a key figure in at least two international legal incidents and became widely despised in the South following the Civil War.

It would be the misfortune of a Southerner who fled to London to learn first-hand how wrong Hester could be.

Joseph Hester was born in 1840 in Granville County, North Carolina, to Methodist minister Benjamin Buxton Hester and his wife Charity, one of eight children and apparently their most difficult. As a boy, he shot and killed a colt and when an older brother confronted him about it, he threatened his sibling with a gun and then ran away from home. After several months of wandering, young Joe became a cabin boy on a merchant ship, the USS *Congress*. In early 1861 Hester enlisted and served as master's mate aboard the Confederate raider CSS *Sumter*, which captured Union ships near Cuba and off the coast of Brazil before sailing to Spain for repairs. While the ship was lying at Gibraltar, Hester entered the cabin of a fellow sailor who had been left in charge of the ship temporarily and shot him dead. Hester insisted he did so because the man was a traitor who was scheming to deliver the *Sumter* into the hands of the Union, whose ships patrolled the Straits of Gibraltar.

Investigators learned the truth: Hester killed the man because he had discovered Hester was stealing supplies. The British, who controlled Gibraltar, arrested him for murder. Raphael Semmes, skipper of the *Sumter*, insisted that he commanded a Confederate ship of war and, according to international agreement, was not subject to British criminal law. A standoff continued until a compromise was reached. The British shackled Hester and placed him aboard HMS *Shannon* destined for Bermuda, from which it was agreed he'd be sent to Charleston for trial. The British were blocked from docking at Bermuda by Union ships, however, and in June of 1863 they simply released their prisoner, who found his way ashore.[1]

The resourceful North Carolinian soon acquired his own schooner to run the blockade outside Confederate ports. With natural charm and persuasion, Hester quickly found some trusting Southern victims willing to pay him to bring them medicine, salt, and other goods, while others beyond the South paid him to deliver cotton and other staples. Hester claimed repeatedly that he had been blockaded and couldn't deliver their cargo — but never refunded their money.[2]

After the war, Hester settled in Raleigh, North Carolina, where, as an apparently embittered Southerner, he openly denounced Yankees, carpetbaggers, and Black people. But money trumped everything for Hester and it was in short supply, so he soon found ways to profit from the misery around him. Hester noted the depressed value of real estate and in 1868 he and some partners incorporated the North Carolina Real and Personal Estate Agency, which was chartered by the state legislature.

Hester's firm operated a scam lottery which sold two-dollar tickets for the chance to win land, homes, buggies, organs, sewing machines, and a wide array of other items, along with cash prizes. In less than two years Hester's operation went bankrupt, and he walked away with large sums and a reputation that was blackened even further. To explain his sudden wealth, he announced that his grandmother in England had left him a large sum in her will and he had to depart to deal with it, leaving his embarrassed partners to take the heat.

When North Carolina organized a militia to deal with postwar violence, Hester saw another opportunity and suddenly reappeared. He managed to persuade the governing authorities that he could track down fugitives for whom they had offered rewards, especially those sought under the Ku Klux Act of 1871. *The Weekly Sentinel* of Raleigh noted Hester's sudden conversion to the federal cause and didn't mince words about the high-profile "scalawag" fresh from his real estate lottery scam, calling him a "shrewd, plausible, unblushing scoundrel . . ."[3]

Hester became a deputy marshal for the State of North Carolina and was often referred to as Detective Hester. He impressed his Republican superiors by arresting individuals he claimed were active members of the Ku Klux, but his methods were called into question by local newspapers, especially when their friends were among those apprehended. In Fayetteville, the *Eagle* complained about the mid-1871 arrest of the sons of a prominent and respected citizen, who were "held in custody in a most degrading manner by this fellow Hester, who it seems, has become a ready tool for all the base ends of Radicalism." The *Eagle* reminded its readers that Hester had already "fleeced the people of North Carolina out of thousands" and had been expelled from a lodge of Freemasons in Raleigh.[4]

Hester added to his unsavoury reputation as he infiltrated the new white racist organization. At one point, he found a bundle of Ku Klux gowns in the woods and persuaded a number of his cronies to don the robes for a photograph in which he posed as the central figure, with a rope around his neck. During 1871, the image appeared in the Republican-friendly *Harper's Weekly* magazine with the caption: "Hanging of a Respectable Republican of North Carolina by the Ku-Klux Desperadoes."[5] His deceit was intended to fuel Northern disdain for the Klan and provide further opportunities to line his pockets as a detective for hire.

Hester investigated Ku Klux organizations in North Carolina and just across the border in York County, South Carolina, where J.W. Avery and Rufus Bratton were among the leading figures. It's unlikely he became personally acquainted with either Avery or Bratton, however, based on later evidence. Both Yorkville men fled justice late that same year and were believed to be in Canada by early 1872. When Hester learned a reward of $60,000 had been offered for the capture of Avery, the most wanted man in the United States, he grew determined to find him. Hester either offered his services to Major Lewis Merrill, who led the effort against the Ku Klux in York County, or Merrill may have contacted Hester, who was operating just across the state line. Regardless, by early 1872 Hester was on the trail of both Avery and Bratton. Ironically, a man who had managed to get away with murder was in pursuit of others who were trying to do the same. His primary target was Avery because of the big reward on his head.

While little is known about Avery's route to Canada, Bratton's travels were recounted in 1921 by a descendant of Lewis Grist, longtime *Yorkville Enquirer* editor and friend of Avery and the Brattons. James D. Grist's account of Bratton's "adventures" appeared in a Charleston paper and the *Enquirer*.

In Grist's telling, Bratton first went to the home of his sister, Sophia, the wife of Dr. James O'Bannon in Barnwell in southwest South Carolina. When he learned federal authorities were on his trail, Bratton moved to Selma, Alabama, where he reconnected with an old friend from York County, Dr. William Barron. In Selma, he began thinking about his future and with Barron made plans to purchase vast tracts of land believed to contain coal and iron deposits. He adopted the name of an uncle, James Simpson, in a bid to avoid detection. But after a few months there, contacts in the Alabama Ku Klux warned him that United States authorities had learned of his whereabouts. Bratton promptly fled to Memphis, Tennessee, where he reunited with his brother, John. The brothers decided to separate and Rufus opted to leave the country entirely, following the paths of his friends from Yorkville, the Manigaults, the Mazycks, and Avery, to Canada.[6]

Bratton appeared at the door of Gabriel Manigault in London on May 21, 1872. His first requirement was accommodation and Manigault directed Bratton to the boarding house of Sarah Hill on nearby Wellington Street, where other Southerners had been welcomed. Bratton was still using the alias James Simpson and Manigault did his best to show him around, but cautioned him to keep his eyes open because there was always a chance someone might be monitoring his movements. He showed Bratton a letter he'd obtained from the Canadian department of justice that explained the legal protections for a political refugee in the country and what to do if someone tried to arrest him. Manigault, a trained lawyer, retained the letter in the event someone attempted to take him back to the South.[7] He likely shared the legal advice in it with all expatriates he welcomed to town.

On May 24, the Queen's Birthday and public holiday, Bratton attended a lacrosse game on the cricket grounds and upon returning to his boarding house was watched by two shadowy figures. It seemed his presence in the city had been noted by persons unknown.[8] Years later, the *Yorkville Enquirer* said Bratton generally kept up his guard in his new surroundings:

> While feeling that he was reasonably safe from capture by the United States authorities he was nevertheless always careful and cautious. A heavy Colt's revolver which perhaps he carried on many a Ku Klux raid was ever in his pocket and he knew how to use it. This pistol was carried for some time after his arrival in Canada.[9]

Bratton was a lover of nature and enjoyed afternoon strolls in the leafy neighbourhood around his boarding house. On June 4, he forgot to take along his trusty Colt. In telling his children later about the events of that day, he thanked God he'd left it at home or there might have been bloodshed. About 4 p.m. Bratton was walking along Waterloo Street when two horse-drawn carriages drove up quickly, and a man hopped from one of them and approached him. The man said he had a warrant for his arrest, then grabbed Bratton and struggled to subdue the lanky and bearded doctor, who resisted. Another man joined in and the only witness to the struggle, eight-year-old Mary Overholt, said she saw something placed over Bratton's face, which immediately took the fight out of him. It is generally believed to have been a cloth soaked in chloroform. The men bundled Bratton into a cab for the short trip to the Great Western Railway station on York Street, where Bratton and his captor boarded a westbound train for Detroit.

Bratton, it was soon learned, had been abducted in a scheme that had been orchestrated by Joe Hester. He had found a willing accomplice in Isaac B. Cornwall, the assistant clerk of Middlesex County Court in London, whom he persuaded to make the arrest sought by United States President Grant. Cornwall, apparently intrigued by Hester's mission, failed to ascertain whether the American detective had obtained necessary and correct extradition papers. Hester, never much for legal niceties, hadn't.

While on the train headed for Detroit, Cornwall discovered he had the wrong man. The arrest warrant was for J.W. Avery, not Bratton. Cornwall and Bratton arrived in Detroit where Hester, who had been on the same train, joined them and found an American official willing to amend the arrest warrant. Hester had stayed out of sight until crossing the border, likely aware that he had no authority on the Canadian side. Because Bratton was also a wanted man, the change was agreed to. With that, Cornwall returned to London and Hester took his prisoner south.[10]

⌣

It took the *London Advertiser* and *London Free Press* several days to report the abduction on Waterloo Street, which became the talk of the town. On June 7, the *Advertiser* headlined it "A Case of Kidnapping. Flagrant Outrage by United States Detectives." It reported:

Dr. Bratton's friends here assert that he has been guilty of no crime, and that he has been taken away for political reasons only. However this may be, and no matter of what crimes he may have been guilty, his removal in this manner, without warrant or authority from our laws, is an outrage which calls for the promptest action. We have no doubt that when the matter is laid before the United States Government, as it will be without delay, Dr. Bratton will be restored. If he has committed any crime there is a proper method pointed out by our laws for his extradition.[11]

The "friends" of Bratton included Gabriel Manigault and Alexander Mazyck, who swung into action. On June 10, the same day that Charles Hutchinson, clerk of Middlesex County Court, dismissed his deputy Cornwall for his role in the affair, Manigault filed a charge alleging abduction. Cornwall was promptly taken into custody. Beforehand, Cornwall told a reporter for the *Advertiser* that Hester had shown him an arrest warrant for murder that seemed valid and insisted that no violence or chloroform had been used in apprehending the suspect.[12]

Alexander Mazyck also became involved. Through his sources he learned that Hester had been in London for some time before Bratton arrived in town and had been able to gain access to mail at the post office over the course of three weeks. On June 6, Mazyck sent a letter of complaint about the local post office to Alexander Campbell, the Postmaster General of Canada:

I have very satisfactory reasons to believe that a United States detective, who has been in London for some time, but has just left it, has been habitually admitted into the interior rooms of the Post Office, generally going in by the back way and apparently spending some hours there daily; and also to believe that the correspondence of some persons, and especially members of my household and their connections and friends, has been subjected to some sort of inspection by him, to what extent, of course, I have not the means of knowing.[13]

Mazyck went on to say that all users of Canada's post office "have a right to know that their correspondence is liable to this sort of examination" and if such activity was considered acceptable by Campbell. If not, he said, something should be done about "such a gross abuse of public confidence." In a reply weeks later, Post Office Secretary William White in Ottawa said Campbell "regrets to find that there was a serious breach of Post Office Regulation . . . the notice he has taken of the matter will have the effect of preventing the occurrence of any similar irregularities in the future." The official admission of wrongdoing came far too late to help Bratton in any way.

———

In Detroit, where the new arrest warrant was prepared, neither Hester nor officials there heeded the protests of their prisoner. They had a Southerner in custody who was wanted for Ku Klux activities back in South Carolina, including murder, and that was good enough for them. With the new paperwork completed, Hester and Bratton boarded a southbound train. At Leavittsburg, Ohio, they stopped so Bratton could send a telegram to friends in London explaining his absence. He said he'd been abducted, chloroformed, and taken to Detroit and was a prisoner on his way south.

In Virginia, he somehow managed to escape the clutches of Hester and spent the night in the woods. The next morning Bratton made his way to the nearest train depot, where, to his chagrin, Hester was waiting. After a strained exchange of pleasantries, Bratton submitted to the detective and they resumed their southbound journey.[14] Upon arriving in Yorkville on June 10, Bratton was taken before a circuit court judge and formally indicted for conspiracy and the murder of Jim

Williams under the Ku Klux Act. He was released when friends posted the security of $12,000, a large amount for the day, and he was ordered to appear in court in Columbia on the first Monday of August.[15]

———

Back in London, word of Bratton's abduction by an American agent on a local street in broad daylight quickly spread far beyond the city. Newspapers were full of outrage at the blatant violation of Canadian sovereignty and called for the federal government to act. On June 11, Liberal leader Edward Blake rose in the House of Commons to ask whether Prime Minister John A. Macdonald was aware of the situation and if Ottawa was prepared to take up his case. Macdonald said he was seeking further details about the incident and been communicating with the British ambassador in Washington as well as the imperial government in Britain.[16]

A preliminary hearing into the abduction charge facing Cornwall began June 13 before a police magistrate. The first witness called was Gabriel Manigault, who had filed the charge. Manigault recalled that Bratton, whom he had known since their service in the Confederate Army, arrived at his London home in a cab on May 21. He was using the name James Simpson and was looking for accommodation, so Manigault took him to Sarah Hill's nearby boarding house.

> He visited us frequently, spending whole evenings with us, and walked around the city a good deal, so much so that I told him there were Yankee detectives here, and he had better not show himself too often. I gave him a copy of a paper in my possession, which was in reply to a letter of mine to the Minister of Justice, which gave the fullest legal directions what a political refugee in Canada should do, if arrested, in order have himself brought before a Canadian court. I saw Dr. Bratton last on the 2nd of June, at my house. He was at that

time living at Mr. [sic] Hill's, and had taken up residence here, intending to remain until after the elections
in the United States.[17]

Under cross-examination by Cornwall's lawyer, Manigault
said many Southerners had assumed false names when they fled to
Canada to escape arrest by the military authorities and avoid subsequent trials conducted without proper civil process. "I am certain
he never committed murder," Manigault testified. "I am convinced
that many in that part of the country were sent to the penitentiary
who committed no crime, and it was for that reason I told him not to
expose himself." And he insisted Bratton never belonged to any white
supremacist organization.

The hearing also heard from Bratton's landlady Sarah Hill,
who said Bratton's departure was completely unexpected, and then
from the cab driver who witnessed the abduction and carried the
men to the train station afterward. Eight-year-old Mary Overholt
testified she saw Cornwall take down Bratton and place something
over his face to subdue him. Edwin Moore, co-proprietor of the
Tecumseh House Hotel, said Hester checked into the hotel about
six weeks before the abduction and explained he was looking for
several parties he would not name. He showed Moore a badge
with the word "detective" on it. The hotelier said he saw Hester
in the company of Cornwall several times during his stay. Charles
Hutchinson, Cornwall's former boss, told court that Cornwall
admitted to him he made the arrest on behalf of Hester, believing
the suspect to be J.W. Avery, for whom a warrant had been issued
under the extradition treaty between Canada and the United States.
Hutchinson recalled Hester appearing at his office on a number of
occasions, most often to see Cornwall. After three days of evidence,
Cornwall was committed for trial.[18]

The British brought pressure to bear on the Grant administration
in Washington about the violation of Canada's sovereignty by Hester.
The Americans, realizing it was a flagrant act and anxious to mend
relations with Canada and Britain, put up no fight and Bratton was

released. It was announced: "Our Government will send him back to Canada without delay and indemnify him for the arrest."[19] Bratton arrived back in London on July 14, just in time for Cornwall's trial, and he remained out of sight.

The very next day, the trial began before Judge William Elliott in a packed Middlesex County courtroom. The first witness was the cab driver, Robert Bates, who was hired by Cornwall on the day of the abduction and witnessed much of what transpired. He stoutly denied any involvement in the physical confrontation, insisting he acted only as a driver. The second witness then strode into the courtroom, much to the dismay of Cornwall and his lawyer. It was Bratton.

This dramatic turn of events elicited gasps from the large crowd of spectators. The slim, dark-haired Bratton carefully recited the events of June 4, when he was walking on Waterloo Street and saw a cab stopped at a distance and two men nearby. One of the men, whom he recognized as Cornwall, walked toward Bratton and when he was within six feet sprang on him, grabbed him by the shoulder, and said he was under arrest. Cornwall would not produce any warrant or explain to Bratton why he was being arrested. In the ensuing struggle, both men fell to the ground, where Cornwall knelt on him. Cornwall called to the cab driver for help and he held Bratton as Cornwall handcuffed him, then both men placed him in the cab. Cornwall read him the warrant, but Bratton said the man named in it was not him, to which Cornwall replied they were going to Windsor where a commissioner who dealt with extradition issues would be consulted and Bratton could seek legal counsel.

Bratton said Cornwall took him to the train station, but the Pacific Express train to Windsor was late arriving, so they drove around nearby streets to kill some time. The two men then boarded the train, and a few hours later Bratton said he unexpectedly found himself in Detroit, where Hester suddenly appeared and announced: "You go with me now." Bratton balked at the demand, insisting: "No. I am under Canadian law, now; that warrant does not allow you to detain me here, and I, under protest, refuse to obey you; neither your government, or you, sir, have a right to detain me here, and if you do, you will pay for it."

Upon hearing that assertion, courtroom spectators "made demonstrations of approval, which the Court immediately suppressed." It was abundantly clear that Dr. Bratton had garnered public sympathy. Bratton testified that Cornwall stayed overnight in Detroit and returned to London the following day. Bratton said he'd seen Hester the day before his abduction at a local religious celebration, then near the scene of the abduction itself, and yet again at the London train station when he and Cornwall boarded the Pacific Express. Bratton testified that while in Detroit Hester produced a new arrest warrant from the United States government, alleging conspiracy and murder, signed by President Grant. This one was made out in Bratton's name.

Cornwall's trial heard several more witnesses, but the evidence from Bratton was particularly damning. The lawyer for Cornwall argued that no abduction had been proved and that Bratton had travelled to Detroit of his own accord. Judge Elliott was having none of it. He said Cornwall was a court official who was well-versed in criminal law and was likely motivated to act by financial gain. He convicted Cornwall and sentenced him to three years in prison.[20]

Not long after the trial, an 18-page pamphlet about Bratton and the case was published. The author was likely Bratton himself, with significant help from Gabriel Manigault. It was clearly an attempt to undo damage the case had done to his reputation in London. It was called "A Statement of Bratton's Case, Being Explanatory of the Ku-Klux Prosecutions in the United States," and its introduction explained: "We undertake to prove that Dr. Bratton was, in Canada, a political refugee, nothing more . . ."

The document dealt at great length with the morality and questionable legality of the Ku Klux Act, under which Bratton had been charged, and it described life in South Carolina during recent turbulent years. It argued Bratton would never have received a fair trial because of the unconstitutional powers that had been granted judges and because juries consisted of Blacks and political enemies. "But we take this opportunity of saying that Dr. Bratton denies having been a member of the Ku-Klux, or any other secret society than the Masonic." Bratton, because of the loss of rights under military rule and the suspension of habeas corpus, was one of about 150 white men who felt compelled to flee York County, it claimed. Joe Hester came in for heavy criticism in the pamphlet, which observed he was still working for the government of North Carolina despite his willingness to flout the law. The pamphlet concluded by inviting anyone interested in seeing the documents on which it was based to do so at a London law firm. It provided no name for its author, other than "TRUTH," at the end.[21]

Bratton had originally planned to remain in London only until after the 1872 presidential election, hoping President Grant's Republicans would go down to defeat, bringing an end to their radical measures to reform the South and punish people like himself. American authorities who had been embarrassed by the Hester-arranged abduction never followed up with formal extradition procedures for Bratton. But the charges under the Ku Klux Act remained alive, at least for the time being. It was becoming clear to Bratton that Grant would

Dr. J. Rufus Bratton of Yorkville, South Carolina, was wanted for Ku Klux terrorism and implicated in the death of a Black militia leader when he fled to Canada in 1872. He became the centre of an international incident when he was abducted on the streets of London and returned to his home to face trial. Following the diplomatic row that ensued, Bratton returned to London and established a thriving medical practice. He was a 32nd-degree Freemason and was accepted into a London lodge of the secret fraternal organization. Bratton was a member of the Scottish Rite Masons and is depicted in that uniform in this 1872 image taken in London. (COURTESY OF THE HISTORICAL CENTER OF YORK COUNTY, CULTURE AND HERITAGE MUSEUMS, SOUTH CAROLINA)

be returned for a second term as president, so the doctor brought his wife Mary and their six children to live in London. That move likely lay behind the decision to publish the 18-page document intended to restore his reputation.

The Brattons found a comfortable home on Piccadilly Street, several blocks from the Manigaults and Mazycks, and Bratton began practising medicine from an office downtown on Dundas Street.[22] Regulations governing medical doctors of the day were not particularly onerous, and with Bratton's education, experience, and hands-on work during the Civil War, he was readily accepted by the medical fraternity and his practice thrived. Several of his sons attended Talbot Street School during their years in London.[23]

Bratton, a Presbyterian and 32nd-degree Mason, also became active in the secret fraternal organization's Kilwinning Lodge in London. Freemasonry today is the largest such organization in the world, with more than three million members. It has a long history, having evolved from the guilds of stonemasons who crafted cathedrals in the Middle Ages. It employs rites and trappings of ancient brotherhoods and religious orders, but has faced much criticism over the years from organized religion, particularly the Roman Catholic Church, even though Freemasonry espouses brotherly love, charity, and truth. It became popular because it allowed prominent, like-minded men to socialize and work together. Over the years, however, some lodges have been accused of prejudice against Jews, Catholics and non-white people, and in Anglo-Saxon countries its members are mainly white Protestants.[24] A key feature of Freemasonry is its secrecy, especially when one member greets another, though this was played down by the Freemasons of Ontario: "The so-called Masonic 'Secrets' are confined to modes of recognition by which a visitor can prove himself to be a Mason and thereby become eligible to enter a lodge in which he was otherwise not known."[25] As a Mason, Bratton found that doors were opened to him almost immediately by well-to-do and well-connected Londoners. With its exclusive nature, its rituals and secrecy, Freemasonry had much in common with the Ku Klux organization that Bratton knew so well back in Yorkville. And he had risen to the top ranks in both.

———

From their vantage point in London, the sons and daughters of South Carolina stayed abreast of developments back home. The Brattons, Manigaults, and Mazycks were hoping for some signs their home state would return to life as they had known it and that the subjugation by occupiers from the North would come to an end, along with their hated Reconstruction. Federal troops remained in South Carolina, however, with the Republicans firmly in control. Democrats pinned their hopes on regaining power in the state following the election of 1876, but that was going to be a challenge because of demographics. A special state census conducted in 1875 determined there were 74,193 white men over the age of 21, compared to 110,735 Black men.[26] (Women, of course, were many years away from being enfranchised.) Black voters heavily favoured the Republicans, the party of Lincoln that had set them free. The Democrats knew the numbers were against them in the lead-up to the 1876 vote. They nominated Wade Hampton for governor, South Carolina's highest ranking officer during the Civil War, and several other former Confederate officers to contest the election.

The Democrats decided they needed to suppress the Black vote, using threats, coercion, and even bribes. They established hundreds of gun clubs and, while armed, their members appeared at Republican political rallies they tried to disrupt. It has been estimated as many as 290 gun clubs were organized as the election approached, with membership of about 15,000 men.[27] As this army of the Democrats grew, the state's Republican leadership lamented what amounted to a return of the Ku Klux, but could do little to curb it because of tepid support from Washington. Hampton endorsed a plan of "bloodless coercion" and rallied his supporters in a cross-state march and rally that mobilized Democrats and stoked their commitment to a return of white supremacy.

A grassroots organization known as the Red Shirts had been created to generate enthusiasm among white voters and further intimidate the Black population. The Red Shirts attracted many of the same gun-toting white supremacists who earlier had joined or supported the Ku Klux, which the government believed had been driven out of existence by late 1871. Despite their slogan of "force without violence," the Red Shirts often resorted to violence. The worst episode came in Edgefield, South Carolina, where local Red Shirts killed 30 Black militiamen and a state senator, several of them in cold blood.[28] Edgefield and Yorkville were the scenes of parades and rallies that attracted thousands of supporters of Hampton and the Democrats.

On October 13, Hampton rode into Yorkville at 11 a.m. at the head of a parade organized for the occasion, which included 600 men on horseback. He received a tumultuous welcome from a crowd estimated at 3,000 as he climbed a heavily decorated stand erected for the event. The former Confederate general told the crowd that Democrats were showing strength in several states in advance of the November 7 vote. "They tell us that the system of oppression and misrule — of Grantism — with which the whole country has been afflicted for the past eight years, is going down, and shall go down," he said, appealing to the widespread sense of grievance among his listeners. Hampton accused Governor Daniel Chamberlain of corruption and of seeking additional troops from Washington to help him cling to power. He said Chamberlain deserved a cell in the penitentiary, not another term as governor.

Hampton rested for a spell at the home of a supporter as a vast crowd continued to mill about in town. After a display of fireworks and a rendition of "Dixie," at 7 p.m., he again addressed the crowd, which remained until proceedings adjourned four hours later. "Thus ended the largest and most enthusiastic political gathering ever held in York County," the *Yorkville Enquirer* said in its lengthy report. It added that "notwithstanding the immense crowd in town, from early morn till late in the night, not an accident or disturbance occurred to mar the proceedings."[29] The stoutly Democratic paper was no doubt hoping to contrast the orderly scene in Yorkville with the disturbances that marred Republican rallies. Hampton had momentum and effectively tapped into the widespread resentment of Republican rule and the continued subjugation of the South.

During October, Governor Chamberlain ordered the disbanding of all rifle clubs, a move he hoped would encourage federal intervention. "Insurrection and domestic violence exist in various portions of the State," Chamberlain said in a letter to President Grant. By mid-October, about 1,100 soldiers and officers were dispatched to keep order in South Carolina.[30] On election day in November, armed Democrats showed up at polls and tried to prevent Black men from voting. And they reminded them their Republican government had done little to protect Black people from threats and violence. The intimidation and voter suppression combined with a strong turnout of white voters to help the Democrats win a narrow victory, attracting 92,261 votes to 91,127 for the Republicans. Democrats engaged in ballot-box stuffing, repeated voting, voting by out-of-state persons, and other tactics to drive up their numbers. Red Shirts rode from one polling place to another, casting ballots wherever they went.

With widespread evidence of fraud, the Republican-controlled State Board of Canvassers took control, declaring invalid all votes cast in Edgefield and Laurens counties, Republican strongholds that had solidly and unexpectedly backed Democrat Hampton. The move gave Republicans control of the state's House of Representatives, the body that could determine the outcome of the election. Democrats walked out in protest, then declared themselves a quorum, forced their way into the State House, and began to conduct public business. The situation was bizarre. For four months South Carolina had two separate legislatures, each holding its own debates and passing laws. Hampton and Chamberlain both claimed the governorship.

Federally, the race for president had been exceptionally close as well. Republican Rutherford B. Hayes had a razor-thin victory over Democrat Samuel Tilden but was not declared president until late February 1877, when a bipartisan election commission finally pronounced him the victor. By April in South Carolina, Chamberlain realized a conciliation-minded federal government under new president Hayes was unlikely to help him remain in office and resigned as governor. He was replaced by Hampton.[31] The federal campaign of the Republicans had been worrisome for the besieged Chamberlain because Hayes had promised to withdraw federal troops that were still posted in Louisiana and South Carolina. The election of Hayes and the departure of Chamberlain marked an important turning point for South Carolina, as historian Richard Zuczek has observed, arguing that conservative white Carolinians were back in charge and Reconstruction (and the Civil War) was finally over.[32]

Developments in South Carolina no doubt came as good news for refugees from that state still living in Canada and prompted many to begin making plans to return. Even those who were wanted on Ku Klux Act charges, like Bratton in London and J.W. Avery in Niagara, were heartened in 1877 when the federal government dropped all outstanding warrants and charges. For them specifically, that came in circuit court in Yorkville in early September when a judge agreed to an official request to remove "State vs. J.R. Bratton and others; murder" from the court docket.[33] Avery was among the others. Meanwhile, the Manigaults and Mazycks were comfortable in London and had no plans to return to the South.

Despite his key role in an international incident that embarrassed his government, Joe Hester continued to receive assignments from Washington and North Carolina. With help from his Republican friends in high places, he became Marshal for Eastern North Carolina, but also undertook investigations for the post office and the federal Department of the Interior. In Washington, he became involved in property development and in Virginia in a mineral-water bottling company. Hester also patented a device for curing tobacco and another for "improvements on pen holders and writing pens." He suffered a stroke in Washington in 1891 at age 51, and died there 10 years later.[34]

Life was good in London for Dr. J. Rufus Bratton. He developed a thriving medical practice, was active in the Freemasons, and

This imposing monument to Confederate Civil War dead can be found at the entrance to Rose Hill Cemetery in York (formerly Yorkville), South Carolina. (KMS PHOTOGRAPHY)

he and his family enjoyed safe and comfortable refuge as turmoil and violence ravaged their home state during the death throes of Reconstruction. The result of the November election and subsequent return of political control to Democrats, who were determined to turn back the clock on Black rights, held strong appeal for Bratton and other white people. By 1878, he decided it was time to return to Yorkville. On October 9, Bratton was feted by a large gathering of Freemasons. The *London Free Press* reported on the event, at which "the brethren of the city took this opportunity of expressing their fraternal feeling and good personal esteem for him on his leaving the jurisdiction." Bratton responded to the salute with a reply that "was an elegant and feeling one."

On October 30, he attended a farewell dinner held at a local restaurant where "substantial refreshments were served." Words of praise were lavished upon the guest of honour, who was given a "past principal's jewel" of the Masons and an engraved silver-headed cane. "To both of the presentations the doctor replied in a feeling manner, expressing the happiness which he had experienced during his sojourn here and his regret in parting with them now." Toasts were repeatedly proposed, songs sung and humorous addresses given as Bratton and his Canadian friends said their farewells. At 11 p.m. all joined in singing "Auld Lang Syne" to conclude the memorable event.[35]

On November 18, 1878, shortly after his 57th birthday, Bratton returned home with little fanfare, the *Yorkville Enquirer* carrying only this brief item: "Dr. J. Rufus Bratton, who for several years past has been residing in Canada, returned with his family Monday evening last to his old home in Yorkville."[36] He rejoined the local Freemasons and re-established his medical practice. His later years were quiet ones compared with the turbulent times after the Civil War, when he'd been a leading figure in the Yorkville area. Bratton's reputation as a medical doctor was excellent and in 1881 he became a member of the State Board of Health and then chairman, a post he held until his death. He also served as president of the South Carolina Medical Association in 1891 and 1892.[37]

Rufus Bratton died in 1897 at the age of 75 and was buried at Bethesda Presbyterian Church Cemetery south of Yorkville. The Yorkville lodge of the Freemasons played a prominent role at his funeral and its members were joined by those from lodges in neighbouring Rock Hill, Chester, and other communities. His substantial headstone took note of his accomplishments in medicine and his four

This is the headstone for Dr. J. Rufus Bratton, a leader of the Ku Klux organization in Yorkville, who fled to Canada to avoid prosecution of crimes related to his activity with the white supremacists. He was readily accepted in London, Ontario, where he practised medicine for a number of years and was a member of the Freemasons. His marker is located several miles south of Yorkville in an area where his family once owned plantations. (KMS PHOTOGRAPHY)

years as a surgeon for the Confederate Army. Part of the inscription reads: "They serve God well who serve his creatures."

In its lengthy story to mark Bratton's passing, the *Yorkville Enquirer*, still unabashedly racist, conceded that after the Civil War, "Dr. Bratton was one of those who became convinced, and who acted upon the conviction, that the only defense which could be secured for home and fireside, was through the Ku-Klux organization, and with this he became directly or indirectly connected."[38] The paper confirmed what everyone in Yorkville and York County had known, a connection that Bratton had spent so much time and effort denying whenever it was used against him. His service to the Confederacy during the war was noted, along with his Christian charity in helping others in need. It termed his life "wonderfully correct." Many Black people and others aware of dark chapters in the doctor's past would disagree with that latter assertion. And for good reason.

Bratton's seven years in the attic began with unexpected drama, but life for him soon settled down. He successfully practised medicine, had a safe refuge for his family, and made many friends who accepted him and were sad to see him return to his native state. Like many thousands of others from south of the border, Black and white, sojourners or transplants, Bratton and his family took full advantage of a welcoming place not terribly foreign nor far from their homeland. It was just so convenient.

More than a century after Bratton returned to South Carolina, another attempt was made to honour him in the Ontario city he had chosen as his refuge. The historic sites committee of London Public Library proposed commemorating Bratton's brazen kidnapping from the streets of London by placing a plaque on a wall of St. Joseph's Hospital, located near the incident. The committee said the event was worth noting because it marked the first time that Ottawa and Britain had been called upon to defend Canadian sovereignty following Confederation. The notion proved unexpectedly controversial, however, once Bratton's background was learned. In early 1985 the library's board of directors voted down the plan when it was pointed out that Bratton, a leading figure in the Ku Klux, had been implicated in the killing of a Black man back in York County and was a prominent white supremacist.[39]

The attitude toward Bratton and his past had hardened in a city that so readily accepted him during his lifetime.

CHAPTER FOURTEEN

TRAFFICKING IN HATE

The deaths of Rufus Bratton, J.W. Avery, and other purveyors of hate did not mark the end of white supremacy in the South. Far from it. Nor did the federal government's largely successful efforts to extinguish the Ku Klux organization through the suspension of legal rights, prosecution, and jail sentences. Haters kept hating and some sought to export hate to America's northern neighbour, which had provided refuge for KK leaders in the 1870s. Would Canada's willingness to tolerate such persons extend to their beliefs with the passage of time? An answer would come about 50 years later.

Bratton's story lived on and became the basis of the 1915 film *The Birth of a Nation*, which reignited public hatred for Black people and triggered the founding of the Ku Klux Klan, which still exists to this day in the United States. The KKK also tapped into resentment of growing immigration during the 1920s and boasted four million American members anxious to reassert white supremacy.[1]

A determined effort was made by the Klan to expand into Canada, where *The Birth of a Nation* attracted large crowds to movie houses, as it did south of the border. Klansmen had mixed success in their recruiting efforts but found relatively barren ground in Ontario in the 1920s, despite widely publicized outdoor rallies, cross burnings, and a bizarre nighttime salute by hooded Klansmen at the Toronto cenotaph outside city hall. They faced unexpected competition in a province they felt would be receptive to their message because of its significant

Black population. By the onset of the Great Depression, the Klansmen and their message of hate had returned to their base in the South.

Not only was the main character in *The Birth of a Nation* loosely based on Bratton, but the town in which the story takes place, Piedmont, was modelled on his hometown of Yorkville, South Carolina. The silent film's cinematography was stunning for its day, experts have agreed. But so was its blatant racism. The film, by D.W. Griffith, was a three-hour-long blockbuster, produced for $110,000 (although promotional ads claimed $500,000) and featuring 18,000 people and 3,000 horses. It was hailed for its ground-breaking camera and editing techniques, such as closeups, cutaways, and cameras that moved alongside the action during a cavalry charge by the Klan. It pandered, however, to white racists willing to pay a premium price for tickets. The tone for its message was set with a title card in the opening scene, which read: "The bringing of the African to America planted the first seed of disunion." Another card referred to "Aryan birthright" and the need for racial purity in America. At one point, Griffith shows a Southern legislature filled with Black representatives depicted as boorish and leering oafs.[2]

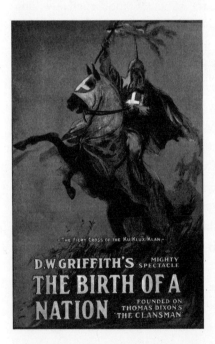

The ground-breaking silent film The Birth of a Nation *of 1915 is blamed for reigniting white supremacy in the South and causing the creation of the Knights of the Ku Klux Klan, nearly 45 years after its predecessor, the Ku Klux, was put down. The film depicted the Klan as saviours of the white race and Black people as ignorant and violent threats to white people. The film was widely condemned for its message but praised for its innovative cinematic techniques.* (FACING HISTORY AND OURSELVES)

Director Griffith was the Kentucky-born son of former Confederate Colonel Jacob Griffith, commander of the First Kentucky Cavalry. The filmmaker and sometime actor found his way to New York, where he directed more than 400 films for the Biograph Company between 1908 and 1913. Most were one-reel efforts lasting about 12 minutes. But the innovative Griffith yearned for more challenge and moved to Mutual Films to direct more substantial films.

During 1913 he latched onto a project that would alter the course of filmmaking and see Griffith hailed as a pioneering genius in the new medium. For one of his first projects, he decided to adapt to the screen *The Clansman*, a book and play written by Thomas Dixon Jr. Born in 1864 in Shelby, North Carolina, Dixon was the son of a Baptist minister in the impoverished town, about 30 miles northwest of Bratton's Yorkville. After a delayed start to his schooling, Dixon proved to be a gifted student. He entered law school and was elected to the state assembly at age 20. He became a Baptist minister and led large congregations in New York and Boston, before leaving to become a full-time lecturer and novelist.

Dixon began writing and speaking about the Ku Klux in a bid to redress what he felt were injustices inflicted on the South by Northerners. He wrote about 20 novels and plays, and appeared in several stage productions and films. Dixon was profoundly conservative in politics and religion, opposing equal rights for Black people because he feared it would lead to intermarriage, a prospect he found distasteful. In 1905, he published *The Clansman: A Historical Romance of the Ku Klux Klan*, which Dixon claimed was "the true story of the Ku Klux Klan Conspiracy, which overturned the Reconstruction regime." He sought to romanticize the white supremacists, who included his father, thereby rewriting history. The inconvenient truth for him was that the Ku Klux didn't bring about an end to Reconstruction at all. The organization had been driven out of existence by late 1871, six years before Reconstruction was finally abandoned. Dixon became a popular but controversial figure because of his book, which he quickly turned into a play that toured throughout the South.

The Clansman story opens with the surrender of Confederate General Robert E. Lee to Union General Ulysses S. Grant at Appomattox Courthouse and covers the years following. One of the leading characters is former Confederate Colonel Ben Cameron, a member of the KK. Dixon's tale is about the corruption of Reconstruction and the violence that grips the town of Piedmont, South Carolina, where four vicious Black men attacked a white woman and her daughter. At another point in his story, the Ku Klux puts on trial a Black man whose advances on a white woman prompted her to leap to her death. The organization, Dixon wrote, defended the honour of helpless women and children, upheld the United States Constitution, and restored order. His hero Cameron, one of the KK leaders, marries the daughter of a Northerner in a romantic twist at the end through which Dixon suggests the North and South can reunite and that the South can rise again.[3]

The novel and stage play received both praise and damnation for characterizing the Ku Klux as heroes and portraying Black people as depraved beasts. Despite blistering criticism, the play drew standing-room-only crowds during its run in several southern cities. As controversy swirled, Dixon felt compelled to issue a statement that said, in part:

> My play is an attempt to build a lighthouse of historic facts on the sands of Reconstruction. Its scene is the past. Its purpose is present and future. I am seeking to unite the nation in a knowledge of the truth. We can never have a real union unless we know one another . . . I am not reviving bitter memories of a dead past. I am sounding the first notes of movement for the supremacy of the Aryan race in the modern world.[4]

There it was for all to see: Dixon's blunt declaration of white supremacy. Other white people no doubt rejoiced at that latter statement and embraced it. Dixon insisted that "every scene and incident of my story is founded on fact." He said his father, a native of York County, South Carolina, and one of his brothers had been members of the Ku Klux. His uncle, Leroy McAfee, who lived in Yorkville, had been a Confederate Colonel and was active in the Klan there. It was to McAfee that Dixon dedicated *The Clansman*. When Dixon was young, he frequently visited his uncle in Yorkville and became well acquainted with the town and its characters. He said he made Yorkville the model for the town of Piedmont. Rufus Bratton, who had been dead for eight years, was widely believed to be his model for hero Ben Cameron, whose surname Dixon was borrowed from the woman his Uncle Leroy married.[5]

For its part, the *Yorkville Enquirer* termed the play a "passing sensation" and "thrilling tale," and dug into its back issues upon learning about the town's connection to *The Clansman*. It concluded that Dixon "has not overdrawn or distorted the situation as it existed in York." But it acknowledged the KK should not receive "all the credit for the salvation of the white race during those times."[6] The *Enquirer* said it doubted there would ever be another effort like Reconstruction, which it claimed was intended to assert the supremacy of Black people over white ones. "White supremacy, especially so far as the negro race is concerned, is a quality that has been fixed by the immutable laws of God," it argued.[7] With that assertion, the *Enquirer* embarked on serial publication of excerpts from *The Clansman*, pointedly noting in an advertisement: "Much of the story is based on events that actually occurred in York."[8] The newspaper knew what appealed to its readership.

———

Thomas Dixon spent his formative years living with the angry reaction of white people to the attempt by outsiders to fundamentally alter the relationship between the white and Black populations, and his writing reflected that antipathy. The Civil War failed to change the attitude of white people toward Black people, and during its aftermath Reconstruction only worsened the situation. The South to which Rufus Bratton, J.W. Avery, John C. Breckinridge, and others returned was still coming to grips with the return to power of leaders who had wielded political and economic influence before the Civil War. In South Carolina, the white minority was determined to reassert itself and undo the changes imposed on its way of life by the hated Northerners. A first priority was to curb the rights granted Black people under what were termed the Civil War Amendments to the United States constitution, the first such amendments passed in 60 years. The 13th Amendment banned slavery and involuntary servitude. The 14th Amendment defined a person under law as anyone born in the United States or a naturalized citizen. The 15th Amendment prohibited governments from denying any United States citizen from voting because of race, colour, or past servitude.

It wasn't long after ratification of the 13th Amendment in 1865 that Southern legislatures began limiting newfound rights for Black people. Collectively these became known as "Jim Crow" laws, the name taken from a minstrel show character, and many of them would remain on the books for 100 years. Violators faced arrest, fines, jail terms, violence, and even death. To administer the legal system and enforce the law, former Confederate soldiers were employed as police officers and judges, effectively stacking the system against Black citizens.[9] Because big cities in the South were slower to adopt such discriminatory legislation, Black people flocked to them from the countryside. In response, white urbanites began to push for similar marginalization of Black people, and before long they were banned from city parks and white neighbourhoods, and segregation was imposed in theatres, restaurants, bus and train stations, at water fountains, in washrooms, swimming pools, elevators, and other places where people gather. Intermarriage or cohabitation of white and Black people was strictly forbidden in most states in the South, and signs were sometimes posted at town and city limits warning Black travellers they were not welcome. Racial discrimination was rampant. The Brattons, Averys, and Breckinridges easily adapted to the postwar South, where white Southerners were determined to turn back the clock and return Black people to a subservient role.

As time passed and Southerners came to grips with their loss to the North and what flowed from that, they began to romanticize the "lost cause." They insisted the Civil War had not been about slavery at all, but about the rights of individual states to chart their own course within the Union. They found a champion in William Archibald Dunning, a New Jersey native and prominent academic. As a political science and history professor at Columbia University, Dunning was a leading authority on political theories and the Reconstruction period. Dunning insisted his work was "grounded on the ideals of impartiality and historical accuracy."[10] In 1898, he published his first volume on the topic of Reconstruction, *Essays on the Civil War and Reconstruction and Related Topics*, for which he drew praise from historians and political scientists alike. His work has been termed a "perilous validation of discrimination" and it inspired a slew of his students to adopt his racist approach in the growing "Dunning School" of historians. Dunning opined: "The freedmen were not, and in the nature of the case could not for generations be, on the same moral, and intellectual plane with the whites." Such sweeping assertions were never provided with any sort of academic explanations. But that didn't stop the accolades for Dunning and his work, and he was elected president of the American Historical Association in 1913, a post once held by Teddy Roosevelt.

———

While Dunning was rising to the top ranks among American historians, Dixon published *The Clansman* and began trying to produce a film about it. In 1914, the project was taken up by D.W. Griffith, a filmmaker who shared Dixon's views about the superiority of the white race.[11] His grandly titled *The Birth of a Nation* produced millions at the box office and may have been the most profitable film of all time.[12]

"People were primed for the message," acknowledges Paul McEwan, a film studies professor who has written extensively about the film. "Hard to argue this was a distortion of history when the history books at that time said the same," he added, clearly referring to the Dunning School of Reconstruction history.[13] Another modern observer, Richard Brody, writing in *The New Yorker*, lamented that Griffith's original work of art carried such a troubling message. "The worst thing about *The Birth of a Nation* is how good it is," he said, contrasting its abhorrent racism with the ground-breaking cinematic techniques.[14] McEwan agreed that the film was "disgustingly racist yet titanically original." The film sparked violence against Black people in many places and riots in theatres that led to it being censored before showings in several cities, including New York.[15]

A photograph which was used to promote The Birth of a Nation. *The costumes worn in the film became the model for those adopted by the modern Ku Klux Klan.* (THE HOLLYWOOD REPORTER)

Shortly after *The Birth of a Nation*'s official launch in Los Angeles on February 8, 1915, *Clansman* author Dixon persuaded an old friend and classmate, United States President Woodrow Wilson, to screen it at the White House. Wilson was a fellow white supremacist who *The Birth of a Nation* expert McEwan said "re-segregated the civil service." The president knew the first-ever showing of a film at the White House would be seen as an endorsement and is reported to have said afterward: "It is like writing history with lightning. And my only regret is that it is all so terribly true."[16] A quote from Wilson was used on a title card in the film about white reaction to Black violence. It read: "The white men were roused by a mere instinct of self-preservation . . . until at last there had sprung into existence a great Ku Klux Klan, a veritable empire of the South, to protect the Southern country."

In Georgia, preacher William Joseph Simmons was recovering from injuries sustained in a car crash when he became intrigued by the widespread success of *The Birth of a Nation*. Simmons would become the founder of the Knights of the Ku Klux Klan, a new organization with old racist roots, which officially incorporated "Klan" in its name. He was inspired by the costumes, headgear, and other paraphernalia from the old Ku Klux he saw depicted in Griffith's film, and he adopted much of it for his men. Simmons sensed an opportunity to establish a modern organization based on white supremacy at a time when America was welcoming large numbers of newcomers from faraway lands, a trend that was engendering resentment and friction.

Ongoing migration of Black people to cities like Chicago, Boston, and Philadelphia only added to the tensions of the day. Simmons learned the film would debut in Atlanta on December 6, 1915, and he saw that as an opportunity to unveil his modern KKK organization. Ten days beforehand, on Thanksgiving Day, he and a group of 15 followers climbed Stone Mountain outside Atlanta to burn a large cross. The event was termed "impressive" on the front page of the *Atlanta Constitution*. "The new secret organization is founded with a view to taking an active part in the betterment of mankind . . . ," it reported.[17] Simmons declared an upcoming event would give his new organization a terrific boost.

When word spread of the cross burning, Simmons placed a newspaper advertisement promoting the KKK, and on the opening night of *The Birth of a Nation* he and his men donned white sheets and Confederate uniforms and rode on hooded horses down Peachtree Street, firing salutes in front of the movie house. Similar displays came in other southern cities, where theatre ushers sometimes wore white sheets and Klansmen distributed literature before and after the show. Simmons turned the movie into a recruiting tool. Crowds packed the Atlanta Theater throughout its run, and on opening night they applauded and cheered. *Constitution* reviewer Ned McIntosh gushed over Griffith's film: "It makes you laugh and moves you to hot tears unashamed . . . It makes you actually live through the greatest period of suffering and trial this country has ever known." The film was accompanied by a 30-piece orchestra that performed an original score. McIntosh insisted the film was true to the facts and dismissed its critics:

'The Birth of a Nation' is built to arouse your emotions, and it does it. It is designed to educate you, and it does so more than many hours studying books. It is not designed to arouse your prejudices, and if you are fair-minded and not predisposed, it will not do so.[18]

That was a big "if" on the part of the reviewer. The times were becoming increasingly racist and the film encouraged white supremacists. Fair-minded persons were becoming scarce, especially in the South and in big cities. Protests by the National Association for the Advancement of Colored People were raised, but they failed to accomplish much. *The Birth of a Nation* was shown well into the 1920s, when sound was added, and it continued to be an effective recruiting tool for the Klan, whose membership climbed into the millions.[19]

This newspaper advertisement promoted the opening of The Birth of a Nation *in Atlanta in 1915. The debut in Atlanta was hailed by white supremacists there who seized on the opportunity to launch the modern Ku Klux Klan. Within a few years, the Klan tried to move into Canada, where it met with limited success.* (ATLANTA CONSTITUTION, DECEMBER 5, 1915)

Recruiting for the KKK was first noted in Ontario in 1922 when an organizer, known as a "kleagle," ventured into the Niagara peninsula from his base in Buffalo. This was likely J.P. Martin, who was testing the Canadian market, which he believed was similar to the American one, with the addition of ongoing religious conflict between Protestants and Catholics. There was some racial segregation and an influx of immigrants, especially to Toronto and southern Ontario, whose industries were booming following the First World War. The strongly British character of Toronto and the lower part of the province was changing and becoming more diverse, to the dismay of the establishment. Local officials had long supported the Loyal Orange Lodge, a Protestant, pro-Britain fraternal organization, which took its name from Prince William of Orange, who defeated the Catholic King James II at the Battle of the Boyne on July 12, 1690. In so doing, William III reclaimed the British monarchy for Protestantism.[20]

By 1920, the Orange Order had about 100,000 members spread across Canada, with Ontario and New Brunswick particular hotbeds. Like other fraternal organizations, it is a secret society, but its main secrets relate to annual passwords and the signs that Orangemen employ to recognize and greet one another. At the turn of the century, Toronto was sometimes referred to as the "Belfast of Canada" because of its sectarianism and the prevalence of Orange Order members in its government. From 1850 to 1950, almost every mayor of Toronto was a member. Orangemen were heavily represented in the Conservative Party provincially and federally, and at least four Canadian prime ministers, including Sir John A. Macdonald, had orange-coloured sashes denoting membership. The others were Sir John Abbott, Sir Mackenzie Bowell, and John Diefenbaker, all Conservatives. Bowell was particularly avid. He joined the Orangemen in 1842, became president of the Belleville lodge by 1860, and from 1870 to 1878 he served as Grand Master of British North America.[21]

Southwestern Ontario was believed by Klan organizers to be fertile ground for its message, given its still-significant Black population, although their numbers had fallen off somewhat after the First World War. Those who remained were increasingly targeted by racists motivated by their underlying intolerance and reports of racial problems elsewhere. With its proximity to population centres in the United States, southwestern Ontario was often influenced by trends and attitudes that developed across the border. The region was not immune from the growing racism that followed the release of *The Birth of a Nation*.

By early 1923, the first organized recruiting drive by the Klan was well underway in Ontario, about the same time the organization was reaching a peak in the United States. Its kleagles held recruiting meetings in the province and sold memberships and official Klan robes and regalia. The arrival of the KKK was condemned by many public officials and ridiculed by newspapers as a typical American scheme to raise money with a cynical appeal to white Protestants. As early as 1922 newspapers had condemned any attempt by American outsiders to incite hatred or violence among Canadians. In noting the presence of Klan recruiters at the other end of the province in London, the *Ottawa Citizen* said in a lead editorial, "There should be no place in this country for such a body which appeals to racial and religious feeling . . ."[22] The *Welland Tribune-Telegraph* said it appeared the Klan's overarching goal amounted to "a scheme to sell cotton nightgowns to boobs."[23]

One of the recruiters, Irwin Roy Hignett, a native of Lancashire, England, who had migrated to the United States, said he was operating on the authority of Klan headquarters in Atlanta. When the *London Advertiser* found him based in London, Hignett denied any involvement in recruiting and insisted he was merely "resting tired nerves."[24] He stoutly insisted: "I am not here on missionary work. The Knights of the Ku Klux Klan have no plans for extension into Canada . . . I am still in London and expect to be here for some time."

Soon afterward, newly elected London Mayor George Wenige issued a sternly worded warning on March 15, 1923, in response to what he called "propaganda" about the Klan he'd seen in a newspaper:

> Gentlemen of foreign extraction in this municipality who may be planning local organization had first better give the matter serious thought. Canadians do not tolerate men with bloody hands walking unafraid in their midst. Justice in this Dominion is swift and sure . . .

I will use every power of my office to rid this city of verminous missionaries of an order that seeks to terrify citizens who may differ from these so-called Knights of the Ku Klux Klan in race, color, religion or ability to succeed . . .

London is not going to be safe for the Ku Klux Klan or any other hooded order. And any non-Canadian who may seek to establish it here will be deported as an undesirable alien so far as it lies in the hands of the mayor of this city to bring it about.[25]

The mayor could not deport anyone, as Wenige (pronounced WENN-ig) would have known. But the shot across the bow of the Klan was noteworthy. It wasn't appreciated, apparently, because the following day Wenige received a death threat from the Klan relayed to him by the *London Free Press*. The provincial response came from Attorney General William Raney, who said the Klan was not welcome in Ontario.

Hignett's continued presence in London may have been behind efforts to intimidate the area's Black population in 1924, when outdoor Klan meetings were held during the summer in a large wooded area near the village of Dorchester, just east of London. Cross burnings were reported at the village fairgrounds. In Bryanston, a hamlet just north of the city, the Klan threatened a local man by saying they'd burn a cross on his front lawn because he was believed to be consorting with a Black woman. His fellow residents armed themselves with guns to defend their neighbour and dissuade the Klan from any such plan. The would-be terrorists got the message and didn't follow through.[26] That same summer, two cross burnings were reported a week apart in Erieau, along the Lake Erie shoreline of Kent County, which had a sizeable Black population. It was believed at least one of the burnings was intended as a threat to local people who had provided bail for a man charged with a serious offence.[27]

In Hamilton, a Klan recruiter named Almond Charles Monteith was finding success. The city was not known for its tolerance of non-white people, and discrimination extended beyond Black people to immigrants from Italy and China as well. Police and some Hamiltonians believed Chinese laundries were involved in opium trafficking and prostitution. Overtly racist city police proposed the Chinese adopt "reasonable" names to assist them in identifying suspects.[28] The provincial police were more concerned about Monteith than local officers, and one night in November of 1924 they raided the Orange Lodge Hall on James Street North and arrested him while he was administering Klan oaths.

A Canadian born near London, who sometimes resided in Niagara Falls, New York, Monteith readily admitted he was an organizer for the KKK. He was charged with carrying a loaded revolver at the ceremony, and police also found on his person a list of 32 men and women he had inducted, Klan correspondence, and 36 white robes and hoods. They also discovered a list of recent expenses, including a notation about $200 Monteith had spent to burn crosses. Orange Lodge officers expressed surprise that Monteith was on their premises and blamed their janitor, with whom Monteith had been boarding, for renting the room to him.[29] Monteith was later convicted on the gun charge and jailed.

By early 1925, with the Ontario Provincial Police monitoring their activities, the Ku Klux Klan of Canada established an office in downtown Toronto and claimed by May to have 1,102 members, of whom 793 had paid dues. A spokesperson claimed as many as 7,000 persons in Toronto were members of the organization, a highly inflated figure no doubt intended for public consumption. About the same time, the Klan was beset by internal division, and some members broke away to form the Ku Klux Klan of the British Empire, with the result the two groups competed vigorously for recruits that year.[30] And each embellished their success.

On April 23, 1925, the *London Advertiser* reported the "Ku Klux Klan of Kanada" would hold its maiden local meeting that same night in Ulster Hall downtown. Before that gathering, the *London Free Press* reported that Police Chief Robert Birrell had no plans to interfere, saying "so long as they maintain order and in no way violate the laws of the land . . . they are at liberty to organize or hold meetings."[31] About 75 people attended, said a reporter who managed to obtain an invitation, noting that only 50 of the attendees paid the $10 initiation fee. The featured speaker of the evening was an American, whose name was not provided, who claimed to be a minister and former president of a university. He said the greatest human sin in the eyes of the Klan was not murder or arson, but the "pouring of white blood into the veins of mud races."

On August 2, 1925, a KKK rally attracted more than 200 participants to Federal Square in London, where J.H. Hawkins, who called himself the "Imperial Klailiff," explained the Klan's views on race: "We are a white man's organization and we do not admit Jews and colored people to our ranks . . . God did not intend to create any new race by the mingling of white and colored blood, and so we do not accept the colored races." Another Klan leader said a key goal of the Klan was "to keep the white race pure."[32] On August 7 a rally began in west-central Toronto after which Klan members in full regalia climbed into cars and drove through the Jewish district of the city, centred on Queen Street and Spadina Avenue. Two days later, 150 persons attended a gathering at Parkdale Assembly Hall where several dozen members were signed up at a ceremony that was convened by six figures clad in white robes and hoods while a cross burned in the background.[33]

During the summer of 1925, the pace of KKK gatherings and cross burnings had picked up, particularly in areas where the descendants of freedom seekers who had escaped discrimination in the South were most numerous. Crosses were burned in Dresden, Chatham, St. Thomas, Ingersoll, and London. A meeting of 1,000 in Woodstock saw controversy arise about the two separate and rival Klan organizations and their relationship with the Orange Lodge. It was reported the gathering ended in "disorder."[34] On October 14, more than 1,000 men and women from across southwestern Ontario flocked to the

Donnybrook Fairgrounds in Dorchester for the first open-air rally of the Ku Klux Klan in Canada. Some attendees wore white hoods, while others had masks. About 100 candidates were sworn in as members while four crosses were set on fire, one towering 50 feet high with a 15-foot crossbar.[35]

The Klan and its rallies, cross burnings, and various controversies filled newspapers during 1926 as its recruiting efforts attracted new members. On January 21, the *London Free Press* reported the first Canadian Ku Klux Klan funeral had taken place at Woodland Cemetery in that city. Alexander Milliken, a member of the Drumbo Klan, near Woodstock, was laid to rest by his fellow Klansmen, who marched single file around the open grave led by the "King Kleagle," who carried a fiery electric cross and a sword while singing "Nearer, My God, to Thee." The ceremony concluded with a salute to the Union Jack, after which the Klan dispersed. It was a rather small event with only family and some close friends allowed to attend.[36] On the evening of March 5, in Toronto, about a dozen white-robed Ku Klux Klan members laid a wreath at the cenotaph outside city hall, and after a brief ceremony they left a cross of purple poppies at the base of the memorial to the war dead. A *Toronto Star* photographer captured the bizarre scene, in which hooded Klansmen are saluting.[37] The purpose of the event was never made clear, but it was effective at keeping the Klan and its recruiting efforts in the news.

On the Victoria Day weekend, Klan members gathered on a hillside outside of Barrie, a town where recruiting had been going well. A crowd estimated at 2,000 witnessed a cross burning and were addressed by several Klan leaders as new members signed up. Two weeks later, a Northern Irish Protestant immigrant who was initiated at that Victoria Day event attempted to blow up St. Mary's Roman Catholic Church in an explosion that shattered the quiet of the Lake Simcoe community.

The perpetrator was William Skelly, a 30-year-old shoemaker who had migrated to Canada just weeks earlier from Northern Ireland, where strife was rampant between Protestants and Catholics. He placed a stick of dynamite against a wall of the church, blowing a four-foot hole in it. Skelly told police he had been instructed by the Klan to destroy the house of worship.[38] He was convicted and sentenced to five years in prison, while two accomplices received terms of four years and three years.[39] All three were sent to Kingston penitentiary and required to do hard labour. In sentencing the men, Ontario Supreme Court Justice William Alexander Logie described the Ku Klux Klan as "an importation from the United States that Canada can do without."[40]

In late June, about 1,100 Klan members gathered at Belleville in eastern Ontario for a fair and induction ceremony, the largest gathering of its kind in that area. Another large gathering took place in Brockville, and at the end of July, 25,000 attended a Klan event at Kingston at which a large cross was burned just outside city limits and 35 new members were initiated. The rally attracted members from "klaverns" across eastern Ontario and neighbouring New York State.[41] That summer, Klan gatherings were held in London, Toronto, Ottawa, Smiths Falls, Perth, Prescott, Picton, and elsewhere.

By late 1926 and early 1927, however, the KKK was in decline and the British Empire Klan was gone, leaving only the first Canadian Klan. In the United States, the organization was also losing members. One of the last large events in Ontario was a September 4, 1927, parade in St. Thomas with two open-air meetings in Pinafore Park. About 200 men and women dressed in full regalia rode horses draped in white, and the procession was led by the Elgin Regimental Band.[42] That same year, a group of hooded Klansmen attempted to enter Hyatt Avenue United Church in London because they wanted to express their appreciation for anti-Catholic sentiments expressed by Benny Eckhardt, a local fundamentalist who was now preaching in nearby Nilestown. They were stopped at the door by Reverend R.J. McCormick, who denied them entry unless they removed their hoods and gowns.[43] The Klan continued for several more years in Ontario, but its peak had passed. By the end of the Depression, it had withered away.

In Ontario, especially, the Ku Klux Klan might have been more successful had it not been for competition from a group whose anti-Catholic bigots wielded the levers of political power and populated the social elite in the province. The Loyal Orange Lodge was firmly entrenched and the Klan was seen by them, and many Ontarians, as American intruders. The KKK gained its greatest traction in communities with a significant Black population, but less support elsewhere. Acclaimed historian Allan Bartley, author of *The Ku Klux Clan in Canada*, focused on the Klan's rise and fall in Ontario and in a 1995 study concluded that the existence of the Loyal Orange Lodge was bad news and an "impediment" for the Klan.[44]

The Klan, Bartley noted, fared better in Saskatchewan, for instance, because the Orange Order was not as "robust" there. The Orangemen controlling Ontario had a long tradition of Protestant and pro-British rhetoric and traditions, unlike the imported and brash newcomer with its robes and burning crosses. The Lodge, Bartley said, "was a bastion of respectability in 1920s Ontario" while the KKK had the "whiff of criminality" to it and seemed to be a commercial endeavour, at least in part.

Ontario prided itself on its orderly society in the British tradition and retained a profound distrust for Americans and their ways. The War of 1812, the threats of annexation from William Seward, and the Fenian raids had all contributed to a sense of wariness, and memories north of the border were long. The Loyal Orange Lodge had effectively cornered the market on bigotry and presented a challenge the KKK never faced in Atlanta or other places where it successfully stoked intolerance and touted white supremacy.

Yet again, Americans who crossed the international border were presented with new opportunities — and challenges — in the oh-so-convenient attic. Over the course of many decades their northward migration for a wide variety of compelling reasons had been generally well received in Canada. For some of their notions it was another story.

EPILOGUE

Geography and history made neighbours of Canada and the United States. The old axiom says that good fences make for good neighbours, but the two countries share the longest undefended border in the world without needing them. That has been a blessing — most of the time. At other times, not so much. For some who crossed the border in the years surrounding the Civil War, it was a life-saving or life-altering experience, particularly for those who came from the South. Some Southerners, white and Black, remained in Canada for only a brief time, while others put down roots.

Throughout history, Canada and the United States have been friends, with a few notable exceptions. The War of 1812, when the Americans were promised that the taking of Canada militarily would involve little more than marching across the border, was the nadir of our long relationship. In the decades following that conflict, which ultimately resolved so little, the United States grew to become a formidable power and war hawks began demanding that Washington get back to the unfinished business of annexing British North America. Legislation to end slavery in Upper Canada and Britain acted as an inducement for Black immigrants to make their way across the border, often along the Underground Railroad. The Civil War generated a stream of skedaddlers, plotters, spies, buyers, and others. In its aftermath followed citizens, Confederate leaders, angry white supremacists, and fugitives from justice.

The first Americans to seek refuge under the Union Jack were settlers anxious to remain loyal to the British Crown, the loyalists. One prominent loyalist was Boston preacher Mather Byles, who was steadfast in his opposition to the American Revolution. He was witty and popular, and when asked to explain his lack of support for the Patriot cause, is said to have responded: "Which is better — to be ruled by one tyrant three thousand miles away or by three thousand tyrants one mile away?"[1] He particularly disliked the undisciplined violence of some revolutionary leaders. Byles was removed from his church after the British left Boston and was charged with aiding the "enemy" by speaking against the revolutionary cause. Byles was ordered to leave Boston, but the aging clergyman refused and was placed under house arrest with a sentry posted at his door. He once told a visitor to his home who asked about the guard standing outside, "Oh, that is my observe-a-Tory." When town fathers finally discontinued the guard, Byles proclaimed: "I have been guarded, re-guarded and disregarded." The authorities gave up trying to bring him in line and he died in 1788 at age 82.

His son, Mather Byles Jr., was also a preacher and even less willing to submit to American authorities. He left Boston with the British Army and made his way to Halifax, where he became chaplain to the British garrison. Not long afterward, he travelled to England, where he was awarded 120 pounds sterling and granted an annual pension of 100 pounds to compensate his claims for losses suffered as a loyalist. Byles Jr. returned to Canada and accepted the call to become rector of Trinity Church in Saint John, New Brunswick.[2]

Meanwhile, in Schoharie, New York, the American Revolution had turned Adam Vrooman into the black sheep of a large and successful family that overwhelmingly supported the break from Britain. Vrooman was a member of Butler's Rangers in the Mohawk Valley, where Patriots routinely beat and persecuted Tories. After the victory for the revolutionaries, Vrooman, other members of Butler's Rangers, and many like-minded persons migrated to Upper Canada, where loyalists were granted free land.[3] Vrooman settled along the Niagara River, and his name is remembered today for his sale of enslaved woman Chloe Cooley in the cross-border incident that led to Upper Canada legislating a gradual end to slavery before the 18th century ended.

The Byleses, father and son, and Vrooman were far from unique in their devotion to the British Crown. It has been estimated about 250,000 inhabitants of the Thirteen Colonies opposed the American Revolution, some 10 to 15 percent of the entire population. About 70,000 of them fled the breakaway colonies, with 50,000 migrating to Britain's North American colonies of Quebec (which then included current-day southern Ontario) and Nova Scotia. In her "A Short History of the United Empire Loyalists," historian Ann Mackenzie noted the significant impact the loyalists had on later events in Canada: "The Loyalists' basic distrust of republicanism and 'mob rule' influenced Canada's gradual 'paper-strewn' path to nationhood, in contrast to the abrupt and violent upheavals in other countries."[4]

Canada's break was gradual and measured, unlike that of the Thirteen Colonies, who resorted to violence and bloodshed. Canada's severing of ties was gradual and reflected ongoing trust and affection for Great Britain, where leaders were appointed, elected, and groomed to govern, rather than elected by the "mob." No need was felt to take up arms in revolt, with the notable exception of the rebellions of 1837–38, when colonial governors put down armed malcontents promoting republican notions, a development which led Britain to introduce more representative government.

Britain introduced slavery to the United States, but with Britain's forced departure, the states were left to deal with the knotty issue that pitted states against each other. The result was a war with monumental loss of life that brought an end to the "peculiar institution" the British had created, then left behind. And throughout the Civil War, Britain unhelpfully meddled by siding with the South, despite its opposition to slavery, which it outlawed years earlier.

To this day, the United States struggles with racism. Is history repeating itself in recent times, or is this merely part of a continuum? During the 2020 presidential election, unmistakable signs of white supremacy emerged and it was clear that much remained to be done to deal with racial inequality. The continued killing of unarmed Black men suspected of minor offences by white police officers further fuelled the Black Lives Matter movement, and some white people, feeling threatened, responded poorly. Republicans, in particular, feared the loss of white privilege as immigration was changing the face of their country to one that was more brown and Black. Racists were encouraged by Donald Trump, widely regarded as one of the worst presidents ever to hold that office. White supremacists sensed Trump's green light for their hatred and continued to spew their venom well after he left office.

Following the Civil War, when Andrew Jackson (another bad president) held power, white people in southern states like South Carolina feared the emergence of political clout for Black people, who far outnumbered white people. Back then, legislators began enacting voter suppression laws, and the Ku Klux embarked on a reign of terror to keep Black men from exercising their newfound franchise, property, and other rights. Echoes of that turbulent past reverberated in recent times when Republican governments in southern states, notably Texas, Georgia, and Florida, enacted laws that would have the effect of discouraging voting in heavily Black electoral districts. Legislatures in those states made it harder for some to vote than to buy a gun, a surefire recipe for further trouble in a country where grievance often leads to gunfire. Some observers noted the voter suppression measures amounted to a new round of Jim Crow laws like those passed to subjugate Black people after the Civil War.

Republican (mainly white) regimes of today realize they've lost the numerical superiority of the white race, and desperately have sought to cling to power. They have come to fear the ballot box and democracy, and will do whatever they can to influence elections. Gerrymandering, the insidious practice of redrawing electoral boundaries, is highly politicized, with bizarre geographical configurations as a result. In effect, politicians choose their voters, rather than let voters choose their politicians. Other efforts are aimed at making it harder to vote for Black people and other minorities by limiting hours and where polling stations were established.

Such tampering with democracy has led to a lack of respect for it, and many Americans rallied behind authoritarian figures like Donald Trump. The Proud Boys, the Oath Keepers, and even the Ku Klux Klan took heart in that growing tendency and exploited it for all it's worth. The fear of losing power and then playing to that fear among citizens have led to wars of misinformation in an era of the Internet and multiple sources of information, many of which are more interested in building audiences by capitalizing on a sense of white grievance than in reporting truth. Trump provided red hats to his followers for his Make America Great Again campaign. The colour red is often associated with passion, and Ku Klux terrorists were once helped by the Red Shirts organization. A sea of red hats was evident when insurrectionists, including the Proud Boys and Oath Keepers, stormed the United States Capitol on January 6, 2021. With the ongoing support in America for authoritarian and racist figures, the evidence is clear that nearly 160 years after the end of the Civil War their country remains divided along the fault line of colour.

Canada can claim no moral superiority on the issue of race. History shows that where large Black populations settled, discrimination festered. In Chatham, where about one-third of the population was Black at one point, school boundaries were gerrymandered to eliminate Black students from school districts. In Windsor, Chatham, and London, separate schools for Black students were either instituted or proposed. And racism lingered for many years, providing some fuel to recruiting efforts launched by the Ku Klux Klan in the 1920s. Had it not been for the already entrenched Loyal Orange Lodge, with its deep-seated prejudices and political control, the KKK might have been more successful in its efforts, at least in Ontario.

Leaders of the post–Civil War Ku Klux organization found acceptance in London and Niagara in the persons of Dr. Rufus Bratton and Major J.W. Avery, both fugitives from justice and wanted for the murder of a Black man. Confederate President Jefferson Davis was accorded welcomes worthy of a hero in Montreal, Toronto, Niagara, and elsewhere. Sympathy for the South was widespread in Canada, likely because of the adage that the enemy of my enemy is my friend. The issues of slavery and racism took a back seat.

Motivations to seek refuge in America's attic ranged from the deep-seated desire for freedom of enslaved people willing to undertake a long and dangerous journey to a foreign land, to a more immediate and reactive one of white people fleeing prosecution for their activities undertaken during and after the Civil War. Some who chose flight merely wanted to avoid fighting in the war, while others were deserters who disdained it. The skedaddlers were reviled on the American side of the border, the same way draft dodgers from the Vietnam War were regarded a century later. Many Americans who escaped to Canada eventually returned home, but only when they felt it was safe to do so. They included Confederate notables Jefferson Davis, John C. Breckinridge, Jubal Early, George Pickett, James Mason, Jacob Thompson, Clement Clay, and others. Even avid Ku Klux leaders like J.W. Avery and Rufus Bratton repatriated themselves in time. Others, like the Manigault and Mazyck families, opted to remain and live out their days in the country next door.

Many Black people, including Josiah Henson, remained in the Chatham area, while their great champions Harriet Tubman and Mary Ann Shadd returned to the United States to continue fighting for racial equality. The legacy of Black people who escaped to Canada on the Underground Railroad is still felt today, with their descendants leading productive lives in Kent County in southwestern Ontario and elsewhere. Baseball Hall of Fame pitcher Ferguson Jenkins, who was born in Chatham, can trace his ancestry on his mother's side to free Black people who fled the Frankfort area of Kentucky. Famed sculptor Artis Lane, born in North Buxton, is descended from freedom seekers who travelled the Underground Railroad. Lane's bronze bust of Sojourner Truth is on display in Emancipation Hall at the Capitol Visitor Center in Washington, D.C., the first statue there to represent a Black woman. And her bust of her great-great-aunt, Mary Ann Shadd, can be found in a Chatham Park. Her father, Abraham Shadd, took up residence near Buxton and became the first Black elected to political office in Canada. Peter Butler III, descended from formerly enslaved people who settled at Wilberforce, just north of London, became Canada's first Black police officer.

The most temporary of all residents were the buyers, spies, crimps, and others who were paid to transact their business across the border. The Confederate spy operations based in Montreal and Toronto were substantial and well-funded efforts, but they ceased with the surrender of Confederate General Robert E. Lee at Appomattox Court House.

Canada's acceptance of the formerly enslaved, fugitives from justice, and high-placed Confederates who faced potential execution as traitors was often an irritant in British-American relations and, later, Canadian-American relations. The *Trent* and *Chesapeake* affairs illustrated the former, accompanied by the sabre-rattling of U.S. Secretary of State William Seward, while the latter involved the abduction of Rufus Bratton from the streets of London in 1872. Overall, however, there was great value in having a place to which those who had run afoul of American law and the authorities could flee. President Abraham Lincoln was loath to prosecute Confederate leaders as war criminals or traitors, fearing he'd make them martyrs for the Southern cause and undermine efforts to reconcile with the South. He was willing to let them escape. Canada provided that escape room, a pressure-relief valve, from which many Confederate leaders and Lincoln's successors benefited.

Had the attic refuge offered by Canada not been available, the history of the Civil War and the years preceding, during, and after it might have been different. Asylum north of the border for Confederate leaders solved a knotty problem for the triumphant Union side, for instance. Trials of alleged traitors and death sentences for some would have made repairing the battered republic even more difficult than it proved to be.

The flight by loyalists from New York State, Black people from Cincinnati, freedom seekers from Southern states, and free Black people from Northern ones was well established by the time profound differences led to bloodshed. Then followed a northward flight of white men unwilling to wage war. Some migrants sought nothing more than safety, but other transplants included plotters, spies, fugitives from justice, and people upset at losing the way of life they had known.

Confederates made extensive use of a friendly and helpful ally in the backyard of their enemy as a base of operations against the North, and as a hideout.

Evidence of the connection between Canada and the Civil War era takes many forms. In Canada, that includes not just historical markers and associated sites, but headstones in cemeteries and at least a couple of monuments.

All provide tangible and important reminders of Canada's unique and important role during troubled times for its southern neighbour.

NOTES

CHAPTER I

1. Michael Power and Nancy Butler, *Slavery and Freedom in Niagara* (Niagara-on-the-Lake, ON: Niagara Historical Society, 1993), 20, https://digitalcommons.buffalostate.edu /magazines-books/12/, accessed December 10, 2020.

2. Grace Vrooman Wickersham and Ernest Bernard Comstock, *The Vrooman Family in America: Descendants of Hendrick Meese Vrooman Who Came From Holland to America in 1664* (Dallas: No publisher given, 1949), 33–34, 63–66, https://babel .hathitrust.org/cgi/pt?id=wu.89062511381&view=1up&seq=5, accessed December 11, 2020.

3. "Butler's Rangers," Niagara Falls Museums, https:// niagarafallsmuseums.ca/discover-our-history/history-notes /butlersrangers.aspx, accessed November 11, 2020.

4. "Adam Crysler," Archives of Ontario, http://ao.minisisinc .com/SCRIPTS/MWIMAIN.DLL/118022389/AUTH_JOIN /HEADING/Crysler,~20Adam,~201732-1793?JUMP, accessed December 5, 2020.

5. Much of the personal and military history of Hardison is gleaned from the application of his widow, Jane Hardison, for a military pension because of his service in the Revolutionary War. Her husband died in 1823 and by the early 1850s she

needed money. She supplied affidavits about their marriage and his military career, but she had limited knowledge because they married in 1800, well after his time of service. Her affidavits were supplemented by those of a relative, a fellow soldier and a confidant. This material can be found in the United States Revolutionary War Pensioners, 1801–1815, 1818–1872, at ancestry.com, accessed December 1, 2020. The accounts in the affidavits are confirmed and augmented by reference to online recitations of the various battles mentioned.

6. Biographical information from the records of Holy Trinity Church in Chippawa, held at Fort Erie Public Library local history archives: http://www.fepl.ca/localhistory/files /original/1022be42a16b57fd49dd3763cebo6bfb.pdf, accessed December 10, 2020.

7. "Chloe Cooley and the Act to Limit Slavery in Upper Canada," by Natasha L. Henry, *The Canadian Encyclopedia*, https://www.thecanadianencyclopedia.ca/en/article /chloe-cooley-and-the-act-to-limit-slavery-in-upper-canada, accessed November 14, 2020.

8. Power and Butler, 18.

9. Power and Butler, 12–14, and Robin Winks, *The Blacks in Canada: A History* (Montreal, QC, and Kingston, ON: McGill-Queen's University Press, 1997, 29–30.

10. Power and Butler, 20.

11. "The Slave in Canada," by The Honourable William Renwick Riddell, Justice of the Supreme Court of Ontario (Washington, DC: The Association for the Study of Negro Life and History, 1920), 58n. Originally published in *The Journal of Negro History*, vol. V, no. 3, July 1920.

12. From the *Canadian Archives*, extracted from the official report Simcoe filed to Westminster following the Upper Canada Executive Council meeting of March 21, 1793, at Navy Hall, quoted in Riddell, 55–56n.

13. "Chloe Cooley . . ." by Henry.

14. "James Somerset, the Boston Runaway Who Ended Slavery in England," New England Historical Society, https://www .newenglandhistoricalsociety.com/james-somerset-the-boston -runaway-who-ended-slavery-in-england, accessed November 14, 2020, and Power and Butler, 23–24.

15. Winks, 26.

16. Riddell, 56–57.

17. Ibid., 58n.

18. Winks, 97.

19. Power and Butler, 36.

20. Winks, 98.

21. "An Act for the Gradual Abolition of Slavery," New York State Education Department, archives, NYSA_13036-78 _L1799_Cho672, https://www.archives.nysed.gov/education /act-gradual-abolition-slavery-1799, accessed December 13, 2020.

22. "Northwest Ordinance," Library of Congress, Research Guides, https://www.loc.gov./rr/program//bib/ourdocs/northwest.html, accessed December 13, 2020.

23. Riddell, 61–62.

24. Power and Butler, 31.

CHAPTER 2

1. Robin W. Winks, *The Blacks in Canada: A History*, second edition (Montreal, QC, and Kingston, ON: McGill-Queen's University Press, 1997), 1, quoting from *Jesuit Relations and Allied Documents: Travels and Explorations of the Jesuit Missionaries in New France, 1610–1791*, specifically the original edition published in 1632 where the quotation appears on pp. 58–60.

2. "Olivier Le Jeune," by Dorothy Williams, *The Canadian Encyclopedia*, https://www.thecanadianencyclopedia.ca/en /article/olivier-le-jeune, accessed December 16, 2020.

3.   "Slavery in the French Colonies: Le Code Noir (the Black Code) of 1685," Library of Congress, blog, https://blogs.loc.gov/law/2011/01/slavery-in-the-french-colonies/, accessed December 15, 2020.

4.   Winks, 5.

5.   Michael Power and Nancy Butler, *Slavery and Freedom in Niagara* (Niagara-on-the-Lake, ON: Niagara Historical Society, 1993), 11.

6.   "A Short History of the United Empire Loyalists," by Ann Mackenzie, *United Empire Loyalists' Association of Canada*, http://www.uelac.org/, accessed May 24, 2021.

7.   Ibid., 112–113.

8.   "Fugitive Slave Acts," History.com, https://www.history.com/topics/black-history/fugitive-slave-acts, accessed December 17, 2020.

9.   Power and Butler, 12, quoting Jason H. Silverman, *Unwelcome Guests: Canada West's Response to Fugitive American Slaves, 1800–1865* (Millwood, NJ: Associated Faculty Press, 1985), 5.

10.   Power and Butler, 44.

11.   "Abolition of the Slave Trade Act," National Archives of the United Kingdom, www.nationalarchives.gov.uk/slavery/pdf/abolition.pdf, accessed December 17, 2020.

12.   "The Slave Trade," National Archives, https://archives.gov/education/lessons/slave-trade.html, accessed December 17, 2020.

13.   Winks, 144–145.

14.   "The Black Settlement in Oro Township," County of Simcoe Archives, https://www.simcoe.ca/Archives/Pages/black.aspx, accessed November 14, 2020.

15.   Winks, 155.

16.   Nikki M. Taylor, *Frontiers of Freedom: Cincinnati's Black Community, 1802–1868* (Athens, OH: Ohio University Press, 2005), 20.

17.   Ibid., 52.

18.   "Cincinnati Riots of 1829," by Douglas Edelstein, BlackPast.org, December 4, 2017, 3, https://www.blackpast.org

/african-american-history/cincinnati-riots-1829/, accessed December 18, 2020.

19. Benjamin Drew, *The Refugee: or the Narratives of Fugitive Slaves in Canada Related by Themselves, with an Account of the History and Condition of the Colored Population of Upper Canada* (Boston, MA: J.P. Jewett and Company; New York, NY: Sheldon, Lamport and Blakeman, 1856), 244–245, quoted in *Ontario's African-Canadian Heritage: The Collected Writings of Fred Landon, 1918–1967*, Karolyn Smardz Frost, Bryan Walls, Hilary Bates Neary, Frederick H. Armstrong, eds. (Toronto, ON: Natural Heritage Books, 2009), 44.

20. Edelstein, 4.

21. Taylor, 61–64.

22. Winks, 156.

23. Landon, 85.

24. Victoria Purcell, *Wilberforce Beginnings: The Wilberforce Colony and Butler Family Legacy* (Victoria, BC: First Choice Books, 2010), 6.

25. Landon, 62.

26. "Underground Railroad," by Natasha L. Henry, *The Canadian Encyclopedia*, https://www.thecanadianencyclopedia.ca/en/article/underground-railroad#, accessed December 19, 2020.

27. Ibid.

28. "Freedom Crossing," Historic Lewiston, New York, http://historiclewiston.org/freedomcrossing/, accessed December 7, 2020.

29. "Underground Railroad," *Encyclopedia of Detroit*, https://detroithistorical.org/learn/encyclopedia-of-detroit/underground-railroad, accessed December 20, 2020.

30. Fugitive Slave File 5, held at Fort Malden Museum, Amherstburg, Ontario, quoted in Carole Jenson, University of Windsor, M.A. Thesis, 1966, "History of the Negro Community in Essex County 1850–1860," 8, https://scholar.uwindsor.ca/etd/6429, accessed December 2, 2020.

31. "To 'Canada' and Back Again: Immigration From the United

States on the Underground Railroad (1840–1860)," by Western
University's MA Public History Students, Western University,
London, Ontario, found at Canadian Museum of Immigration
at Pier 21, https://pier21.ca/research/immigration-history
/to-canada-and-back-again-immigration-from-the-united-states
-on-the-underground-railroad-1840.

32. Josiah Henson, *Father Henson's Story of His Own Life*
(Boston, MA: J.P. Jewitt, 1858), quoted in Landon, 51.

33. Landon, 195.

34. "1837," MaritimeHistoryoftheGreatLakes.com, https://www
.maritimehistoryofthegreatlakes.ca/documents/hgl/default
.asp?ID=s030, accessed December 24, 2020.

35. "Navy Island," Niagara Falls Museums, https://
niagarafallsmuseums.ca/discover-our-history/history-notes
/navyisland.aspx, accessed December 24, 2020.

36. Francis Bond Head, *A Narrative* (London, UK: J. Murray,
1839), 392, quoted in Landon, 193–194.

CHAPTER 3

1. Letter from Tom Elice (Ellis) to Mary Warner, dated July 9,
1854, Archives of Ontario, F 4536, 10029559.

2. "The Story of Josiah Henson, the Real Inspiration for 'Uncle
Tom's Cabin,'" by Jared Brock, *Smithsonian Magazine*, May
16, 2018, https://www.smithsonianmag.com/history/story
-josiah-henson-real-inspiration-unlce-toms-cabin-180969094/,
accessed December 27, 2020.

3. Josiah Henson, *The Life of Josiah Henson, Formerly a Slave,
Now an Inhabitant of Canada* (Boston, MA: Arthur D. Phelps,
1849), 58–59.

4. Ibid., 66–67.

5. "Josiah Henson," *Dictionary of Canadian Biography*, http://
www.biographi.ca/en/bio/henson_josiah_11E.html, accessed
November 2, 2020.

6. "Uncle Tom's Cabin Historic Site," Ontario Heritage Trust, https://www.heritagetrust.on.ca/en/properties/uncle-toms-cabin, accessed October 4, 2020.

7. "The Story of Josiah Henson . . . ," by Brock, *Smithsonian Magazine*.

8. Harriet Beecher Stowe, *The Key to Uncle Tom's Cabin: Presenting the Original Facts and Documents Upon Which the Story is Founded, Together With Corroborative Statements Verifying the Truth of the Work*, Chapter 6, http://www.gutenberg.org/files/54812/54812-h/54812-h.htm, accessed December 30, 2020.

9. *Ontario's African-Canadian Heritage: Collected Writings of Fred Landon, 1918–1967*, eds. Karolyn Smardz Frost, Bryan Walls, Hilary Bates Neary, and Fred Armstrong (Toronto, ON: Natural Heritage Books, 2009), 99–100.

10. Robin W. Winks, *The Blacks in Canada: A History* (Montreal, QC, and Kingston, ON: McGill-Queen's University Press, 1997), 210.

11. Landon, 100.

12. Winks, 213.

13. "The Founding of the Elgin Settlement," Presbyterian Church in Canada Archives, https://presbyterianarchives.ca/2017/02/02/part-4-the-founding-of-the-elgin-settlement/.

14. Landon, 101.

15. Winks, 211–212.

16. "Henry Walton Bibb," *Dictionary of Canadian Biography*, http://www.biographi.ca/en/bio/bibb_henry_walton_8E.html, accessed November 18, 2020.

17. "Henry Bibb: A Force For Abolition of Slavery," by Nancy Stearns Theiss, *Louisville Courier-Journal* (Kentucky), February 10, 2015, https://www.courier-journal.com/story/news/local/oldham/2015/02/10/henry-bibb-force-abolition-slavery/23170113/, accessed November 18, 2020.

18. "Henry Bibb, A Colonizer," by Fred Landon, *Journal of Negro History*, vol. 5, no. 4, October 1920, 443–446.

19. Mary Ann Shadd Cary, *Dictionary of Canadian Biography*, http://www.biographi.ca/en/bio/shadd_mary_ann_camberton_12E.html, accessed December 27, 2002.

20. Winks, 200.

21. Ibid, 202.

22. "Josiah Henson," *Dictionary of Canadian Biography*.

23. Ibid.

CHAPTER 4

1.   Elijah Leonard, *The Honorable Elijah Leonard: A Memoir* (London, ON: Advertiser Printing, 1894), 47–48.

2.   "Fugitive Slave Act of 1850," by Natasha L. Henry, *The Canadian Encyclopedia*, https://www.thecanadianencyclopedia.ca/en/article/fugitive-slave-act-of-1850, accessed December 24, 2020.

3.   "The Chatham Slave Case," *Toronto Globe*, October 8, 1858, 2.

4.   *The Eldon House Diaries: Five Women's Views of the 19th Century*, eds. Robin S. Harris and Terry G. Harris (Toronto, ON: The Champlain Society, 1994), 85.

5.   "Fugitive Slave Acts," History.com, https://www.history.com/topics/black-history/fugitive-slave-acts, accessed December 17, 2020.

6.   "Fugitive Slave Act of 1850," by Natasha L. Henry.

7.   "Compromise of 1850," and "The Fugitive Slave Act of 1850," History.com, https://www.history.com/topics/abolitionist-movement/compromise-of-1850, accessed December 17, 2020.

8.   "Harriet Tubman, the Moses of her People," Harriet Tubman Historical Society, http://www.harriet-tubman.org/moses-underground-railroad, accessed December 25, 2020.

9.   "Harriet Tubman," History.com, https://www.history.com/topics/black-history/harriet-tubman, accessed December 26, 2020.

10. "Frederick Douglass," History.com, https://www.history.com

/topics/black-history/frederick-douglass, accessed December 26, 2020.

11. *Ontario's African-Canadian Heritage: Collected Writings of Fred Landon, 1918-1967*, eds. Karolyn Smardz Frost, Bryan Walls, Hilary Bates Neary, Frederick Armstrong (Toronto, ON: Natural Heritage Books, 2009), 209-210.

12. Frederick H. Armstrong, *The Forest City: An Illustrated History of London, Canada* (London, ON: Windsor Publications, 1986), 83–86.

13. "The Crash of 1857," Civil War, http://www.civilwar.com /causes/economic/148575-the-crash-of-1857, accessed January 6, 2021.

14. Armstrong, 86.

15. "Making a Living: African Canadian Workers in London, Ontario, 1861–1901," by Tracey Adams, *Labour Magazine*, Spring 2011, 14.

16. Benjamin Drew, *The Refugee: Or the Narratives of Fugitive Slaves in Canada* (Boston, MA: John P. Jewett and Company, 1856), 295, 297.

17. *The Refugees from Slavery in Canada West. Report to the Freedmen's Inquiry Commission*, by S.G. Howe (Boston, MA: Wright and Potter, 1864), 69, 70, 102, 104.

18. Robin W. Winks, *The Blacks in Canada: A History* (Montreal, QC, and Kingston, ON: McGill-Queen's University Press, 1997), 371.

19. Drew, 321–322.

20. Ibid., 341.

21. From a memorial plaque in Victoria Park, London, near the site of the integrated school in the British garrison barracks, erected in 2008 by the Congress of Black Women, London Chapter, the London Heritage Council and the City of London.

22. "Refugees from Slavery in Canada West," *Report of the Freedmen's Inquiry Commission*, by S.G. Howe (Boston, MA: Wright and Potter, 1864), 51–52.

23. Landon, 147.

24. Osborne P. Anderson, *A Voice From Harper's Ferry* (Boston, MA: Printed for the Author, 1861), 9.

25. Landon, 197.

26. "John Brown. American Abolitionist," *Encyclopedia Britannica*, https://www.britannica.com/biography/John-Brown -American-abolitionist, accessed January 5, 2021.

27. Oswald Garrison Villard, *John Brown 1800–1859: A Biography Fifty Years After* (London, UK: Constable and Company, 1910), 752.

28. Anderson, 46.

29. "John Brown," History.com, https://www.history.com/topics /abolitionist-movement/john-brown, accessed January 5, 2021.

30. Landon, 198.

31. Winks, 268.

32. Anderson, 13.

33. "John Brown. American Abolitionist," *Encyclopedia Britannica*, https://www.britannica.com/biography/John-Brown -American-abolitionist, accessed January 6, 2021.

34. "Dred Scott decision," *Encyclopedia Britannica*, https:// britannica.com/event/Dred-Scott-decision/Reception-and -significance, accessed January 6, 2021.

35. *New York Tribune*, March 10, 1857, 4.

36. *New York Tribune*, March 11, 1857, 4.

37. "The Slavery Question," *New York Times*, March 9, 1857, 4.

38. "The Dred Scott Case — The Nationality of Slavery," *Daily Constitutionalist and Republic* (Augusta, GA), March 15, 1857, 2.

39. "The Anderson Case," by Deidre Rowe Brown, Law Society of Ontario, https://lso.ca/about-lso/osgoode-hall -and-ontario-legal-heritage/exhibitions-and-virtual-museum /historical-vignettes/legal-history/the-anderson-case, accessed January 9, 2021.

40. John Boyko, *Blood and Daring: How Canada Fought the Civil War and Forged a Nation* (Toronto, ON: Alfred A. Knopf Canada, 2013), 19–59.

41. Winks, 270.

42. "This Day in History: September 22. Lincoln Issues
     Emancipation Proclamation," History.com, https://www
     .history.com/this-day-in-history/lincoln-issues-emancipation
     -proclamation, accessed December 30, 2020.

43. "The Story of Josiah Henson . . ." by Brock, *Smithsonian
     Magazine*.

CHAPTER 5

1.   Amanda Foreman, *A World on Fire: Britain's Crucial Role
     in the American Civil War* (New York, NY: Random House,
     2012), 36–37.

2.   Ibid., 37–38.

3.   John Boyko, *Blood and Daring: How Canada Fought the
     American Civil War and Forged a Nation* (Toronto, ON:
     Alfred A. Knopf Canada, 2013), 62–63.

4.   "William Seward's Foreign War Panacea Reconsidered," by
     Niels Eichorn, *The Journal of the Civil War Era*, March 23,
     2018, https://www.journalofthecivilwarera.org/2018/03
     /william-h-sewards-foreign-war-panacea-reconsidered/,
     accessed January 21, 2021.

5.   Boyko, 65.

6.   Foreman, 46.

7.   Boyko, 67.

8.   Foreman, 53.

9.   "John C. Breckinridge: Nationalist, Confederate, Kentuckian,"
     by Lowell H. Harrison, *The Filson Club History Quarterly*,
     vol. 47, no. 3, April 1973, 127–128.

10. "United States Presidential Election of 1860," by Michael
     Levy, *Encyclopedia Britannica*, https://www.britannica.com
     /event/United-States-presidential-election-of-1860, accessed
     January 21, 2021.

11. "Causes of the Civil War," History.com, https://history.com

/topics/american-civil-war/american-civil-war-history, accessed
January 20, 2021.

12. "The Union Gone," *Charleston Mercury* (South Carolina),
November 7, 1860, 1.

13. Christopher Dickey, *Our Man in Charleston: Britain's Secret
Agent in the Civil War South* (New York, NY: Crown, 2015),
172–173.

14. Foreman, 61,

15. Dickey, 174.

16. "Lords Proprietors of Carolina," *South Carolina Encyclopedia*,
https://www.scencyclopedia.org/sce/entries/lords-proprietors
-of-carolina, accessed January 23, 2021.

17. "The First to Secede," by James Loewen, *American Heritage*,
https://www.americanheritage.com/first-secede, accessed
January 23, 2021.

18. "Secession," *South Carolina Encyclopedia*, https://www
.scencyclopedia.org/sce/entries/secession, accessed January 23,
2021.

19. "The 20th Day of December, in the Year of Our Lord, 1860,"
Charleston Mercury, December 21, 1860, 1.

20. "The Union is Dissolved," *Charleston Mercury*, December 21,
1860, 2.

21. "Secession," *South Carolina Encyclopedia*.

22. Dickey, 190.

23. "March 4, 1861: Abraham Lincoln Inaugurated," *This Day in
History*, History.com, https://www.history.com/this-day-in
-history/Lincoln-inaugurated, accessed January 26, 2021.

24. Foreman, 64.

25. "Fort Sumter," Bordewich.

26. Edward Lining Manigault, Jr., *The Manigault Family of South
Carolina: Its Ancestors and Descendants* (Morrisville, NC:
Lulu Press, 2006), 18.

27. "Sea Coast Defences," Library of Congress, https://www.loc
.gov/resource/g3911r.cw0365000/, accessed January 22, 2021.

28. Boyko, 67–70.

29. "Fort Sumter," Bordewich.
30. "Must We Have War?," *Charleston Mercury*, April 17, 1861, 1.
31. Boyko, 75–76.
32. Foreman, 92–93.
33. "Anticipated Collision at Fort Pickens," *New York Herald*, April 17, 1861, 1.
34. Boyko, 75–76.
35. Robin W. Winks, *The Civil War Years: Canada and the United States* (Montreal, QC, and Kingston, ON: McGill-Queen's University Press, 1998), 46.
36. Foreman, 99, 102.
37. Boyko, 86–87.

CHAPTER 6

1. Lois E. Darroch, *Four Went West to the Civil War* (Kitchener, ON: McBain Publications, 1985), 80.
2. Claire Hoy, *Canadians in the Civil War* (Toronto, ON: McArthur and Company, 2004), 4–5.
3. Darroch, 109
4. A.N. Wolverton, *Dr. Newton Wolverton: An Intimate Anecdotal Biography of One of the Most Colorful Characters in Canadian History* (Bolton, ON: Leopold Classic Library, 2017), 23–26.
5. Hoy, 7, with a very similar version in Wolverton, 28.
6. Wolverton, 33–38.
7. "The Civil War: The Senate's Story," The United States Senate, https://www.senate.gov/artandhistory/history/common/civil_war/WarBegins.htm, accessed February 1, 2021.
8. "The First Battle of Bull Run," History.com, https://www.history.com/topics/american-civil-war/first-battle-of-bull-run, accessed January 25, 2021.
9. "The Civil War: The Senate's Story."
10. "Canadians Serving in the Civil War," by Norman Shannon,

Historynet.com, https://www.historynet.com/canadians-serving
-civil-war.htm, accessed January 29, 2021.

11. Hoy, vi.

12. "American Civil War and Canada," by John Boyko, *The Canadian Encyclopedia*, https://www.thecanadianencyclopedia.ca/en/article/american-civil-war, accessed February 3, 2021.

13. Hoy, 30, 59–60.

14. Arthur Rankin Biography, *Dictionary of Canadian Biography*, http://www.biographi.ca/en/bio/rankin_arthur_12E.html, accessed January 30, 2021.

15. *Montreal Gazette*, October 7, 1861, 2, quoted in John E. Buja, *Arthur Rankin: A Political Biography* (Windsor: MA thesis, University of Windsor, 1982), 98.

16. Buja, 98–99.

17. *Toronto Globe*, October 7, 1861, as extensively quoted in "Arrest of Mr. Arthur Rankin, M.P.P.," *Detroit Free Press*, October 8, 1861, 1.

18. Robin W. Winks, *The Civil War Years: Canada and the United States* (Montreal, QC, and Kingston, ON: McGill-Queen's University Press, 1998), 72–75.

19. "Resignation of Col. Rankin," *Detroit Free Press*, December 28, 1861, 1.

20. "A Field for Investigation," *Detroit Free Press*, April 2, 1862, 1.

21. "Arthur Rankin Biography," *Dictionary of Canadian Biography*.

22. Company E, 16th Arkansas Infantry Regiment, Confederate States of America, http://www.couchgenweb.com/civilwar/16inf_f&s.html, accessed February 6, 2021.

23. Roster of Confederate Soldiers of Georgia 1861–1865, Ancestry.com.

24. Hoy, 63–69.

25. "Dr. Solomon Secord monument to remain on Kincardine's main street," by Liz Dadson, *The Kincardine Record*, https://kincardinerecord.com/story.php?id=6354, accessed January 29, 2021.

26. "When Johnny (Canuck) Comes Marching Home Again . . ." by Tyrell.

27. John Boyko, *Blood and Daring: How Canada Fought the American Civil War and Forged a Nation* (Toronto, ON: Alfred A. Knopf, 2013), 26.

28. "Anderson Abbott," *Dictionary of Canadian Biography*, http://www.biographi.ca/en/bio/abbott_anderson_ruffin_14E.html, accessed January 30, 2021.

29. "Doctor of Courage," by Alice Taylor, *University of Toronto Magazine*, February 3, 2015, https://magazine.utoronto.ca/campus/history/doctor-of-courage-alexander-augusta-civil-rights-hero/, accessed April 9, 2021.

30. "How Black Canadians Fought for Liberty in the U.S. Civil War," by Richard Reid, *Toronto Star*, January 31, 2015, https://www.thestar.com/opinion/commentary/2015/01/31/how-black-canadians-fought-for-liberty-in-the-american-civil-war.html.

31. Hoy, 144.

32. Boyko, 141–142.

33. "Soldier Girl: The Emma Edmonds Story," by Tom Derreck, *Canada's History*, https://www.canadashistory.ca/explore/women/soldier-girl-the-emma-edmonds-story, accessed February 7, 2021.

34. S. Emma E. Edmonds, *Nurse and Spy in the Union Army: The Adventures and Experiences of a Woman in Hospitals, Camps and Battle-fields* (Hartford, CT: W.S. Williams & Co., 1865), 2001 reprint by Applewood Books, Bedford MA, 18–19.

35. Boyko, 108–112.

36. Boyko, 110, quoting Louise Chipley Slavicek, *Women and the Civil War* (New York, NY: Doubleday, 2009), 27.

37. Edmonds, 358–360.

38. Hoy, 37–38.

39. "Soldier Girl."

40. "Soldier Girl," and Boyko, 108.

41. Boyko, 108.

1. "Substitutes (Civil War), by David A. Norris, *Encyclopedia of North Carolina*, https://www.ncpedia.org/substitutes-civil-war, accessed February 7, 2021.

2. "Conscription," by Sacher.

3. James W. Geary, "Yankee Recruits, Conscripts, and Illegal Evaders," in *The Civil War Soldier: A Historical Reader*, eds. Michael Barton and Larry M. Logue (New York, NY: New York University Press, 2002), 62, and Peter Levine, "Draft Evasion in the North during the Civil War, 1863–1865," *The Journal of American History*, vol. 67, no. 4, March 1981, 817.

4. Levine, 828.

5. "Racial Rhetoric: The *Detroit Free Press* and its Part in the Detroit Race Riot of 1863," by Matthew Kundinger, *University of Michigan Journal*, https://michiganjournalhistory.files.wordpress.com/2014/02/kundinger.pdf, accessed February 16, 2021.

6. "Conscription," by John M. Sacher, *Essential Civil War Curriculum*, https://www.essentialcivilwarcurriculum.com/conscription.html, accessed February 7, 2021.

7. Robin W. Winks, *The Civil War Years: Canada and the United States* (Montreal, QC, and Kingston, ON: McGill-Queen's University Press, 1998), 202.

8. John Boyko, *Blood and Daring: How Canada Fought the American Civil War and Forged a Nation* (Toronto, ON: Alfred A. Knopfl 2013), 129, and Claire Hoy, *Canadians in the Civil War* (Toronto, ON: McArthur and Company, 2004), 129. Canadian historian Boyko puts the figure at 12,000, including military deserters, while Hoy says the total was closer to 20,000.

9. "Drafting in the States," *Toronto Globe*, August 11, 1862, 2.

10. "The Stampede to Canada," *Buffalo Evening Post*, August 9, 1862, 2.

11. "The Rush for Canada," *Detroit Free Press*, August 12, 1862, 1.

12. "Man Shot at Niagara Falls," *Buffalo Commercial*, August 12, 1862, 3.

13. "Cowards Running," *Detroit Free Press*, August 12, 1862, 2.

14. "Amicable Relations," *Detroit Free Press*, August 14, 1862, 1.

15. "The Exodus From the North," *Buffalo Courier*, August 14, 1862, 3.

16. "The Falls Hotels and Runaways," and "Arrested on Suspicion of 'Canada,'" *Buffalo Commercial*, August 14, 1862, 3.

17. "Latest from the Sneaks," *Buffalo Courier*, August 16, 1862, 3.

18. Untitled item, *Buffalo Evening Post*, August 15, 1862, 2.

19. "No Passes for Visiting Canada," *Detroit Free Press*, August 10, 1862, 3.

20. "Runaways Stopped," *Buffalo Weekly Express*, August 19, 1862, 3.

21. "The Escapade to Canada," *Detroit Free Press*, August 19, 1862, 1.

22. "Skedaddling to Canada and Back," by Kathy Warnes, *Meandering Michigan History*, https://meanderingmichiganhistory.weebly.com/skedaddling-to-canada-and-back.html, accessed February 15, 2021.

23. Boyko, 129.

24. Hoy, 131.

25. "Luring Canadian Soldiers into Union Lines During the War Between the States," by Marguerite B. Hamer, *Canadian Historical Review*, 77, June 1996, quoted in Hoy, 134.

26. Hoy, 129.

27. Hoy, 127, 133–134.

28. Winks, 193.

29. *Toronto Leader*, July 15, 1862, quoted in Raney, 24.

30. Raney, 24, 27.

31. Boyko, 140–141.

32. "Reconstruction," History.com, https://www.history.com/topics/american-civil-war/reconstruction, accessed March 17, 2021.

33. Raney, 31.

34. Boyko, 144.

35. Raney, 29–30.

36. Ella Lonn, *Foreigners in the Union Army and Navy* (Baton Rouge, LA: Louisiana State University Press, 1951), 451.

37. "Life in the British Army," *The Royal Engineers*, http://www.royalengineers.ca/DailyLife.html, accessed February 17, 2021.

38. Quoted in Hoy, 135.

39. Boyko, 117.

40. Raney, 24–25.

41. Boyko, 118.

42. "A Long March — Adventures of a Deserter from the British Army," *Detroit Free Press*, January 6, 1863, 1.

43. Raney, 27–28.

CHAPTER 8

1. Ian Radforth, *Royal Spectacle: The 1860 Visit of the Prince of Wales to Canada and the United States* (Toronto, ON: University of Toronto Press, 2004), 7, 17–22.

2. "The Diary of H.C.R. Becher, *Ontario Historical Society Papers and Records*, vol. XXXIII (Toronto, ON: Ontario Historical Society, 1939), 133–134.

3. "Old Tecumseh House Is Closing Career of Great Interest," *London Advertiser*, September 16, 1929, 1.

4. Miller, 97–98.

5. Armstrong, 99–100.

6. Frederick H. Armstrong, *The Forest City: An Illustrated History of London, Canada* (Windsor, ON: Windsor Publications, 1986), 84–87.

7. "Tecumseh Opened in 1858," by L.N. Bronson, *London Free Press*, December 26, 1958, 6.

8. Orlo Miller, *This Was London: The First Two Centuries* (Westport, ON: Butternut Press, 1988), 95.

9. Gary May, *Hard Oiler: The Story of Early Canadians' Quest*

for *Oil at Home and Abroad* (Toronto, ON: Dundurn Press, 1998), 33–34.

10. "Some Effects of the American Civil War on Canadian Agriculture," by Fred Landon, *Ontario Agricultural History*, vol. VII, no. 4, October 1933.

11. Diary of H.C.R Becher, 136.

12. "Military Roots: They Run Deep in London," by Jane Foy, *London Free Press*, November 1, 1980, B1.

13. Miller, 105–106.

14. "Manitoba History: Frank Cornish — The Man," *Manitoba Historical Society*, http://www.mhs.mb.ca/docs/mb_history/09/cornish.f.shstml, accessed February 25, 2021.

15. "Fugitive Slaves in London Before 1860," by Fred Landon, *Transactions of the London and Middlesex Historical Society, Part X* (London, ON: London and Middlesex Historical Society, 1919), 36–37.

16. *The Carty Chronicles of Landmarks and Londoners*, edited by Catherine B. McEwen (London, ON: London and Middlesex Historical Society, 2005), 80.

17. Robin Winks, *The Civil War Years: Canada and the United States* (Montreal, QC, and Kingston, ON: McGill-Queen's University Press, 1998), 277.

18. *Carty Chronicles*, 80.

19. "Laure 'Doucette' Larendon: Beauregard's Daughter," EmergingCivilWar.com, https://emergingcivilwar.com/2019/03/27/laure-doucette-larendon-beauregards-daughter/, accessed September 24, 2010.

20. John Boyko, *Blood and Daring: How Canada Fought the American Civil War and Forged a Nation* (Toronto, ON: Alfred A. Knopf, 2013), 153–155.

21. Amanda Foreman, *A World on Fire: Britain's Crucial Role in the American Civil War* (New York, NY: Random House, 2010), 596.

22. Adam Mayers, *Dixie & the Dominion* (Toronto, ON: Dundurn, 2003), 41.

23. Foreman, 597.

24. Mayers, 67–68.

25. Boyko, 170.

26. Foreman, 658.

27. "Fugitive Slaves in London Before 1860," Landon, 38.

28. Ibid., 59.

29. Foreman, 659–663.

30. Mayers, 89.

31. "Confederacy's Canadian Mission: Spies Across the Border," HistoryNet.com, https://www.historynet.com/confederacys -canadian-mission-spies-across-the-border.htm, accessed February 26, 2021.

32. Boyko, 174.

CHAPTER 9

1. Robin Winks, *The Civil War Years: Canada and the United States* (Montreal, QC, and Kingston, ON: McGill-Queen's University Press, 1998), 299.

2. Ibid., 182, 303.

3. Mayers, 129–130, 203–205.

4. John Boyko, *Blood and Daring: How Canada Fought the American Civil War and Forged a Nation* (Toronto, ON: Alfred A. Knopf, 2013), 190–191.

5. Adam Mayers, *Dixie & the Dominion* (Toronto, ON: Dundurn, 2003), 140–146.

6. Boyko, 186–189.

7. Winks, 346.

8. Claire Hoy, *Canadians in the Civil War* (Toronto, ON: McArthur & Company, 2004), 333.

9. "Clement Claiborne Clay," *Encyclopedia of Alabama*, http:// encyclopediaofalabama.org/article/h-2951, accessed March 5, 2021.

10. Mayers, 186–188.

11. Hoy 348–349.

12. Frank H. Heck, *Proud Kentuckian John C. Breckinridge, 1821–1875* (Lexington KY: University Press of Kentucky, 2009), 133.

13. Hoy, 348.

14. Mayers, 158.

15. "Lincoln Assassin John Wilkes Booth's Canadian Connection," by Andy Blatchford, *The Canadian Press*, https://globalnews.ca/news/1611968/lincoln-assassin-john-wilkes-booths-canadian-connection/, accessed March 6, 2021.

16. "Civil War Timeline 1864," TheCivilWar.com, https://thecivil-war.com/civil-war-timeline/civil-war-timeline-1864/, accessed March 11, 2021.

17. "This Day in History: April 3," History.com, https://history.com/this-day-in-history/confederate-capital-of-richmond-is-captured/, accessed March 11, 2021.

18. Amanda Foreman, *A World on Fire: Britain's Crucial Role in the American Civil War* (New York, NY: Random House, 2012), 779.

19. Doris Kearns Goodwin, *Team of Rivals: The Political Genius of Abraham Lincoln* (New York, NY: Simon and Schuster, 2005), 732.

20. Winks, 362.

21. "The Fiend in Gray," by Jane Singer, *Washington Post*, June 1, 2003, https://www.washingtonpost.com/archive/lifestyle/magazine/2003/06/01/the-fiend-in-gray/818f9565-ca66-4ccc-b70d-c5023229966a/.

22. Hoy, 235.

23. Boyko, 252.

24. "Yellow Fever Plot of 1864 Targeted Lincoln, U.S. Cities," CivilWarProfiles.com, https://www.civilwarprofiles.com/yellow-fever-plot-of-1864-targeted-lincoln-u-s-cities/, accessed March 12, 2021.

25. "The Fiend in Gray," Singer, and "Luke Pryor Blackburn," at FindAGrave.com, https://www.findagrave.com/memorial/10042/luke-pryor-blackburn#view-photo=30798639, accessed March 13, 2021.

26. "Fort Sumter: Restoration of the Stars and Stripes," *New York Times*, April 18, 1865, 8.

27. Foreman, 770–771.

28. Hoy, 352–353.

29. Mayers, 208–209.

30. Boyko, 251–255.

31. "Assassination," *The Atlantic*, July 1865, https://www .theatlantic.com/magazine/archive/1865/07/assassination /308768/, accessed March 9, 2021.

CHAPTER 10

1. Sherman Zavitz, *It Happened at Niagara: Stories from Niagara's Fascinating Past* (Niagara Falls, ON: Lundy's Lane Historical Society, 2008), 57–69.

2. Ibid., 91–92.

3. "Niagara-on-the-Lake as a Confederate Refuge," by Nicholas Rescher (Niagara-on-the-Lake, ON: NAP Publications Inc. with the co-operation of the Niagara Historical Society, 2003), 4–5, 23–24.

4. William C. Davis, *Breckinridge: Statesman, Soldier, Symbol* (Baton Rouge, LA: Louisiana State University Press, 1974), 554.

5. "Niagara-on-the-Lake as a Confederate Refuge," 8.

6. Davis, 555.

7. Virginia Mason, *The Public Life and Diplomatic Correspondence of James M. Mason, With Some Personal History* (Roanoke, VA: Stone Printing, 1906, reprint 2012 Forgotten Books), 586–587.

8. Davis, 582.

9. Rescher, 8.

10. "The Secret Service of the Confederacy," by John W. Headley, Signal Corps Association, http://www.civilwarsignals.org/pages /spy/confedsecret/confedsecret.html, accessed April 9, 2021.

11. Goodwin, 713.

12. George T. Denison, *Soldiering in Canada: Recollections and Experiences* (Toronto, ON: George N. Morang and Company, 1901), 59.

13. Ibid., 69.

14. "When Jefferson Davis Visited Niagara," by A.J. Clark, *Ontario Historical Society Papers and Records*, vol. XIX (Toronto, ON: Ontario Historical Society, 1922), 88.

15. "A Speech by Jefferson Davis," *New York Times*, June 12, 1867, 5.

16. Clark, 89.

17. *Niagara Mail*, June 5, 1867, quoted in Rescher, 13.

18. "Jefferson Davis in Canada — Rebel View of His Reception," *New York Times*, June 13, 1867, 5.

19. "Jeff Davis at Toronto," *New York Times*, June 7, 1867, 1.

20. "From the Archives: Jefferson Davis and Family Found Refuge in Montreal," by John Kalbfleisch, *Montreal Gazette*, November 25, 2017.

21. "Freshly Defeated in the U.S. Civil War, Confederate Leader Jefferson Davis Came to Canada to Give the Newly Founded Country Defence Tips," by Tristin Hopper, *The National Post*, July 25, 2014.

22. Varina H. Davis, *Jefferson Davis, Ex-President of the Confederate States of America: A Memoir by his Wife* (New York, NY: Belford, 1890), 804.

23. Ibid., 799.

24. "Imprisonment and Trial of Jefferson Davis," Encyclopedia.com, https://www.encyclopedia.com/history/dictionaries-thesauruses-pictures-and-press-releases/davis-imprisonment-and-trial, accessed March 14, 2021.

25. Mason, 588.

26. Mayers, 216.

27. The Reappearance of Davis," *New York Times*, April 15, 1881, 4.

28. "Personal," *Toronto Globe*, May 30, 1881, 2.

29. William Kirby, *Annals of Niagara* (Toronto, ON: Macmillan, 1927), 301.

30. *Niagara Mail*, February 10, 1869, 590, quoted in Rescher, 16.

CHAPTER 11

1. Amanda Foreman, *A World on Fire: Britain's Crucial Role in the American Civil War* (New York, NY: Random House, 2012), 787.
2. "The Economic Costs of the American Civil War: Estimates and Implications," by Claudia Goldin and Frank Lewis, *Journal of Economic History*, 35 (1975), 299–326, quoted in EH.net, *Economic History Association*, https://eh.net/encyclopedia /the-economics-of-the-civil-war/, accessed March 16, 2021.
3. "The Origin of the American Civil War," by Gerald Gunderson, *Journal of Economic History*, 34 (1974), 915–950, quoted in EH.net, *Economic History Association*, https:// eh.net/encyclopedia/the-economics-of-the-civil-war/, accessed March 16, 2021.
4. "The Economics of the Civil War," by Roger L. Ransom, EH.net, *Economic History Association*, https://eh.net/encyclopedia /the-economics-of-the-civil-war/, accessed March 16, 2021.
5. Richard Zuczek, *State of Rebellion: Reconstruction in South Carolina* (Columbia, SC: The University of South Carolina Press, 1996), 2, 6.
6. "Ku Klux Klan," *South Carolina Encyclopedia*, https:// scencyclopedia.org/sce/entries/ku-klux-klan/, accessed October 24, 2020.
7. Zuczek, 18.
8. West, 5.
9. West, 40–41.
10. "The Ku Klux Klan — What is it?," *Yorkville Enquirer*, April 28, 1868, 3.
11. "Robert Scott Kingston," *South Carolina Encyclopedia*, https:// www.scencyclopedia.org/sce/entries/scott-robert-kingston/, accessed March 27, 2021.
12. Budiansky, 115–116.

13. West, 2.

14. Budiansky, 115–116, and West, 72.

15. "How Many U.S. Presidents Owned Enslaved People?" by Evan Andrews, History.com, https://www.history.com/news/how-many-u-s-presidents-owned-slaves, accessed March 25, 2021.

16. "Reconstruction," History.com, https://www.history.com/topics/american-civil-war/reconstruction, accessed March 17, 2021.

17. Ibid., 70–71.

18. Diary of Dr. James Rufus Bratton (Transcription by J.L. West, York County Public Library, Rock Hill, SC), Part 1, p. 9, quoted in West, 3.

19. West, 32–33.

20. "Barn Burnt," *Yorkville Enquirer*, March 24, 1870, 2.

21. "The United States Court, Friday, December 29, 1871," *Columbia Daily Phoenix* (South Carolina), December 30, 1871, 2.

22. "The Trial of the Ku Klux," *Yorkville Enquirer*, December 21, 1871, 3.

23. West, 124.

24. "J.W. Avery," *Yorkville Enquirer*, April 6, 1871, 3.

25. Zuczek, 95–97.

26. "A Conference — The Ku-Klux Law," *Yorkville Enquirer*, May 18, 1871.

27. "Testimony of the Joint Select Committee to Inquire into the Condition of Affairs in the Late Insurrectionary States," (Washington, VA: Government Printing Office, 1872), 1391, https://archive.org/details/reportofjointselo8unit, accessed March 29, 2021.

28. Ibid., 1348.

29. Ibid., 1365.

30. Zuczek, 98–101.

31. "Great Stampede of Ku-klux Conspirators," *New York Times*, October 31, 1871, 1.

32. Samuel Brooks Mendenhall, *Tales of York County* (Rock Hill, SC: Reynolds & Reynolds, 1989), 52.

33. "A Breeze in the United States Court, on Monday," *Columbia Daily Phoenix*, January 3, 1872, 2.

34. Eric Foner, *Reconstruction: America's Unfinished Revolution 1863–1877* (New York, NY: Harper and Row, 1988), 458.

35. Zuczek, 104.

36. Ron W. Shaw, *Rendition on Wellington Street: London Ontario's Unrepentant Confederates, the Ku Klux Klan* (Carleton Place, ON: Global Heritage Press, 2018), 129.

37. *Yorkville Enquirer*, May 2, 1872, 3.

38. "Communication From Maj. Avery," *Yorkville Enquirer*, September 5, 1872, 4.

39. House purchase details kindly shared by Niagara historian Douglas Phibbs, based on transfer deed number 14739 in the Niagara North Land Registry Office in St. Catharines.

40. Richard Zuczek, *State of Rebellion: Reconstruction in South Carolina* (Columbia, SC: University of South Carolina Press, 1996), 206–207.

41. "Major J.W. Avery," *Yorkville Enquirer*, November 8, 1877, 2.

42. Miranda Riley, Royal Military College Museum, Canadian Armed Forces, Kingston, Ontario.

CHAPTER 12

1. "Morgan's Raid," Ohio History Central, https://ohiohistorycentral .org/w/Morgan%27s_Raid, accessed March 8, 2022.

2. *The Carty Chronicles of Landmarks and Londoners*, edited by Catherine B. McEwen (London, ON: London and Middlesex Historical Society, 2005), 80.

3. Ron W. Shaw, *Rendition on Wellington Street* (Carleton Place, ON: Global Heritage Press, 2018), 85.

4. "Reform. The Labors of Meseroll and Linton at London, Ont.,

and the Results," *Jackson Citizen Patriot* (Michigan), July 17, 1877, 4.

5. "The Debates and Proceedings of the Third Session, Forty-Second Congress," (Washington, VA: Congressional Globe, 1873), 716.

6. Shaw, 84, and Daniel J. Brock, *Fragments From the Forks: London Ontario's Legacy* (London, ON: London and Middlesex Historical Society, 2011), 133.

7. Shaw, 83.

8. "General Assembly of the State of South Carolina, 1877," (Columbia, SC: Calvo & Patton State Printers, 1877), 284.

9. "Railroad Commissioner Thomas Replies to Mr. Earle," *The Watchman and Southron* (Sumter, SC), October 28, 1891, 2.

10. Shaw, 81.

11. "Carolina — The French Huguenots," https://www.carolana .com/Carolina/Settlement/french_huguenot_settlers.html, accessed September 14, 2020.

12. "The Oaks Plantation," Historical Marker Database, https:// www.hmdb.org/m.asp?m=16383, accessed April 19, 2021.

13. "Springfield Plantation," Historical Marker Database, https:// www.hmdb.org/m.asp?m=29489, accessed September 16, 2020.

14. "The Huguenots in South Carolina, 1680–1720," by Carol Merchant, Dissertations, Theses, and Masters Projects, College of William and Mary, 1973, https://dx.doi.org/doi:10.21220 /s2-djrf-sg53, accessed September 21, 2020.

15. "The Manigault Family," Joseph Manigault House, Charleston Museum brochure.

16. Edward Lining Manigault, Jr., *The Manigault Family of South Carolina: Its Ancestors and Descendants* (Morrisville, NC: Lulu Press, 2006), 18–19.

17. "The Gullah: Rice, Slavery, and the Sierra Leone–American Connection," by Joseph A. Opala, https://glc.yale.edu/gullah -rice-slavery-and-sierra-leone-american-connection, accessed April 5, 2021.

18. "Rice History," Carolina Aromatic Rice Plantation, https://www
.carolinaplantationrice.com/history/, accessed April 4, 2021.

19. "Letter Addressed to Governor M.L. Bonham, of South
Carolina, on the defenses of Charleston," by Gabriel
Manigault, dated September 12, 1863, https://babel.hathitrust
.org/cgi/pt?id=dul1.ark:/13960/tojtogk7t&view=1up&seq=2,
accessed April 20, 2021.

20. "Hospital Yorkville," Samuel Brooks Mendenhall, *Tales of York
County* (Rock Hill, SC: Reynolds and Reynolds, 1989), 40.

21. "School Notice," *Yorkville Enquirer*, September 21, 1865, 3.

22. "Yorkville Female College," *Yorkville Enquirer*, November 15,
1866, 3.

23. "Departure," *Yorkville Enquirer*, May 6, 1869, 2. Also printed
May 10 under the headline "Carolinians Going to Canada," in
the *Charleston Daily Courier*, May 10, 1869, 1.

24. "A Statement of Dr. Bratton's Case, Being an Explanation of
the Ku-Klux Prosecutions in the Southern States (London, ON:
Free Press, 1872), 13.

25. "Edward Middleton Manigault," The Johnson Collection,
Spartanburg, South Carolina, https://thejohnsoncollection.org
/middleton-manigault/, accessed April 23, 2021.

26. "Starvation Ends Life's Search for Spiritual Beauty," *Fresno
Morning Republican* (California), September 9, 1922, 9.

27. Gabriel Manigault, *The United States Unmasked: A Search
into the Causes of the Rise and Progress of These States*
(London, ON: J.H. Vivian, 1878), 3.

28. Ibid., 66.

29. Ibid., 156.

30. G. Manigault, formerly of South Carolina, *A Political Creed:
Embracing Some Ascertained Truths in Sociology and Politics*
(New York, NY: Wynkoop and Hallenbeck, 1884), 93.

CHAPTER 13

1.   Ron W. Shaw, *Rendition on Wellington Street* (Carleton Place, ON: Global Heritage Press, 2018), 52–53.
2.   "Hester's History," *Indiana State Sentinel* (Indianapolis, Indiana), February 16, 1876, 7.
3.   "Buzzards of a Feather," *The Weekly Sentinel* (Raleigh, North Carolina), December 28, 1875, 1.
4.   "Arrests and Infamous Despotism," *Fayetteville Eagle* (North Carolina), August 24, 1871, 2.
5.   "Hester's History," 7.
6.   "Dr. Bratton's Adventures as Member of Original Ku-Klux Klans," by James D. Grist in *Charleston Sunday News*, *Yorkville Enquirer*, February 1, 1921, 1.
7.   "The Kidnapping of Dr. Rufus Bratton," by Fred Landon, *The Journal of Negro History*, vol. 10, no. 3, July 1925, 330.
8.   "The Bratton Kidnapping," by H. Orlo Miller, secretary of the London and Middlesex Historical Society, *The Canadian Science Digest*, April 1938, 127.
9.   "Dr. Bratton's Adventures . . ." by Grist.
10. Landon, 331.
11. "A Case of Kidnapping," *London Advertiser*, June 7, 1872, 3.
12. "The Kidnapping Case," *London Advertiser*, June 11, 1872, 3.
13. "Post Office Espionage," *Ottawa Citizen*, October 12, 1872, 3.
14. Jerry L. West, *The Reconstruction Ku Klux Klan in York County, South Carolina, 1865–1877* (Jefferson, NC: McFarland Publishing, 2002), 129.
15. "United States Court," *Charleston Daily News*, June 12, 1872, 4.
16. Landon, 332.
17. "The Kidnapping Case," *London Advertiser*, June 13, 1872, 3.
18. "The Kidnapping," *London Advertiser*, June 15, 1882, 3.
19. "The Canadian Abduction Case," *Norfolk Virginian*, June 22, 1872, 3.
20. "The Abduction of Dr. Bratton," *Yorkville Enquirer*, August 1, 1872, 4. This account is from a fine and full report of two days

of trial coverage provided by the *London Free Press* in its issues of July 16 and 17, 1872.

21. "A Statement of Dr. Bratton's Case, Being Explanatory of the Ku-Klux Prosecutions in the United States," by "Truth" (London, ON: Free Press Printing, 1872).

22. "Dr. Bratton's Adventures . . ." by Grist.

23. "1872 London Kidnapping Linked with KKK Activities," by Fred Landon, *London Free Press*, May 23, 1964, 34.

24. "Freemasonry," *Encyclopedia Britannica*, https://www.britannica.com/topic/order-of-Freemasons, accessed May 3, 2021.

25. "Freemasonry in London and Area," https://masonic.on.ca/about-freemasonry/, accessed May 3, 2021.

26. "Election of 1876," *South Carolina Encyclopedia*, https://www.scencyclopedia.org/sce/entries/election-of-1876/, accessed May 3, 2021.

27. Richard Zuczek, *State of Rebellion: Reconstruction in South Carolina* (Columbia, SC: University of South Carolina Press, 1996), 169.

28. "Red Shirts," *South Carolina Encyclopedia*, https://www.scencyclopedia.org/sce/red-shirts/, accessed May 3, 2021.

29. "Hampton. Grand Demonstration by the York Democracy," *Yorkville Enquirer*, October 19, 1876, 2.

30. Zuczek, 177–178.

31. "Election of 1876," *South Carolina Encyclopedia*.

32. Zuczek, 201.

33. "Circuit Court," *Yorkville Enquirer*, September 12, 1878, 2.

34. Shaw, 131–132.

35. "Key Figure in Kidnap Incident Honored by Masons," by L.N. Bronson, *London Free Press*, July 17, 1985, D5.

36. "Return of Dr. Bratton," *Yorkville Enquirer*, November 21, 1878, 2.

37. "Bratton Family of Physicians," Historic Brattonsville Culture and Heritage Museums of York, South Carolina. https://chmuseums.org/history, accessed November 6, 2020.

38. "Death of Dr. Bratton," *Yorkville Enquirer*, September 4, 1897, 2.

39. "Klan Connection Kills Plaque for Kidnap Site," *London Free Press*, April 18, 1985, C2.

CHAPTER 14

1. "Rebirth of the Klan," History.com, https://www.history.com /topics/reconstruction/ku-klux-klan, accessed May 5, 2020.

2. "The Worst Thing About 'Birth of a Nation' Is How Good It Is," by Richard Brody, *New York Magazine*, February 1, 2013, https://www.newyorker.com/culture/richard-brody/the-worst -thing-about-birth-of-a-nation-is-how-good-it-is, accessed May 5, 2020.

3. "The Clansman: An Historical Romance of the Ku Klux Klan," Documenting the American South (DocSouth), University of North Carolina, https://docsouth.unc.edu/southlit/dixonclan /summary.html, accessed May 6, 2021.

4. "Dixon's Clansman," *Yorkville Enquirer*, October 17, 1905, 2.

5. "Nelson Cameron, Ex-Slave, 81 years, recollection in *Federal Writer's Project: Slave Narrative Project*, vol. 14, South Carolina, Part 1, Library of Congress, https://www.loc.gov /resource/mesn.141/?, accessed May 12, 2021.

6. "The Clansman," *Yorkville Enquirer*, October 31, 1905, 2.

7. "The Clansman," *Yorkville Enquirer*, October 20, 1905, 2.

8. "The Clansman. Thrilling Tale of the Reconstruction Period," *Yorkville Enquirer*, October 31, 1905, 4.

9. "Jim Crow Laws," History.com, https://www.history.com /topics/early-20th-century-us/jim-crow-laws, accessed May 10, 2021.

10. "William Archibald Dunning: Father of Historiographic Racism, Columbia's Legacy of Academic Jim Crow," by Tommy Song, *Columbia University and Slavery*, 5, https://columbiaandslavery

.columbia.edu/content/william-archibald-dunning-father
-historiographic-racism-columbias-legacy-academic-jim-crow,
accessed May 7, 2021.

11. "The Birth of a Nation," by Michael Soper, *Charlotte Observer*
    (North Carolina), July 14, 1963, 51.

12. "D.W. Griffith, American Director," *Encyclopedia Britannica*,
    https://www.britannica.com/biography/D-W-Griffith, accessed
    May 12, 2021.

13. "How 'The Birth of a Nation' Revitalized the Ku Klux Klan,"
    History.com, https://www.history.com/news/kkk-birth-of-a
    -nation-film, accessed May 13, 2021.

14. Brody, "The Worst Thing . . . ."

15. "D.W. Griffith," *Encyclopedia Britannica*.

16. "How 'The Birth of a Nation' . . ."

17. "Klan is Established with Impressiveness," *Atlanta
    Constitution*, November 28, 1915, 1.

18. "'Birth of a Nation' Thrills Tremendous Atlanta Audience," by
    Ned McIntosh, *Atlanta Constitution*, December 7, 1915, 7.

19. "How 'The Birth of a Nation' . . ."

20. "Orange Order in Canada," *The Canadian Encyclopedia*,
    https://www.thecanadianencyclopedia.ca/en/article/orange
    -order, accessed May 15, 2021.

21. "Sir Mackenzie Bowell," *The Canadian Encyclopedia*, https://
    www.thecanadianencyclopedia.ca/en/article/sir-mackenzie
    -bowell, accessed June 15, 2021.

22. Quoted in Allan Bartley, *The Ku Klux Klan in Canada: A
    Century of Promoting Racism and Hate in the Peaceable
    Kingdom* (Halifax, NS: Formac Publishing, 2020), 39.

23. Quoted in "A Public Nuisance: The Ku Klux Klan in Ontario
    1923–27," by Allan Bartley, *Journal of Canadian Studies*, vol.
    30, issue 3, Fall 1995, 156–174.

24. "Disclaims Title of 'Grand Serpent,'" *Toronto Globe*, March
    15, 1923, 5.

25. "No Klansmen Need Apply," George Wenige letter of March 15,
    1923, found in *London Free Press: From the Vault. A*

Photo-History of London to 1950, by Jennifer Granger (Windsor, ON: Biblioasis, 2017), 252.

26. Bartley, 40–41.

27. "Kent County People Warned That Such Practices Will Cause Arrest," *Toronto Globe*, August 13, 1924, 3.

28. John Weaver, *Crimes, Constables and Courts: Order and Transgression in a Canadian City, 1816–1970* (Montreal, QC, and Kingston, ON: McGill-Queen's University Press, 1995), 115–116, quoted in Bartley, 41.

29. "Ku Klux Rears Head in City of Hamilton With 32 Initiations," *Toronto Globe*, November 19, 1924, 1.

30. Bartley, 62.

31. "The Ku Klux Klan in London, Ontario," by John Lisowski, *The Historian*, vol. 24, 2015, London and Middlesex Historical Society, 44.

32. Lisowski, 44.

33. Bartley, 67.

34. Bartley, "A Public Nuisance . . ."

35. Lisowski, 45.

36. Ibid.

37. "Ku Klux Klan Lay Wreath at Cenotaph," *Toronto Star*, March 6, 1926, 3.

38. "Ku Klux Klan Accused of Dynamite Outrage in the Town of Barrie," *Toronto Globe*, June 22, 1926, 1.

39. Bartley, 76–78.

40. "Notes and Comments," *Toronto Globe*, October 16, 1926, 4.

41. Bartley, 99.

42. "Impressive Parade of Ku Klux Klan," *Toronto Globe*, September 5, 1927, 2.

43. Lisowski, 46.

44. Bartley, "A Public Nuisance . . ."

EPILOGUE

1. "Mather Byles, the Witty Loyalist Even the Patriots Liked," New England Historical Society, https://www .newenglandhistoricalsociety.com/mather-byles-bostons-witty -loyalist-even-patriots-liked, accessed May 23, 2021.

2. "Mather Byles," *Dictionary of Canadian Biography*, http://www .biographi.ca/en/bio/byles_mather_5E.html, accessed May 26, 2021.

3. Grace Vrooman Wickersham and Ernest Bernard Comstock, *The Vrooman Family in America: Descendants of Hendrick Meese Vrooman Who Came From Holland to America in 1664* (Dallas: No publisher given, 1949), 33–34, 63–66, https:// babel.hathitrust.org/cgi/pt?id=wu.89062511381&view=1up &seq=5, accessed December 11, 2020.

4. "A Short History of the United Empire Loyalists," by Ann Mackenzie, *United Empire Loyalists' Association of Canada*, http://www.uelac.org/.

SELECTED BIBLIOGRAPHY

BOOKS

Anderson, Osborne P. *A Voice From Harper's Ferry*. Boston, MA: Printed for Author, 1861.

Bartley, Allan. *The Ku Klux Klan in Canada: A Century of Promoting Racism and Hate in the Peaceable Kingdom*. Halifax, NS: Formac Publishing, 2020.

Boyko, John. *Blood and Daring: How Canada Fought the Civil War and Forged a Nation*. Toronto, ON: Alfred A. Knopf Canada, 2013.

Davis, Varina H. *Jefferson Davis, Ex-President of the Confederate States of America: A Memoir by his Wife*. New York, NY: Belford, 1890.

Davis, William C. *Breckinridge: Statesman, Soldier, Symbol*. Baton Rouge, LA: Louisiana State University Press, 1974.

Edmonds, S. Emma E. *Nurse and Spy in the Union Army: The Adventures and Experiences of a Woman in Hospitals, Camps and Battlefields*. Hartford, CT: W.S. Williams & Co., 1865, reprint 2001 by Applewood Books, Bedford, MA.

Foner, Eric. *Reconstruction: America's Unfinished Revolution, 1863–1877*. New York, NY: Harper and Row, 1988.

Foreman, Amanda. *A World on Fire: Britain's Crucial Role in the American Civil War*. New York, NY: Random House, 2012.

Heck, Frank H. *Proud Kentuckian John C. Breckinridge, 1821–1875*. Lexington, KY: University Press of Kentucky, 2009.

Henson, Josiah. *The Life of Josiah Henson, Formerly a Slave, Now an Inhabitant of Canada*. Boston, MA: Arthur D. Phelps, 1849.

Henson, Josiah. *Father Henson's Story of His Own Life*. Boston, MA: J.P. Jewitt, 1858.

Hoy, Claire. *Canadians in the Civil War*. Toronto, ON: McArthur and Company, 2004.

Kirby, William. *Annals of Niagara*. Toronto, ON: Macmillan, 1927.

Lonn, Ella. *Foreigners in the Union Army and Navy*. Baton Rouge, LA: Louisiana State University Press, 1951.

Manigault, Edward Lining, Jr. *The Manigault Family of South Carolina: Its Ancestors and Descendants*. Morrisville, NC: Lulu Press, 2006.

Manigault, Gabriel. *A Political Creed: Embracing Some Ascertained Truths in Sociology and Politics*. New York, NY: Wynkoop and Hallenbeck, 1884.

Manigault, Gabriel. *The United States Unmasked: A Search into the Causes of the Rise and Progress of These States*. London, ON: J.H. Vivian, 1878.

Mason, Virginia. *The Public Life and Diplomatic Correspondence of James M. Mason, With Some Personal History*. Roanoke, VA: Stone Printing, 1906, reprint 2012.

Mayers, Adam. *Dixie & The Dominion*. Toronto, ON: Dundurn, 2003.

McEwen, Catherine B., ed. *The Carty Chronicles of Landmarks and Londoners*. London, ON: London and Middlesex Historical Society, 2005.

Mendenhall, Samuel Brooks. *Tales of York County*. Rock Hill, SC: Reynolds and Reynolds, 1989.

Power, Michael, and Nancy Butler. *Slavery and Freedom in Niagara*. Niagara-on-the-Lake, ON: Niagara Historical Society, 1993.

Purcell, Victoria. *Wilberforce Beginnings: The Wilberforce Colony and Butler Family Legacy*. Victoria, BC: First Choice Books, 2010.

Shaw, Ron W. *Rendition on Wellington Street: London's Unrepentant Confederates, the Ku Klux Klan*. Carleton Place, ON: Global Heritage Press, 2018.

Stowe, Harriet Beecher. *The Key to Uncle Tom's Cabin: Presenting the Original Facts and Documents Upon Which the Story is Founded, Together with Corroborative Statements Verifying the Truth of the Work*, 1853, http://www.gutenberg.org/files/54812 /54812-h/54812-h.htm.

Villard, Oswald Garrison. *John Brown 1800–1859: A Biography Fifty Years After*. London, UK: Constable and Company, 1910.

West, Jerry L. *The Reconstruction Ku Klux Klan in York County, South Carolina, 1865–1877*. Jefferson NC: McFarland, 2002.

Wickersham, Grace Vrooman, and Ernest Bernard Comstock. *The Vrooman Family in America: Descendants of Hendrick Meese Vrooman Who Came From Holland to America in 1666*. Dallas, TX, 1949.

Winks, Robin W. *The Blacks in Canada: A History*, second edition. Montreal, QC, and Kingston, ON: McGill–Queen's University Press, 1997.

Winks, Robin W. *The Civil War Years: Canada and the United States*. Montreal, QC, and Kingston, ON: McGill–Queen's University Press, 1998.

Zuczek, Richard. *State of Rebellion: Reconstruction in South Carolina*. Columbia, SC: The University of South Carolina Press, 1996.

ARCHIVAL SOURCES

Buxton National Historic Site, North Buxton, Ontario

County of Simcoe (Ontario) Archives

Historic Brattonsville Culture and Heritage Museums of York, South Carolina

National Archives of the United Kingdom

New England Historical Society

Niagara Falls Museums
Niagara Historical Society
Presbyterian Church in Canada Archives
London and Middlesex Historical Society
Ontario Historical Society
Ontario Heritage Trust

OTHER SOURCES

"A Statement of Dr. Bratton's Case, Being an Explanation of the
Ku-Klux Prosecutions in the Southern States." London, ON:
Free Press, 1872 (pamphlet).
"Abraham D. Shadd," by Joyce Shadd Middleton, Buxton National
Historic Site, North Buxton, Ontario.
Biographical information from records of Holy Trinity Church,
Chippawa, Ontario, held at Fort Erie Public Library local history
archives.
Letter from Tom Elice (Ellis) to Mary Warner, dated July 9, 1854,
Archives of Ontario, F 4536, 10029559.
"Sea Coast Defences," Library of Congress.

NEWSPAPERS

Atlanta Constitution
Buffalo Commercial
Buffalo Courier
Buffalo Evening Post
Buffalo Weekly Express
Charleston Daily News, SC
Charleston Mercury, SC
Charleston Sunday News, SC
Charlotte Observer, NC
Columbia Daily Phoenix, SC

Daily Constitutionalist and Republic, Augusta, GA
Daily Press, Norfolk, VA
Detroit Free Press
Fayetteville Eagle, NC
Fayetteville Weekly Observer, NC
Fresno Morning Republican, CA
Indiana State Sentinel, Indianapolis, IN
Jackson Citizen Patriot, MI
London Advertiser
London Free Press
Louisville Courier-Journal, KY
Montreal Gazette
National Post
New York Herald
New York Times
New York Tribune
Niagara Mail
Norfolk Virginian, VA
Ottawa Citizen
Toronto Globe
Toronto Leader
Toronto Star
Washington Post
The Watchman and Southron, Sumter, SC
The Weekly Sentinel, Raleigh, NC
Yorkville Enquirer, SC

ONLINE RESOURCES

American Heritage
Ancestry.com
Biography.com
Canada's History
The Canadian Encyclopedia

TheCivilWar.com
CivilWarProfiles.com
Dictionary of Canadian Biography
Documenting the American South (DocSouth)
Eh.net (Economic History Association)
EmergingCivilWar.com
Encyclopedia Britannica
Encyclopedia of Alabama
Encyclopedia of Detroit
Encyclopedia of North Carolina
Find-A-Grave.com
HathiTrust Digital Library
History.com
Historynet.com
Journal of Canadian Studies
Journal of Negro History
National Archives (U.S.)
National Archives of the United Kingdom
Newspapers.com
South Carolina Encyclopedia

INDEX

Illustrations indicated by page numbers in italics

Emancipation Day, 33
Emancipation Proclamation,
  85–86, 129, 205
England. *See* Britain
Essex County (ON), 48–49, 64,
  76, 123, 127, 137
extradition, 83–84, 164–65

Fargo, William, 160
Farnsworth, John Franklin, 114,
  127
Fayetteville Eagle (newspaper),
  243
Fenians, 111, 222, 280
Fenwick, William, 141
Finney, Seymour, 48
First Battle of Bull Run (Battle of
  First Manassas), 107, 111–13,
  125
First Michigan Regiment of
  Lancers, 115–16, 117–18
First Nations. *See* Indigenous
  peoples
Fisher, William, 139
Florida, 97, 99, 100, 284
Foner, Eric, 216–17
Foreign Enlistment Act (1819),
  116, 137
Forrest, Nathan Bedford, 201
Forsyth, William, 181
Fort Donelson, 130
Fort Douglas, 158–59
Fort Erie (ON; formerly
  Waterloo), 24–25, 47–48, 53
Fort George, 38, 182

Fort Henry, 142
Fort Lafayette, 167
Fort Malden, 49
Fort Monroe, 167, 188
Fort Moultrie, 100, 102
Fort Niagara, 23, 24, 182, 185,
  190
Fort Sumter, 100–103, 174–75
Fort Ticonderoga, 24
France, 35–36
Frazer, John, 167
Freedmen's Bureau, 202, 203, 206
Freedmen's Bureau Bill (1866), 206
Freemasonry, 254–55, 260
Fugitive Slave Act (1793), 37,
  41, 70
Fugitive Slave Act (1850), 61,
  63, 65, 71, 72, 117
Fuller, James Cannings, 56

Garrison, William Lloyd, 72
Georgia, 97, 99, 284
Georgian (ship), 165
gerrymandering, 284
Gist, William, 95, 97
Grant, Ulysses S., 121, 170, 203,
  206–7, 212–13, 215, 220,
  253–54
Great Britain. *See* Britain
Great Western Railway, 73
"Greek fire," 162, 165
Greeley, Horace, 82, 182
Griffith, D.W., 265, 269. See also
  The Birth of a Nation (film)
Grisley, William, 21, 26–27

lynching, of Jim Williams,
210–12, 215, 216, 248–49,
250–51
Lyons, Richard Bickerton Pemell,
95, 105, 106, 143

Macdonald, John A., 83, 106,
140, *140*, 143, 249, 273
Mackenzie, Ann, 283
Mackenzie, William Lyon, 49–50
Maine, 30–31, 137
Manifest Destiny, 90
Manigault family
assistance for other
Southerners, 217–18
background, 226–30
in London, ON, 15–16, 225,
231–32, 232–34, 234, 235,
236, 237–38, 258
in Yorkville, SC, 230–31
Manigault, Anne Porcher Mazyck
(wife of Gabriel Edward
Manigault), 229, 231, 237, 239
Manigault, Ann "Nancy"
Mazyck (granddaughter of
Gabriel Edward Manigault),
234, 237
Manigault, Arthur M., 103, 229
Manigault, Charles, 231
Manigault, Charlotte (daughter
of Gabriel Edward Manigault),
231, 234, 237–38
Manigault, Charlotte Dayton
(wife of Joseph Manigault),
229

Manigault, Edward (brother of
Gabriel Edward Manigault), 229
Manigault, Edward, Sr. (son of
Gabriel Edward Manigault),
231, 234
Manigault, Edward Middleton,
Jr. (grandson of Gabriel
Edward Manigault), 234,
236–37, *237*
Manigault, Eliza, 231, 234, 238
Manigault, Emma, 231, 233,
238
Manigault, Gabriel
(great-great-grandfather of
Gabriel Edward Manigault),
227–28
Manigault, Gabriel (uncle of
Gabriel Edward Manigault),
228
Manigault, Gabriel Edward
Avery and, 217
background, 98, 229–30
Bratton's abduction from
Canada and, 245, 246,
249–50, 252
in Civil War, 103, 229, 230
death and burial, 239, *239*
family, 231, 234, 236–38
A Political Creed, 238–39
refuge in Canada, 231–32,
234, 235
secession of South Carolina
and, 101, 230
The United States Unmasked,
238

Ku Klux and, 202, 208
Manigault and Mazyck families in, 230–32
mob violence at Rose Hotel,
203–5, 204
monument to Confederate
dead, 259
name, 17
Yorkville Female College, 231
See also Avery, J.W.; Bratton,
Rufus
Yorkville Enquirer (newspaper)
1876 South Carolina elections
and, 256–57
on Avery, 220
background of, 202
on Bratton, 245, 260, 261–62
on *The Clansman* (Dixon),
267
Ku Klux and, 202, 207, 213
on Manigault family, 231–32
Young, Bennett, 162–63,
164–65, 188, 199

Zuczek, Richard, 217, 258

This book is also available as a Global Certified Accessible™ (GCA) ebook. ECW Press's ebooks are screen reader friendly and are built to meet the needs of those who are unable to read standard print due to blindness, low vision, dyslexia, or a physical disability.

At ECW Press, we want you to enjoy our books in whatever format you like. If you've bought a print copy just send an email to ebook@ecwpress.com and include:

Get the
ebook free!*
*proof of purchase
required

- the book title
- the name of the store where you purchased it
- a screenshot or picture of your order/receipt number and your name
- your preference of file type: PDF (for desktop reading), ePub (for a phone/tablet, Kobo, or Nook), mobi (for Kindle)

A real person will respond to your email with your ebook attached. Please note this offer is only for copies bought for personal use and does not apply to school or library copies.

Thank you for supporting an independently owned Canadian publisher with your purchase!